Colonist Fathers, Corporate Sons

*A Selective History
of the Call Family*

COLONIST FATHERS, CORPORATE SONS

A Selective History of the Call Family

BY
HOWARD M. CARLISLE

Photographs without credits courtesy of the Call family.

ISBN 0-9651936-0-8

© 1996 Calls Trust

All Rights Reserved

Printed by Publishers Press
Printed in the United States of America
Cover design by Steve McCrea

It is worthwhile for anyone to have behind him a few generations of honest, hard-working ancestry.

—John Phillips Marquand

Contents

List of Maps & Exhibits ix

Preface: Howard M. Carlisle xi

Chapter 1: Early New England and
Conversion to Mormonism 1

Chapter 2: Anson Call the Colonizer 15

Chapter 3: Starting Anew: Anson Vasco Call I
and Anson Vasco Call II 39

Chapter 4: Anson Vasco Call II:
A Brief Stop in Chesterfield 47

Chapter 5: Anson Vasco Call II: Settlement of Star Valley 55

Chapter 6: Thomas Call:
Continuing the Building Tradition 81

Chapter 7: Early Entrepreneurs:
Reuel and Osborne Call 97

Chapter 8: Development of Maverik and
Related Family Enterprises 123

Chapter 9: Growing Up in Soda Springs
and the Search for Independence 147

Chapter 10: Early Development of Flying J 167

Chapter 11: Growth through Acquisition 187

Chapter 12: Rise to Dominance in Travel Plazas and Diesel 215

Epilogue 247

SOURCES AND BIBLIOGRAPHY 253

INDEX 257

List of Maps & Exhibits

Maps:

Migration of Anson Call Family, 1838-1848 6

Outline of the State of Deseret and Utah Territory in
    the western United States 18

Oregon Trail and Lander Cut-off in western
    Wyoming and southeast Idaho 57
    Also key communities where Anson Vasco Call II resided

Star Valley, Wyoming 61

Map showing locations of Flying J facilities 233

Exhibits:

Exhibit I: Call Family Ancestors through the
              Thomas Call Line Beginning with the First
              American Immigrants 3

Exhibit II: Anson Call Family (parents, wives, and
              children) 36

Exhibit III: Children of Anson Vasco Call Who Resided in
              Chesterfield, Idaho 52

Exhibit IV: Anson Vasco Call II Family (wives and children) 76

Exhibit V: Thomas John Call Family (parents and children) 85

Preface

In 1993 I reached an agreement with Jay Call to write a history of his company, Flying J Inc. I had authored several management books including a business history, and Jay's company offered another opportunity to write about an entrepreneur who started with one retail outlet and, in just over thirty years, expanded it into a billion-dollar corporation based on sales.

As I started interviewing several of Jay's business associates, relatives, and childhood friends, I discovered that he had a rich pioneer and business heritage that deserved far greater examination than I had intended. Five generations back, his ancestor Anson Call had been a leading colonist under Brigham Young. Two generations later, Calls in the same family line were some of the first settlers of Star Valley, Wyoming. Following in these same enterprising tracks, but this time as entrepreneurs, were several of Jay's relatives: Reuel Call, his uncle, became a leading petroleum figure in the western United States, started a company to build airplanes, and founded Maverik, a chain of convenience stores in a five-state area; Reuel's brother and Jay's father, Osborne, parlayed a single service station in Soda Springs, Idaho, into a series of significant businesses before he died in his forties; another relative, Christian Call, was a leader in establishing a major California retail chain, Sav-On Drug; and the Coveys who began Little America and other mountain-states businesses are blood related.

I quickly became fascinated with the prospect of searching through the Call family lineage for related leadership qualities, "building" traits, and other characteristics. I became more intrigued after discovering a largely untapped information gold mine on each of the key figures. Anson Call had written a diary (later published) that is widely considered one of the most important sources on early Mormondom, although little of depth had been written on his life except for a master's degree thesis. Family histories existed on each male colonist in three generations of Jay's ancestral tree as well as on most of their wives (twelve in total since their husbands were polygamists). And Reuel Call, now in his late eighties, was active flying airplanes and running his private corporations, and therefore available for interview.

After stumbling onto this reservoir of historical data relevant to a noteworthy family history but not to a book about a company, I told Jay how unfortunate it would be to have this information and fail to put it into some useful, permanent form for family members. Jay agreed and we planned a publication of a hundred or so pages for distribution to close relatives.

After becoming more aware of Anson Call's contributions and those of his descendants, I became convinced that the material had significance beyond the immediate Call family. It was not only important data on the colonization of the Great Basin and Star Valley, but it contained significant lessons on several diverse subjects such as how to start a business, issues in handling family relations, and methods of supervision.

As the reader will discover, Jay's approach to those in his employ is to make sure they are on the right track and then give them essentially total freedom to pursue the tasks at hand. This is the relationship he developed with me regarding this manuscript. Nearly three years after these initial discussions, almost solely on my initiate, what was once perceived as a small family book has turned into a volume of several hundred pages covering Call family history from the Plymouth Colony in 1620 to the 1995 sales results of Call-dominated businesses.

Jay provided two specific instructions affecting the contents. First, it was not to be a book about him. He tends to shun the spotlight and likes to give credit to others. Initially he insisted that I restrict his accomplishments and those of Flying J's to one chapter. However, as he gained confidence in my ability to analyze events objectively, he agreed to expanding the company-related portion to include happenings and data that I considered significant.

His second directive was to write the book as an independent observer. He wanted a thorough, accurate history, even if major conflicts or human frailties were unveiled that could prove sensitive to certain family members. My job was to summarize and interpret happenings of historical significance, not to support any particular set of values, beliefs, or personalities. Any failings in this regard are mine, not his. In effect, it is my book written at arm's length from the sponsor.

The research rearoused my interest in issues that have long been important to me as a management professor, such as the "nature-nurture" controversy. Do individuals have certain traits because they inherited them from their parents, or does their environment dictate values, skills, interests, and intellect? This led to questions such as the following: Did Anson's success as a colonizer under Brigham Young have any connection to his descendants four generations later being successful entrepreneurs? How did Anson Vasco

II's colonization efforts in Star Valley affect his work habits and values and, in turn, influence his offspring? Where did Reuel Call pick up his early incentive to be an entrepreneur? How did the interaction between Reuel and Osborne influence their business pursuits and those of their children who followed similar careers? What are the sources of Jay's entrepreneurial and management skills? Do Mormon families whose pioneer ancestors suffered through anti-Mormon persecutions have different attitudes and a distinctive mentality because of these experiences?

Hopefully the book will be useful in helping the reader make such judgments. Conclusions regarding the influence of inheritance versus experience are not black and white. Each affects behavior in varying ways depending on the circumstances. I found it most interesting that many values held by early Call pioneers were carried down through several family generations, but this phenomenon could be explained by their home lives, community and religious values, and friends as well as by inheritance. What is unusual is to find such a large group of successful entrepreneurs, most with similar traits, coming from the same three-generation family line. Family ties, whether springing from inheritance or common experiences, are definitely involved.

The reader needs to be forewarned of the book's limited scope. It is not a genealogical, religious, or social history of the Call family. Rather it is an examination of the lives and especially the leadership skills of a select group of successful colonists and entrepreneurs with common blood ties. Although the book's focus is narrow, I have taken special care to consider events within their broader social, cultural, economic, and environmental contexts. The accurate interpretation of history is dependent on such a holistic approach.

By featuring a small select group, my intent is not to belittle or cast as less worthy those family members who have failed to experience comparable business success or who decided to pursue other occupations. Fortunately, people have diverse goals and interests and find a variety of valuable ways to contribute to society. As a business professor specializing in management and leadership, I was naturally inclined to research topics consistent with this expertise.

Also, the roles of the wives and their ancestors are essentially ignored, although their blood lines and influences would likely be equally important. But, as should be obvious, my decision to trace Call family roots back to 1620 made it impossible to track all descendants. Also with my focus on business pursuits, especially events leading to the development of Maverik Country Stores, Inc. and Flying J Inc., my concentration on male family members was inevitable.

As an academician, I found working on this project to be one of my most valuable educational experiences. In previous research, I had never undertaken a study requiring a detailed examination of events over 170 years, especially events that involved some of my own ancestors. Furthermore, many of Jay's associates and most of his close family are still alive, making it possible to obtain data and opinions firsthand. Also, I was given open access to Flying J corporate records, and ample information was available from other sources. This was capped by the freedom given me to move in any direction the research might lead under a schedule that was solely self imposed.

To acknowledge each person who provided support in preparing this manuscript would take several pages. Over 120 individuals gave time for interviews. Members and friends of the Call family have been extremely cooperative as have employees of Flying J. Chapters and portions of chapters have been reviewed by numerous Flying J employees, relatives, family acquaintances, and historians such as Leonard J. Arrington, George S. Ellsworth, F. Ross Peterson, and the late A. J. (Jeff) Simmonds. Primary editing tasks were handled by T.Y. Booth.

To keep the book more readable, I have used footnotes only for information purposes, not to document findings. A bibliography section on sources is included after the last chapter. Those interested in more complete documentation should feel free to contact me at my home in Logan, Utah.

Howard M. Carlisle
March 1996

CHAPTER
1

EARLY NEW ENGLAND AND CONVERSION TO MORMONISM

*T*o trace the early Call family roots in America requires a review of the history of the thirteen colonies followed by the founding and initial trials of the Church of Jesus Christ of Latter-day Saints (Mormon Church). Members of the family were involved in major events leading to both the establishment of the United States government and the early evolution of Mormonism. Going back twelve generations in the family tree from the current generation (the generation that includes the primary owners of Flying J Inc. and Maverik Country Stores, Inc.) to the first Call ancestors' arrival in America encompasses over 350 years. (For a chronological list of the generations, see Exhibit I, page 3). This first family to reach the New World was Thomas and Bennett Harrison Call with their three children, Margaret, Thomas, and John. They emigrated from Kent, England, arriving in Massachusetts in 1637. This was just seventeen years after the Mayflower landed and the pilgrims formed the settlement at Plymouth, placing them among the first 15,000 to emigrate from England to Massachusetts. The family settled in Charleston, a suburb north of Boston. John was only a few months old when the family left England. In 1657 John married Hannah Kettell, and one year later they had a son who took the name of John, later holding the title of Captain John Call. Captain Call and Martha Lowden had seven children, the fifth being Samuel, born June 6, 1698. Thus, there were four generations of Calls in Massachusetts before 1700.

It was Samuel's son, Joseph (born in 1742), who played an important role in the American struggle for independence. In June 1775 Joseph fought in the Battle of Bunker Hill (located in his hometown, Charleston) where British forces defeated the American militia. Joseph then joined the revolutionary army, serving under General George Washington from before the Declaration of Independence on July 4, 1776, until after the Revolutionary War ended in 1783. He later became a Baptist minister and for sixteen years organized churches from Boston up through New England and into Canada. (The only link in the genealogy that might be questionable is the parents of Joseph. Some sources show John as his father. Others indicate Samuel.)

Joseph and Mary Sanderson Call's youngest son (seventh child) Cyril, was born in Woodstock, Vermont, June 29, 1785. On April 6, 1806, he married Sarah (Sally) Tiffany. Sally's ancestors came over on the Mayflower, thus tying the Call line to the first settlers at Plymouth Rock. (Sally's genealogical line traces back to Sarah Cooke. Both of Sarah's parents, John Cooke and Sarah Warren, sailed to America on the Mayflower). Cyril also served in the militia, fighting three years against the British in the War of 1812, known as the "second war of independence." Soon after the war he moved to Ohio, then considered the western frontier. In October 1831 he was

Cyril Call

baptized by Mormon missionaries, thus becoming a member of the Latter-day Saints Church just eighteen months after it was formed. He helped build the Kirtland Temple near his home in Ohio and then took part in the exodus to Missouri when the Saints left Ohio in 1838. As persecution against the Mormons continued, Cyril and his family were forced from Missouri to Nauvoo, Illinois, then to Winter Quarters, Nebraska, and finally to Salt Lake City,

Exhibit I

CALL FAMILY ANCESTORS THROUGH THE THOMAS CALL LINE, BEGINNING WITH THE FIRST AMERICAN IMMIGRANTS

GENERATION	CALL FAMILY	RELEVANT WIFE	BORN	DIED
First	Thomas Call	Bennett Harrison	1597	May 1676
Second	John Call	Hannah Kettell	3/6/1636	4/19/1697
Third	John Call	Martha Lowden	1/20/1658	5/4/1732
Fourth	Samuel Call	Abigail Sprague	6/6/1698	Before 1748
Fifth	Joseph Call	Mary Sanderson	1742	1822-23
Sixth	Cyril Call	Sarah (Sally) Tiffany	6/29/1785	5/23/1873
Seventh	Anson Call	Mary Flint	5/13/1810	8/31/1890
Eighth	Anson Vasco Call I	Charlotte Holbrook	7/9/1834	8/14/1867
Ninth	Anson Vasco Call II	Rosa Emily Stayner	5/23/1855	10/12/1944
Tenth	Thomas Call	Ethel Grace Papworth	8/20/1884	6/11/1976
Eleventh	(Ten children including Reuel and Osborne Call)			
Twelfth	(Numerous grandchildren including Jay, Larry, Bill, and Val Call)			

arriving in 1848. He resided in Bountiful, Utah, until he died on May 23, 1873, at age eighty-seven.

It was Cyril and Sally Tiffany Call's second of thirteen children, Anson Call, who became one of Brigham Young's chief lieutenants in colonizing the Great Basin region of the West—an area nearly 1000 miles square consisting primarily of semi-arid desert. Anson was born in Vermont on May 13, 1810, and at age seven his family moved to Ohio. At twenty-three, he married Mary Flint, the daughter of a wealthy Ohio farmer. Mary was well educated whereas Anson had limited education, having spent most of his early years working on the family farm, in part because of sickness in the family. One year later, in 1834, after three years of studying the Bible and the Book of Mormon, Anson renounced his Methodist faith and joined the Mormon Church, bravely announcing his decision before the local Methodist congregation. He was baptized by William Smith, a brother of Joseph Smith, the Church's founder, and confirmed by David Whitmer, one of the three witnesses to the Book of Mormon. Catching the missionary spirit, Anson quickly made thirty converts including his wife, who, because of her conversion, was disinherited by her father. After accepting Mormonism, Anson moved his family to within thirty miles of the Kirtland Temple and, like his father, helped build that structure. At the time he became well acquainted with the founders of the LDS religion. He had many close contacts with Joseph Smith since the Mormon movement at the time was small. Kirtland, the Church's headquarters, had a population of only 2,000. On one occasion in Kirtland, he offered $500 as bond for Joseph Smith when he was under arrest.

After continued harassment, in 1838 Anson and his father were some of the first Mormons to leave, traveling by steamboat down the Ohio and up the Mississippi and Missouri Rivers to Independence, Missouri. They first purchased land in Caldwell County north of Independence where Missouri officials earlier had given Mormons permission to settle. Anson and Cyril then acquired land and started farms on the Grand River in Daviess County north of Far West, Adam-ondi-Ahman, and other Mormon settlements. Mormons had resided for several years in Jackson County near Independence, Missouri, where Joseph Smith had established a mission backed by a group of converts, primarily from New York State. The city of Independence had special significance for the Mormons since Joseph Smith prophesied that some day it would be the center of Zion. The main purpose of the mission was to convert the local Lamanites—the Book of Mormon term for Indians. Within a few years the area's non-Mormon residents, wary of the growing dominance of Independence and the claim that it was to be the capital of Mormondom, forced the unwanted Saints to relocate on the sparsely settled prairie in the counties to the north.

After Cyril and Anson had their farms laid out on the banks of the Grand River, Cyril returned and brought their families from Kirtland as part of the 500-to-600-strong Mormon migration known as the Kirtland Camp. Continued fear of clashes with the Mormons caused authorities to enlarge the state militia for the purposes of maintaining order and monitoring the expansion of the suspect Mormon community, now stretching over four counties in the northwest section of Missouri.

This antagonism and distrust of Mormons partially resulted from Zion's Camp, a group of 200 armed men that Joseph Smith led from Kirtland in April 1834 to recover property church members had been forced to abandon six months earlier when they left Jackson County. However, when his forces were weakened by cholera (fourteen died), Joseph saw the cause was lost, and he disbanded his small brigade. Even though the Missourians were apprehensive over this show of force, their primary fear was not Mormon military strength or even what they considered their fanaticism and eccentric beliefs. Their biggest concern, after witnessing Mormon communities spring up almost overnight, was that their growing numbers could result in dominant political power.

As violent outbreaks between the Mormons and non-Mormons accelerated in Missouri's northern counties, LDS Church leaders were uncertain over how to proceed. Should they use weapons and match force with force or pursue a course of pacifism? In 1838 the Sons of Dan (generally called Danites), a relatively small secret fraternal organization was established; they were committed to using force to defend the rights of Mormons and to retaliate against aggressors. As the Danites became more active, hostilities increased and the possibility of full-scale combat became imminent. (In an interview in 1885 with Mormon historian B. H. Roberts, Anson acknowledged that he was a Danite.) The situation became inflamed when Governor Boggs, on October 27, 1838, issued a directive that Mormons "must be exterminated or driven from the state." Three days later a mob massacred eighteen Mormon males (two were boys) and wounded thirteen women and children at Haun's Mill, a small Mormon outpost a few miles northeast of Far West.

Given these events, before the end of the year Anson and his family followed the advice of Joseph Smith and abandoned their farms and timberland and gathered in Adam-ondi-Ahman, the Mormon community north of Far West in Daviess County. Anson gave up his home and 700 acres. They loaded their possessions into six wagons, moved into Adam-ondi-Ahman, and prepared for attack. Then, in February 1839, less than a year after arriving in Missouri, the undermanned Saints in Far West and Adam-ondi-Ahman, following a wise decision by their leaders, surrendered their arms and gave up peacefully to the state militia. The commander of the militia then issued an ultimatum which gave the Saints ten days to leave the state or their homes and property would be destroyed. Before departing, Anson tried to obtain payment for corn he had grown on shares the previous summer and to be

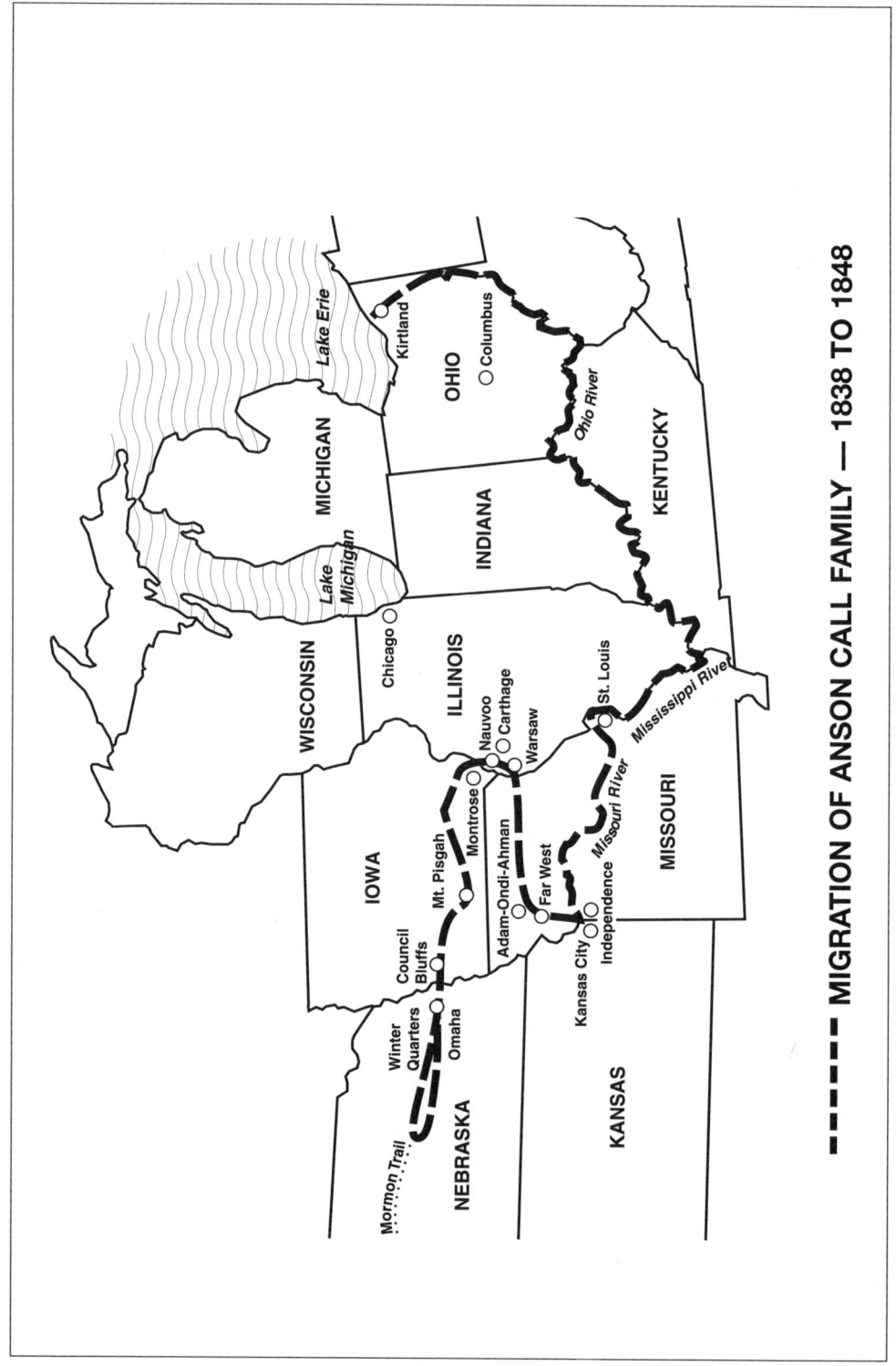

reimbursed for other property he had abandoned. In the process he was captured several times and beaten by mobs. After these experiences, Anson finally gave up hope of receiving compensation. (Two of Anson's beating are recorded in *History of the Church, Period I, Volume III*, written by Joseph Smith and his clerks.)

The actions of Governor Boggs and the militia sent 15,000 Mormons scurrying back across Missouri, uncertain of their destination. They could not escape by going west since they were not prepared for a long journey beyond the frontier. Their hope was that Iowa or Illinois would give them asylum. The migration was difficult since they were again forced to leave in the middle of winter, breaking a trail through snow nearly to their knees. The problems of Anson and his family were compounded when, in February 1839, amid a severe storm, their wagon turned over in a creek destroying part of their already limited food supplies and other possessions. They finally reached the Mississippi River April 25, traversing it at Warsaw, Illinois; they were the first Mormons to do so at this location. There they settled down again, praying they had finally found a safe haven.

Some of their early visitors were Joseph and Hyrum Smith along with Sidney Rigdon, all of whom had recently escaped from the jail in Liberty, Missouri, a community just north of Independence. At the time, Joseph told the group of his plans to build a community upstream in Illinois in a swampy bend of the Mississippi River known as Commerce, later renamed Nauvoo.

In the spring, Cyril rented a farm five miles from Warsaw, and Anson obtained a contract with the local railroad and hired other Mormons to split rails. Most of the Mormon community was engaged in founding Nauvoo, fifteen miles north along the river. In 1842, Joseph Smith counseled Anson to move to Nauvoo. Before moving, however, he was called to serve a six-month proselyting mission in Ohio. Upon his return, he found his family in poverty, a common condition among Mormons at the time. Near Nauvoo, he hurriedly built a small brick home and raised a crop of corn while quarrying stone for the temple. He also served as a member of the Nauvoo Legion, the Mormon military force under General Joseph Smith.

On August 6, 1842, when a new Masonic Lodge (the Rising Sun Lodge of the Ancient York Masons) was being established in Montrose, Iowa, Anson participated in an event that received a prominent place in early Mormon history. On this hot summer day, Joseph Smith raised a glass of water and prophesied that the Latter-day Saints would eventually migrate to the Rocky Mountains, noting that the cold water in his glass tasted much like that of the water in the crystal streams found in those majestic mountains.

He said that several men in the audience were destined to perform great work in the land. Pointing to Anson he proclaimed, "There is Anson. He shall go and assist in building cities from one end of the country to the other." Anson was startled and taken aback by such a declaration, noting, "I queried in my head how it was possible for me to accomplish that great work with the persecution, the poverty, and sickness that I had thus far to contend with." At the time, little did Anson realize the magnitude of his future role in developing the desert regions of the West.[1]

The Call families remained in Nauvoo until after 1844 when unrest among the non-Mormons again erupted, resulting in the martyrdom of Joseph Smith and his brother Hyrum. Since the founding of the church, Joseph was accustomed to being on the run and forced into hiding as a means of avoiding warrants for his arrest and escaping vigilante action. In June 1844, 500 men under Robert Smith, the Carthage justice of the peace, sought to arrest the church leader. According to Joseph, Judge Thomas, the circuit judge of the district, advised him to appoint delegates to visit the different county precincts and seek to negotiate a peaceful settlement. Anson was assigned with David Evans to visit the precincts in the south part of the county under Colonel Williams. After staying overnight with Anson's father in Warsaw, they attempted to locate Colonel Williams but he was not available. An angry crowd of fifty armed men threatened to put the delegates sent by Joseph Smith into the Mississippi River and "make fish bait out of them." They also claimed they would do the same to Judge Thomas if he gave the Mormons encouragement to do other than abide by the wishes of the justice of the peace. They let Anson and David get a head start by mounting their horses, but then chased the pair north toward Nauvoo.

After relating their experience to Joseph, he assigned Anson and David to deliver a letter and obtain an interview with Judge Thomas, who was holding court in Knoxville, eighty miles away. When they arrived, Judge Thomas was reluctant to see them. Finally, under pressure from the pair, he gave them a letter for Joseph stating the following:

> In pursuing your letter I find that you are mistaken in the instructions that I gave you while at Nauvoo. Now, sir, I know of no course for you to pursue to answer to the requirements of the law, but to suffer your-

---

1. It should be noted that some confusion exists over the date this event took place. In the original handwritten diary, Anson lists July 14, 1843. However, in the History of the Church, Volume V, authored by Joseph Smith and his scribes, the date is shown as August 6, 1842.

self to be taken by the officer holding the writ, and go before the justice of the peace who issued the same, and have an investigation of the matter. It is the officer's duty to protect you. This the law requires, and I cannot as an officer of the law give you different instructions.

When Anson and David insisted that Joseph would be killed if he surrendered himself to the Carthage justice of the peace, the judge's response was, "Would it not be better that one or two men be killed than a whole community be destroyed?"

Recognizing the danger their Prophet was in, Anson and David hastily returned to Nauvoo on June 20, 1844, intending to inform Joseph that he should not give himself up. When they arrived in Nauvoo, Joseph's bodyguards would not let them see him. Later that afternoon Joseph's wife, Emma, took the letter, saying that Joseph would receive it, but she refused them admission. It is unlikely Joseph ever read the letter. He had left or was in the process of leaving with Hyrum to hide across the river in Iowa. On June 24, two days later, they gave themselves up to the Carthage justice of the peace and were incarcerated in the Carthage jail, only to be killed by a mob on June 27, 1844. Joseph had been arrested over thirty-five times previously. On this occasion, the charges were for treason and inciting riots.

Anson was one of the guards at the Nauvoo Temple when Joseph and Hyrum were murdered in Carthage jail. As he was leaving his early morning watch, he recalls how Orrin Porter Rockwell came wildly riding through the streets, yelling in language interspersed by profanities common to his speech, that the Prophet had been killed.

During the next year mobs continued to harass the Mormons. Homes and farms in the communities surrounding Nauvoo were frequently burned. In the fall of 1845, Anson was one of a hundred Mormons assigned to assist Sheriff Backenstos in preventing more destruction by those bent on driving them from Illinois. Mormons assisted the sheriff because he could not obtain enough non-Mormon volunteers. Anson got special permission to look after his father's property to the south in Warsaw. However, Anson arrived too late. A mob had moved through the area and set fire to many farmhouses. After a search of the surroundings near Cyril's burning home, Anson found his father and family scattered about hiding in cornfields.

As in Iowa, the primary cause of local anti-Mormon hatred was the continuing fear of their growing power. At the time of Joseph Smith's death, the population of Nauvoo had expanded to between 15,000 to 20,000, making it the largest city in Illinois. Under Nauvoo's charter, the city was essentially a state within a state, having its own laws, police system, courts, and militia. Before Joseph's death, it was again becoming increasingly evident to Mormon leaders that peaceful coexistence with their Gentile neighbors was impossible, and after his martyrdom, the situation became more untenable. As a means of forcing the Mormons to leave, in late 1845 the Illinois legislature revoked Nauvoo's charter and, in the process, nullified the legality of the Nauvoo Legion. Unlike Governor Boggs in Missouri, the Illinois governor did not issue an order requiring the Mormons to leave, but he strongly advised them to, stating that "they will never be able to live at peace with their neighbors in Illinois."

Thus in the fall of 1845, reacting to this strong pressure, the Mormon hierarchy made the decision to abandon Illinois and re-establish their Zion in an unpopulated area of the West, hopefully outside of the territorial United States. This gave them three logical choices—Oregon, California, or the Great Basin region, then still part of Mexico. Anson, along with his fellow Saints, spent the winter of 1845–46 helping make wagons in preparation for the long journey. All of Nauvoo's buildings were converted into workshops, and several thousand wagons were made. Fearing arrest, LDS Church leaders were the first to depart in February 1846. The bulk of the Mormon population had vacated by April. Anson and his family did not leave until May 2, after selling their house for less than one-third of its value. His late departure was likely due to Mary's poor health but he was also one who applied strong pressure for the Mormons to receive compensation for the property they were vacating. Mary had only one functioning lung (attributed to her having tuberculosis as a child), and she had experienced continuing problems since the birth of twins in 1841, one of whom was stillborn. Her health turned worse after the birth of her last child, a boy named Hyrum, on December 3, 1845, just four months before the mass evacuation.

It was extremely difficult for the Saints to abandon this lovely city. It was the largest in the upper Mississippi Valley and represented one of the remarkable achievements in early Mormon history. It was built in six years primarily by a group of 15,000 destitute refugees from Missouri who had fled in disarray with their prophet and other leaders in jail. "Nauvoo the beautiful" was known not merely for its size, but also for its square city blocks, fine buildings, and tree-lined streets.

Anson and his family were fortunate they did not evacuate with the first group in February. Mud, rain, and snow made travel slow, the disease rate high, and daily existence onerous—one of the most trying periods in the entire migration west. Leaving under better conditions in May, Anson took a

Anson Call

Mary Flint Call

more direct route across Iowa rather than going south as did the main contingent under Brigham Young. Cyril had a two-week start on Anson, but his son caught up with him at Mt. Pisgah. Together they met the main body of Mormon immigrants near Council Bluffs. The Calls' journey across Iowa to the Missouri River required approximately six weeks, less than one-half the time taken by the first company. However, Anson and Mary did not escape hardship. Hyrum, their newborn son, died during their travels on June 15. He was buried at Cedar Creek under an oak tree in a grave unmarked except for his name carved into the tree. Cyril Moroni, their second son, age eight, died three weeks later on July 9 after they had crossed the Missouri River at Bellevue, Nebraska, leaving them with just three children.

Although it was now the middle of July, President Brigham Young was still intent on reaching the Rocky Mountains before fall. President Young and Heber C. Kimball each organized a company of seventy-five wagons for this purpose. Brigham Young put Anson in charge of the first ten, a group that included his father Cyril and two of his brothers, Harvey and Josiah. For Brigham to place Anson as head of his first ten wagons was a significant gesture. It displayed the extreme confidence Brigham had in him as a leader, scout, and frontiersman. After proceeding over one hundred miles along the Platte River to Loup Fork, Brigham decided to abandon the journey until spring, primarily because of the delay and physical drain from their arduous trip across Iowa. Also they would be short of forage since the Indians had burned the grass in front of them. At Brigham's direction, the company built a fort of 125 log houses on Running Water River in Nebraska and wintered there.

When spring arrived, President Young instructed the group to return to Winter Quarters (Florence), Nebraska, the primary Mormon community in the region. The populace there suffered from such illness during the winter that writer Wallace Stegner described it as a plague. Hundreds became sick and many died. When Anson arrived, Brigham directed him to take his company across the river, break up the prairie, and plant crops at Pottawatomie, Iowa. The intent was to create a temporary community on Indian lands to serve as a vital supply point in provisioning the wagon trains that would move through in the next two years. It was also to raise funds to pay debts other Mormons had earlier left behind when they withdrew from Iowa. Furthermore, Brigham instructed the men to let the wives and children care for the farms while they sought employment in the surrounding area, thus giving them funds to purchase other provisions required for the trek west. Anson and several close relatives and friends in the fall harvested hay and during the winter worked as colliers supplying coal to the surrounding communities.

Accordingly, a disappointed Anson and others in his charge did not accompany Brigham Young and the first Mormon settlers in 1847 when they moved to the western slopes of the Rocky Mountains by the Great Salt Lake. The first company under Brigham Young consisted of 148 members, 144 of whom were men. Companies that followed later that summer swelled the valley's population to 2,000 in the first year. Six weeks after his arrival on July 24th, Brigham returned to Nebraska to oversee the evacuation of Winter Quarters and to prepare for the mass exodus the next year.

The caravan in 1848 was organized by Brigham Young into three divisions. In total almost 2,500 people and 800 to 900 wagons were involved. Brigham captained the first group of 397 wagons. This time Anson was in charge of twenty wagons under President Young. Leaving in May to cross Nebraska, the companies followed the trail blazed the prior year by Brigham's first pioneer company. Rather than following the Oregon Trail on the south side of the Platte River, this route wound along the north bank. Brigham's reasons for using this alternate course were to avoid possible hostile crowds and benefit from grasslands that were not as heavily grazed. At Fort Laramie, the halfway point, they joined the Oregon Trail, following it to Fort Bridger where the Oregon Trail proceeds northwest and the Mormon Trail turns southwest across the rugged Wasatch Mountains and into the Great Salt Lake Valley.

The trip was made with minimum difficulty compared to most mass migrations of the period. The only injury was when a lady broke her leg by getting it caught under a wagon wheel. The bone was set by Anson and Brigham Young. Anson lost part of his cattle in the notorious stretch of alkali flats and bad water just before Independence Rock in Wyoming. Later, on September 14, they experienced an early snowfall in the Wind River area. However, being less that 200 miles from the valley, the snow could not dampen their spirits. According to his diary, Anson and his family made the memorable descent into the Great Salt Lake Valley with the first company on September 19, 1848, although official Church records place the arrival date as September 20. (Anson and his family were likely part of an advance party, since he was known for constantly wanting to push ahead.) Brigham Young and his fellow travelers were met by a large welcome party, anxious to see their Prophet return. For the Calls, it was a fulfillment of their prayers. After more than a dozen years of being nomads, they were eagerly looking forward to being in a land where they could help build a Mormon empire without fear of violence from apprehensive neighbors.

CHAPTER
2

ANSON CALL THE COLONIZER

*T*hree days after reaching their Mormon homeland, Anson took his wife and three children to North Canyon (now Bountiful) ten miles north of Salt Lake City. The Calls' three children were Anson Vasco (fourteen), Mary Vashta (twelve), and Chester (seven). Bountiful became Anson's base of operations for the next half century. It was the second community settled by Mormons in Utah, formed in 1847 by several immigrants.[1] For a short time after Anson and his relatives arrived, the community was known as Call's Settlement. The name was changed four times between then and 1855 when "Bountiful" became the official title. From 1848 to 1855 the most commonly used name was North Canyon or North Canyon Ward.

Because of their arrival late in the autumn of 1848, Anson did not have time to build a permanent log cabin. He constructed an Indian wickiup, a cone-shaped hut composed of willows and branches for structure overlaid by a mixture of leaves, grass, and mud. When he arrived, Anson's assets consisted of four oxen, four cows, two calves, one pig, one sheep, and six chickens. However, he did not leave all his misfortune on the Mormon Trail or in

---

1. Some historians argue that Holladay was second and Bountiful third.

the Midwest. The hardship was too much for the pig which died within a week. An Indian dog killed his sheep the following day, and his best ox drowned in a spring the day after. Not to be held back, Anson managed to cultivate ten acres before snowfall by rigging up a harness and using his cows and remaining ox to break up the virgin soil.

The winter proved to be one of the family's most difficult trials. The weather was severe, and few of the 2,400 new valley residents that summer came early enough to plant crops. The immigrants in 1848 doubled the valley's population, putting pressure on a food supply that was already limited because of the prior year's sparse harvest. Wheat flour was especially scarce so Anson and his family had a continual diet of corn meal. On one occasion, Mary chastised Anson after he looked at his bowl of corn meal mush and commented, "I refuse to thank the Lord for this old corn meal." Before the winter was over the corn meal was gone and the family was forced to eat parched corn. It was common for families to be on half rations and, even at that, many resorted to consuming thistle roots, camas bulbs, crows, coyotes, and essentially anything considered edible.

At the close of the first winter, Anson built a log cabin, cultivated more land, and planted five bushels of seed. His newly tilled ground required constant care and fighting an infestation of crickets before he harvested 200 bushels of grain. (Anson's fascination with and skill in remembering numbers and other such details make his diaries of unusual historical significance.)

In the fall of 1848, Anson was called as Bishop of the North Canyon Ward (sometimes spelled North Kanyon), the second person to assume this position, and he was finally looking forward to a more normal life on the frontier. After building and abandoning a minimum of six homes with adjoining farmlands in the prior fifteen years, he obviously relished the thoughts of establishing his roots and giving his family a feeling of permanency. With more favorable weather and improvements in his farm, his harvest the second year was five times more productive than in 1849, yielding 1,000 bushels of grain. However, as often happened with early Mormon settlers, he had hardly settled in before he was again on the move at the direction of Brigham Young.

In 1849 when he took up his permanent residence in the Great Salt Lake Valley, President Young unveiled his grandiose plans for the Kingdom of God, stating,

> . . . we shall build a city and a temple to the Most High God in this place. We will extend our settlements to the east and west, to the north

and to the south, and we will build towns and cities by the hundreds, and thousands of Saints will gather in from the nations of the earth. This will become the great highway of nations.

Before the year was out, at Brigham's direction, the colonists established twenty-six towns and, in the process, opened five major valleys to land settlement. Initially, few restrictions stood in the way of Brigham's expansionist plans. The region had few permanent residents other than Indians. This was because of limited fresh water, a scarcity of suitable farmland, and a climate subject to temperature extremes. Furthermore, it was blocked on the east by the rugged Rocky Mountains and on the west by vast deserts and the Great Salt Lake.

In 1847 when the Mormons first settled in the area, it was part of Mexico. At the time the United States was at war with Mexico, but hostilities were terminated February 2, 1848, with the Treaty of Guadalupe Hidalgo. Under the provisions of the treaty, the vast regions known as New Mexico and California were ceded to the United States, and the Rio Grande River was confirmed as the border between Mexico and Texas. Thus before Anson and his family arrived, the Great Basin was already part of the United States.

Ever aggressive, Brigham Young got a jump on the government in Washington by proposing a State of Deseret. In the spring of 1849 this self-proclaimed provisional state was established with "Governor" Brigham Young as head of the executive branch. The provisional State of Deseret extended roughly from the crest of the Sierra Nevada to the crest of the Rocky Mountains, an area measuring nearly a 1,000 miles in both directions. It was a vast untamed region constituting almost one-sixth of the United States. One key feature Brigham insisted be within the state was an outlet to the Pacific Ocean in Southern California, thus providing the Mormon colony a potential route for its converts migrating from abroad. In all, to Brigham, it was a step toward fulfilling his dream to create an independent commonwealth and the first stage of the Kingdom of God.

Within a year, the national Congress aborted Brigham's plans by establishing the Territory of Utah September 9, 1850. (However, the general assembly under Brigham Young did not formally dissolve itself until April 5, 1851.) The Territory of Utah was approximately half the size of the State of Deseret, eliminating entirely the portions in current-day California, Idaho, Oregon, Arizona, and New Mexico. Politicians in Washington were wary of the Mormon failure to differentiate between church and state and wanted to keep the religious sect under control. Besides, the area lacked the 60,000

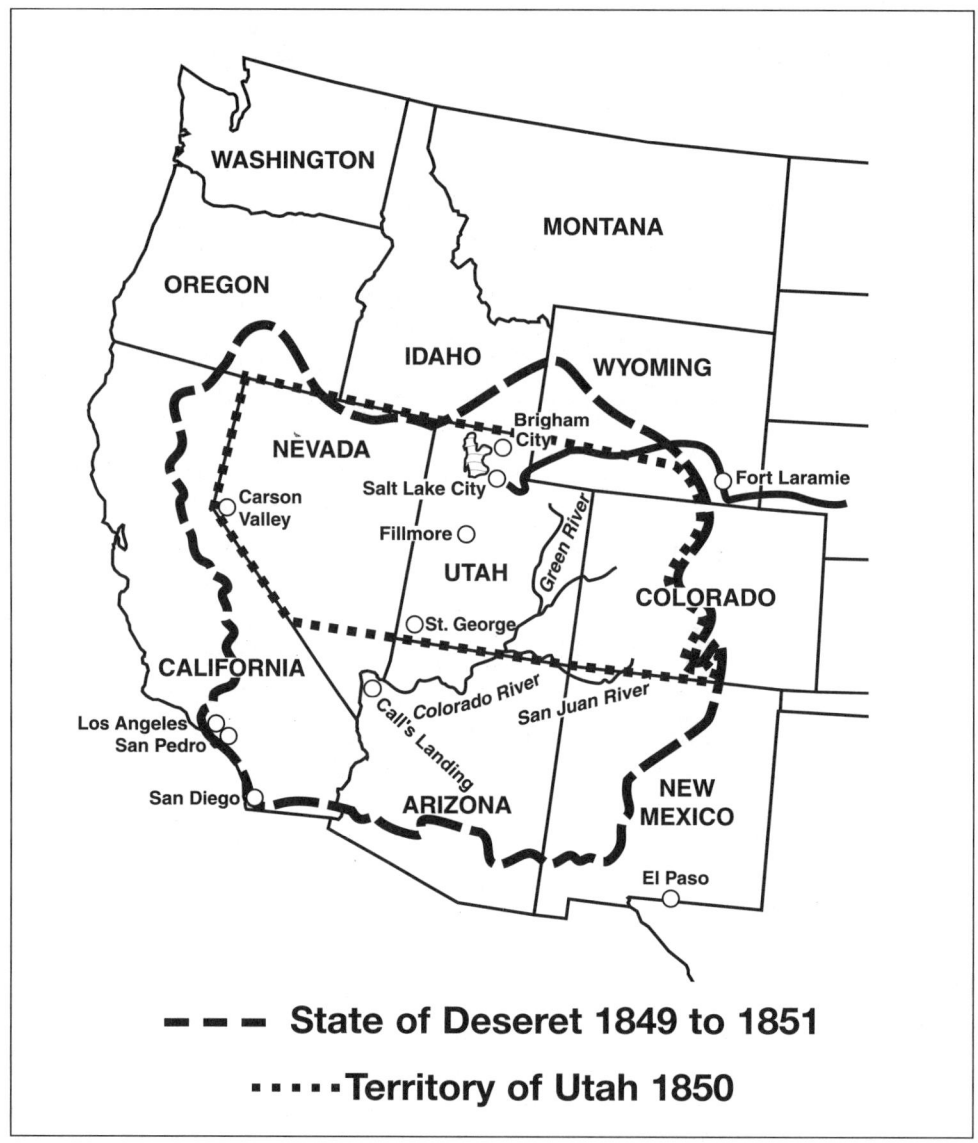

- - - State of Deseret 1849 to 1851

· · · · · Territory of Utah 1850

residents required to apply for statehood. Brigham preferred statehood over territoriality since the citizens of a state elect their officers whereas territorial officials are appointed by the U.S. government. However, in a concession to the Mormon population, President Fillmore appointed Brigham as the first governor.

The U.S. government's reduction of the region under Brigham's control did not dampen his expansionist ambitions. In 1850, at his behest, seventeen more communities were settled. Within a decade the number of Mormon settlements totalled over one hundred, several far outside the Territory of Utah, such as those at San Bernardino, California, and Lemhi, Idaho. Initially, Brigham perceived this kingdom to be exclusively Mormon, warning the Saints not to "have any trade or commerce with the Gentile World." Furthermore, Mormons "who dealt with outsiders would be cut off from the Church." However, increased traffic sparked by the California gold rush brought much needed trade to the "Crossroads of the West," and Brigham eventually changed his mind, although he never quit demanding that his Mormon dominion be self-sufficient.

Anson's role as a colonizer began in 1850 when Brigham Young called him, along with many others, to help develop the Little Salt Lake Valley area in southern Utah and create a central community, later named Parowan, in Iron County. The party, under Apostle George A. Smith (a cousin of Joseph Smith), was composed of one hundred wagons and 138 members, only thirteen of whom were women or children. Anson led the first fifty wagons that left in December. During the journey, the company faced many hardships, including attacks by Indians and temperatures that dipped to 21 degrees below zero on Christmas night. Five days after their arrival on January 12, 1851, the county was organized and Anson was elected justice of the peace. He also served as first presiding elder (branch president) and took the lead in exploring and settling the area. Parowan was the most southerly Mormon community at the time and one of only five cities incorporated by the General Assembly of the State of Deseret on February 6, 1851. In March, Anson returned to Salt Lake City and enlisted fifty-three more settlers to follow him back to the small southern outpost. Parowan never grew to be a large community, but its settlement clearly demonstrated Brigham Young's intention to expand his new Zion into this region.

Before returning to Parowan on April 15, 1851, Anson, like many prominent Mormons, entered into polygamy, marrying Ann Mariah Bowen (sometimes spelled Maria) who was to accompany him on many of his journeys, partially due to Mary's poor health. At the time, Anson was forty and Mariah was seventeen. In 1839, when she was five, her family had become acquainted with Anson as a missionary in Indiana. The family later lived in Iowa across from Nauvoo until her father died in 1847. In 1849, when just fifteen, she drove a wagon with two yoke of oxen the entire length of the Mormon Trail as part of the Orson Hyde company.

Anson's marriage to Mariah reflects how matrimony often occurred at the time. As Anson prepared for his return to Parowan, Brigham Young encouraged him to take his family, but this was not possible due to Mary's

Mariah Bowen Call

health. Accordingly, Brigham told Anson to find another wife that could accompany him. Anson was not sure how Mary would react, but he gave his concurrence to Brigham, noting that he had no one in mind. The conversation took place at the start of general conference prior to Anson making a report on developments in Parowan. As Brigham looked over the audience, he spotted Mariah and suggested that she would be appropriate. The next day Anson was introduced to Mariah in Brigham's office. Three days later, Anson and Mariah were married by Brigham Young. Shortly after, they left with the other settlers for Iron County.

Joseph Smith's revelation making plural marriage a part of the Mormon religion occurred as early as 1831. However, apparently it was a decade later at Nauvoo before he, Brigham Young, and others married additional wives. It was not officially announced as part of Mormon religious teachings until 1852 when the Saints were safely in Utah, a year after Anson married for the second time. A popular misconception is that only 2 or 3 percent of Mormon adults practiced polygamy. In terms of eligible LDS adults, the more accurate figure is 15 to 20 percent (likely 10 percent of the men and 20 to 30 percent of the women), although polygamy totals varied depending on the community and the religious leader in charge. According to the diaries and family histories of Anson's first three plural wives, each marriage resulted from specific direction by Brigham Young. In later years, Anson taught his sons that it was necessary to have a minimum of four wives to attain the highest level in heaven, the Celestial Kingdom. (Anson's wives and children are shown in Exhibit II, page 36.)

Before the summer was over, the First Presidency of the Mormon Church visited Parowan and, noting the progress being made, instructed Anson and Mariah to return to Salt Lake City and enlist another fifty families to start a settlement in the Pahvant (also spelled Pavant) Valley, an Indian name for "close to water." This valley is some 150 miles south of Salt Lake City and 93 miles north and slightly east of Parowan.

This was one of Anson's most important assignments. President (and now Governor) Young, through an act of the territorial legislature dated October 4, 1851, designated the proposed community as the future territorial capital supplanting Salt Lake City. This decision was made in recognition of the Pahvant Valley being situated near the geographic center of the territory whereas Salt Lake City was well to the north. Also, at the time, the intent was to expand more to the south based on the common belief that the land north of Ogden was less suitable for agriculture. The community was named Fillmore after President Millard Fillmore who had recently appointed Brigham Young territorial governor. At the October 1851 LDS General Conference, Anson was designated as president of the colony. He was also made probate judge of Millard County by the territorial legislature that was meeting concurrently. After Anson arrived in Fillmore in October, Brigham Young also installed him as presiding elder (branch president) and Indian agent.

When Anson, Mariah, and his fellow colonists reached the Pahvant Valley, they met an eager President Young, Orson Pratt, and a group of forty Mormons (primarily lawmakers) who were laying out a city plan along Chalk Creek and selecting a site for the territorial capitol building. Under Anson's leadership, his company immediately began to erect several cabins in fort style, arranged in a peculiar triangular shape with Chalk Creek running through one side. Under adverse wintery conditions, Anson and his party completed thirty cabins and a log schoolhouse within ninety days. They then built roads, a grist mill, and a saw mill, and started cultivating a large tract of land. In a letter to Brigham Young dated November 24, 1851 (printed later in the January 24, 1852, issue of the *Deseret News*), Anson explained the difficulties of colonizing the semi-arid lands of the West:

> We have had an addition of three [people] to our camp since you left; have built a corral according to your instructions, including about two and a half acres of ground. We found, upon trial, that the ground was so dry and hard, being also rocky, that it was next to impossible to stockade or picket in our houses with the tools we have to work with; so we have built our houses in close order, having our doors and windows on the outside.

In the first few years, difficulty with Indians forced the settlers to construct a fort of stone and adobe. In August 1852, Anson was elected to represent Millard County in the territorial legislature. In March 1854, with one wing of the state house nearing completion, the fort in place, and the community well established (308 members were in Anson's ward), he was

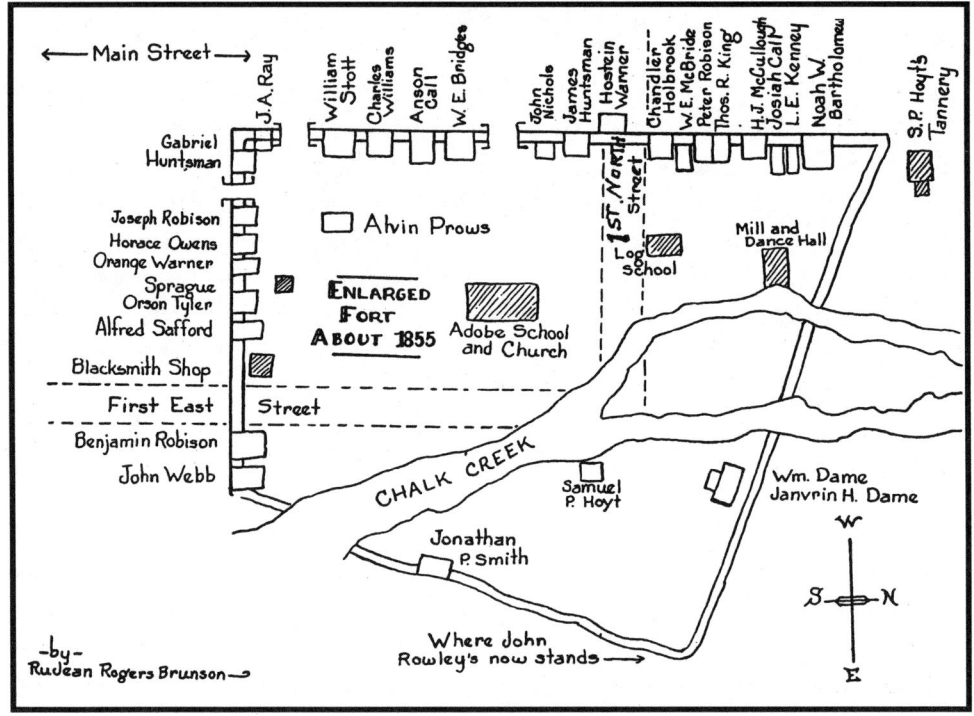

*Layout of original Fillmore fort established by Anson Call.
(Courtesy of Daughters of the Utah Pioneers,* Milestones of Millard, *1951.)*

relieved of his assignment and returned to his Bountiful home.

The fifth meeting of the Utah territorial legislature opened in Fillmore on December 10, 1855, remaining in session for just over a month. In December 1856 the legislature convened in Fillmore, but soon adjourned to reconvene in Salt Lake after Brigham Young abandoned the idea of transferring the capital. The resolution to keep the capital in Salt Lake City was passed primarily due to rapid expansion adjacent to the city along the Wasatch Front.

In the autumn of 1854, Anson launched an undertaking that eventually resulted in a 1,000-acre farm in Box Elder County. It was located six miles north of the closest community, Box Elder Fort, founded three years earlier. When Anson arrived, the community at Box Elder Fort (now Brigham City) consisted of approximately 150 families. It was an area where one of his descendants over a century later would start a company, Flying J, that would grow to be the country's leader in diesel retail sales. A major incentive leading Anson to establish this farm was to provide employment for poverty-stricken converts to the Mormon Church brought from Europe through the Perpetual Emigration Fund. It was also to teach them how to farm in this semi-arid region since most had other occupations and none had experience in this type of farming. The Perpetual Emigration Fund was used to pay transportation for Church members to Utah who were too poor to arrange their own financing. In turn, once settled, they were to repay their travel costs. The Fund was extremely successful, aiding 40,000 converts in their passage to Zion. Thus, Anson's farm in Box Elder County did not result from a Brigham Young colonization directive, such as the Parowan and Fillmore settlements, though Anson gained prior approval from the Church president.

One year later while visiting Anson's Box Elder farm (at the time the most northerly Mormon outpost from Salt Lake City), Brigham Young counseled him to build a fort to protect himself and his workers from possible attack by Indians. Thus Call's Fort was constructed, serving as a refuge for travelers and as security for those living in the area. The fort's stone walls were three feet thick and eight feet high. The interior was 120 feet square, containing an 18-by- 40-foot adobe home for Mariah and their two children, both born earlier in Fillmore. Eventually he had two adobe houses and three log structures. Within the fort was a blacksmith shop and a Burr mill (two circular stones for grinding grain). Subsequently, when the fort became a

Call's Fort monument erected in 1933 on State Highway 69, Honeyville, Utah.

stop on the stage line, he added a tavern and accommodations for travelers. Later his two brothers, Omer and Homer, became part owners.

The small settlement never did develop into a permanent community. In 1855 Anson hired Thomas Harper to manage the farm, and the area south of the fort to Brigham City became known as Harper Ward. The fort is no longer standing. A monument identifying the location is on the west side of State Highway 69 at the southern entrance to Honeyville. The monument, made of stone from the fort, was dedicated July 24, 1933.

With farms in Bountiful and Box Elder County and official matters that frequently required his presence in Fillmore, Anson was constantly on the move at a time when horses were the swiftest means of transportation. His life became more complex in May of 1855 when United States Marshal Joseph L. Heywood, an acquaintance since their days in Kirtland, appointed him as his deputy for the territory. Heywood was a Mormon initially appointed by Brigham Young as the marshal for the state of Deseret. When Utah Territory was established, Heywood was appointed U.S. Marshal for Utah by President Millard Fillmore in 1851 and reappointed by President Franklin Pierce in 1855. Heywood had selected some of the most renowned and feared frontiersmen as his deputies, the first being Orrin Porter Rockwell. Although Anson did not share Rockwell's reputation as a gun-slinging avenger, he was known as someone who could hold his own with the frontiersmen of his day, and he had the courage and skill to enforce the law and provide protection to federal officials and territorial officers. Such a reputation was highly unusual for a man small in stature. Anson was five-feet-five-inches tall and weighed 135 pounds. Most notable in his reputation was his skill in being able to peacefully negotiate with Indian tribes.

Soon after his appointment, Heywood accompanied a federal judge on a visit to Nevada and California, leaving Anson in charge. His task was made more difficult three months later when Judge W. W. Drummond, a Mormon antagonist, arrived in the territory to take charge of the federal courts. Anson's tenure as a deputy did not last long. In 1856 just before the Utah War, officials in Washington were becoming more concerned about the independent theocracy in Utah, and a non-Mormon U.S. Marshal was appointed.

When Anson returned from Fillmore, he stayed active in politics. In 1855 when Utah had only one political party, he was the nominee as the Davis County representative to the legislature. However, four days before the election he withdrew at the request of Church authorities so that a member of the Council of Fifty, John D. Parker, could be elected.

Each year brought new assignments and responsibilities. In the 1856 April General Conference, Brigham Young called Anson to help found a formal mission in Carson Valley, nearly 500 miles west at the foot of the Sierra Nevada. Earlier in 1852, a small settlement known as Mormon Station had been established within this far corner of Utah Territory in Washoe County. Some inhabitants objected to being governed or tried by Mormon law, and a move was initiated to have the area annexed by California. Amid such controversy, in 1854 the Utah Legislature created Carson County. Brigham Young became enamored with the idea of expanding the Carson Valley colony, viewing it as a convenient halfway station for Mormon converts from Europe and the Pacific region who, after sailing to California, would head for settlements in Utah.

The next year, President and Governor Brigham Young appointed Apostle Orson Hyde to oversee development of the county. The following year (1856), was when Anson received his call along with 257 other "missionaries" to reinforce the colony and build up the surrounding area. At this time, Chester Loveland, Anson's brother-in-law (Chester married Fanny, Anson's younger sister), replaced Orson Hyde as head of the Mormon settlement. Chester and his family were part of the Call contingent that had earlier moved back and forth across Missouri and remained in Pottawatomie, Iowa, in 1847 preparing for the spring migration to Utah. His home had been torched by the mob along with Cyril's (Anson's father) in Warsaw, Illinois, in 1844.

In May 1856, Anson left Call's Fort with Mariah and their three children, the youngest being only two months old, and joined 150 other families making the trip across Nevada. Anson took three wagons, four mules, twenty-three head of cattle, and 178 sheep. He reached the Washoe Valley in forty-three days, having lost thirty-four of his sheep and three cattle, mostly as a result of thievery by Indians. He helped survey the Truckee Valley and engaged in other explorations, but did not stay long. It is unclear why Anson started home on September 17, arriving in Bountiful on October 13, although he did note in his diary that little was raised on the farm that year "on account of dry weather and bad management by the man I left." Mariah remained in Carson Valley to look after their stock. With three small children and only a canvas wagon cover as a roof over the log walls of her residence, life was difficult, but Mariah was known as a "woman who could handle a gun and drive horses as good as any man."

Anson hardly had time to rest before Brigham Young called him to aid in a major rescue operation. Earlier in October the Martin and Willie handcart companies were already experiencing cold weather and snow along the Mormon Trail near the current site of Casper, Wyoming, and by the Sweetwater River to the west. In the October General Conference, President Young called for sixty teams and fifteen or twenty wagons to provide supplies to the ill-fated parties. Within two weeks, as the snow deepened in areas to over eighteen inches, those in charge realized that the rescue detachment was only a pittance of what would be needed. In responding to Brigham Young's later urgings to help over 1,000 stranded Saints (three-fourths of whom were women and children), Anson collected thirteen teams and drivers from North Canyon Ward and headed into the snowy mountains. He was to participate in what the most prominent handcart historians describe as "the most heroic mass rescue the frontier ever witnessed."

With a surge of European converts eager to reach the Mormon Zion, most lacking adequate resources to provide for their passage, Brigham Young decided in 1856 that handcarts could be used if supported by some ox-driven wagons and at least a few horses. The first three handcart companies left Iowa City in June of 1856, making the 1,300-mile trip with few more problems than the earlier wagon train companies. These handcart companies enjoyed reasonable weather and arrived in Salt Lake City before October 2. However, the fourth and fifth companies (Willie and Martin), consisting of 1,076 members, experienced a series of delays that proved catastrophic. Initially their chartered ships departed England three weeks late. Then their unexpectedly large numbers plus poor planning caused another three-week delay in Iowa City due to the scarcity of materials to build and provision the necessary handcarts. The wood used to make the handcarts had not been adequately dried, and only thirteen wagons could be constructed or purchased to support their exodus.

The companies did not leave Iowa City until the middle of July, reaching Winter Quarters (now known as Florence, Nebraska) in the middle of August. Thus they had traveled only 277 miles, leaving them a remaining journey of 1,000 miles, which they hoped to complete before snowfall. The Martin company averaged fifteen miles per day, reaching Fort Laramie on October 8 where they expected to find additional provisions, but none had been sent. Then, on October 18, near Casper, Wyoming, they faced blizzards on the Wyoming plains, which can be some of the most treacherous in the West because of high winds. After three days of heavy snow with drifts reaching over two feet deep, travel came to a halt.

Anson and his followers comprised thirteen of the 250 horse and mule teams that participated in the rescue. Because of the cold and deep snow,

Anson's company remained on the Green River for a week before they could continue. They first met the Willie party which now had sufficient food and transportation. Accordingly, Anson volunteered to continue on to assist the Martin company still struggling to cross Rocky Ridge twenty miles east of South Pass and nearly 300 miles from Salt Lake City. Shortly, in Anson's words, "we found them starving and freezing and dying and the most suffering that I ever saw among human beings." Anson was away thirty-three days in the rescue crusade. On some occasions his party traveled less than two miles a day. Several rescuers described it as the most difficult trip of their lives. Of the 1,076 members comprising the Willie and Martin companies, over 220 died en route, making the death toll the largest of any migration west, some five times the total lost in the much-publicized Donner Party tragedy.

Several months later, Anson followed Brigham Young's advice and married two of the handcart survivors—Margaretta Clark and Emma Summers, one from the Martin and one from the Willie company. Both were in their late twenties, and both made the arduous pilgrimage without other members of their families. The handcart survivors did not reach the valley until December, and most lacked accommodations or they were in such poor health they had to be taken in by host families, such as the Calls. However, Margaretta and Emma were not part of the Call household. Anson became acquainted with Emma through her brother George who lived in North

Margaretta Clark Call

Emma Summers Call

Canyon Ward and drove one of the two wagons Anson supplied as part of the rescue operations.

Anson's ties with Margaretta go back to the rescue operation. When Anson found the Martin party in the cottonwood grove at Rocky Ridge, Margaretta was one of the nearly frozen, snow-blind, emaciated passengers placed in his wagon. As he was arranging the load, he noticed Margaretta gnawing on a frozen squash intended for the horses. He could tell she was not responding properly and could not sit up, obviously suffering from extreme hypothermia. Over her objections, Anson and another rescuer forced her to stand and walk back and forth with their support until her circulation improved. In telling the story years after, Margaretta noted that well-bred Englishmen from her homeland would have been much more gentle than Anson, but his persistence saved her life. Just three months later, February 7, 1857, they were married by Brigham Young in his office with Mary serving as a witness. Three weeks after he married Emma.

Anson's two new wives turned out to be devoted, hardworking, accepting mates. The transition was not easy for Margaretta since her prior experience was as a factory worker in England. She learned to be an excellent cook and provided numerous meals for neighbors and those in need. Anson eventually had six children by Margaretta and five by Emma. These wives became permanent residents of Bountiful where their children grew up.

The living arrangement Anson made for his wives in Bountiful is again revealing of polygamist times. Extending in a U shape from his original Bountiful home, he built separate living quarters for each wife and her children. The land within the U was a commons area where the children played together. The families shared the large kitchen, pantry, and laundry facilities, and often jointly prepared lunch or the evening meal. Each wife had a cow and a child assigned to care for it. The first and only store in Bountiful for many years—Call's Davis County Mercantile—was conveniently located. It was part of the compound, enclosed in a small area on the spacious front porch of Mary's home.

When Anson married Margaretta and Emma, Mariah and her three children were still in Carson Valley, Nevada. They returned in July 1857 after selling their cattle and joining a caravan headed by Chester Loveland's son. They came back when Brigham Young instructed Mormons to evacuate the area in anticipation of a possible war with the United States military.

Anson had been involved in essentially every major epoch event in Mormon history since joining the Church in Ohio, and these adventures were to continue with the Utah War. In the fall of 1857 when President James

Buchanan sent Johnston's Army to take control of Utah Territory, enforce national laws, and impose the federal government's will on the Mormons, Anson was adjutant of the South Davis unit of the Nauvoo Legion known as the "Silver Sharps," formed the first week in August of that year. This company, consisting primarily of men over forty-five, held frequent drills on Anson's farmland during September. In November they left to build fortifications in Echo Canyon fifty miles northeast of Salt Lake City. They were among the 800 legion members poised at the mouth of Echo Canyon for over a month during the coldest days of winter waiting to do battle with Johnston's forces—an army of 2,500 troops. Although the Mormons were outnumbered at the fortifications, a large number of males lived in the valley. President Buchanan had given Colonel Johnston a challenging assignment since Utah Territory now had a population of approximately 40,000, at least 8,000 of whom were able-bodied men. A census taken in 1856 listed over 75,000 residents in the territory, but it has since been established that this figure was inflated to support the territory's petition for statehood.

Johnston's advance to Utah was slowed in Wyoming when over fifty military supply wagons were destroyed by a small Mormon detachment under the command of Lot Smith. In the spring, when Brigham Young decided to evacuate Salt Lake City and all communities to the north (threatening a scorched-earth approach), Anson filled five wagons and moved his families and 4,000 pounds of flour south to the temporary village of "Shanghai" in Utah Valley. He returned north at Brigham Young's direction, standing by to burn all the structures and crops if it became necessary. Before the Mormon families evacuated, a pile of straw and kindling was placed in each building. Accordingly the entire community could be set afire in one or two hours. The Calls remained at Shanghai flats from May 6 through July 4 along with approximately 30,000 others until a peaceful settlement was negotiated.

The settlement resulted from several factors: the loss of Johnston's supplies and the potential strength of the Mormon resistance; growing criticism of President Buchanan's actions in Washington; and, above all, Brigham Young's willingness to compromise. The threat of Johnston's Army was the death knell not only for the Mormon colony in Carson Valley as noted, but for several others in outlying locations. When Johnston's forces started marching toward Utah, Brigham Young directed community leaders to dispose of all property, buy guns and ammunition, and return to Utah to help fight the "enemy."

In October 1858, Anson's younger brother, Josiah, was killed by Indians at Chicken Creek near Scipio when he was returning home to Fillmore after visiting Anson in Bountiful. Josiah was part of the initial party under Anson that settled Fillmore. Josiah served as the community's first sheriff and remained with his family as permanent residents after Anson returned to Bountiful. On April 9, 1861, Anson married Josiah's widow, Henrietta Caroline. Although he never lived with her, he provided support in raising her six children.

It was in 1860 that Anson opened the store on his front porch in partnership with his brother-in-law, Joseph Holbrook. Later the store was relocated on Main Street and ultimately merged with the Cooperative Mercantile Institution, a modest form of the Mormon United Order where citizens shared in the ownership. Also in 1860 he sold his farm at Call's Fort to his brother-in-law, Chester Loveland, and purchased another one near Bountiful. Mariah's "permanent" residence had been on the Box Elder County farm. Now with her four children (the last one was born in Utah County while awaiting Johnston's army), she returned to Bountiful. In 1862, two of these children (ages six and ten) died within two months of each other. However, she soon gave birth to two more, one in 1863 and one in 1866, keeping her children at four, all of whom grew to maturity and raised families of their own.

Anson's last colonization assignment was one of his most important. Brigham Young, given his unusual capacity to envision the future and think holistically, was seeking to find a quicker, more efficient means to bring Saints and supplies to his inland empire. For some time he had eyed the lower Colorado River as the solution, sending out an exploration party in 1855. In 1857–58 a small steamboat owned by the United States Army forged upstream from the mouth of the Colorado River to Black Canyon near the current site of Hoover Dam. Brigham quickly perceived this as a means of gaining a much needed waterway to the ocean similar to the access provided by the Mississippi and Missouri Rivers when the Saints were in the Midwest. It was especially inviting since he had recently abandoned Carson Valley and needed a more efficient means to transport goods and people from the West Coast. However, it was not until the October 1864 General Conference that he made his intent clear: "We shall want another path to bring home the Saints, and we want to prepare for it. The Colorado River is only a short way from St. George, and if I lived there I would soon have steamboats passing up the river, and it would serve as an inland station for the other communities and as an outpost to furnish supplies to the immigrants bound for Salt Lake."

Shortly after the conference on November 1, 1864, Brigham Young assigned Anson to "take an exploring company and locate a road to the Colorado River and then explore the river and find a suitable place for a warehouse and build the same, and form a settlement at or near the place of landing." Within two weeks, Anson left with several companies. Some were to form settlements on the road between St. George and the proposed landing, while Anson was to continue on to build the dock and warehouse. Anson and his party crossed the mountains and traveled along the Colorado River, finally selecting a site on a river bend near the mouth of Black Canyon that became known as Call's Landing. The location is one mile downstream from the mouth of Boulder Canyon, the site originally selected for Hoover Dam, and twelve miles above the present dam site. This places the community approximately twenty miles southeast of present-day Las Vegas.

In late December, Anson and his crew laid out forty 100-square-foot lots and began digging the warehouse foundation. The settlement was unique in several respects. No attempt was made to cultivate farmland because of the dry climate and desert sand. Rather than being a colonization effort, Callville was a commercial undertaking. The warehouse venture was funded by several businessmen in Salt Lake City, including Anson.

In March 1865, Anson traveled 450 miles to his Bountiful home and returned with Mary (his first wife), a surveyor, twenty more workers, and supplies. This was the first time Mary had accompanied him as a colonist outside of Bountiful. After the town site was laid out, it was named Callville. In this isolated desert, building materials were scarce. The warehouse was constructed of limestone obtained from a quarry several miles away, but the nearest timber supply was in mountains seventy miles west. The 120-by-30-foot warehouse included a store and a residence for Anson. The walls of the warehouse and other buildings still stand although they are submerged in the waters of Lake Mead.

In 1865, Anson signed an agreement with R.R. Sheath of San Francisco to ship freight down the coast to San Diego and up the Colorado River to Callville. This route proved extremely difficult and, in the end, foolhardy. The steamers had to be equipped with a winch and cable that was then connected to heavy iron rings pounded into the walls of the canyon enabling the boats to be pulled up through what became known as Ringbolt Rapids. The first boat to reach Callville docked on October 8, 1866. With a thriving community and plans for two more warehouses, the future of Callville appeared secure. However, several problems occurred besides the difficulty of navigating the Colorado. A suitable road was never developed to St. George due to the lack of open passes through the perilous mountains ringing the commu-

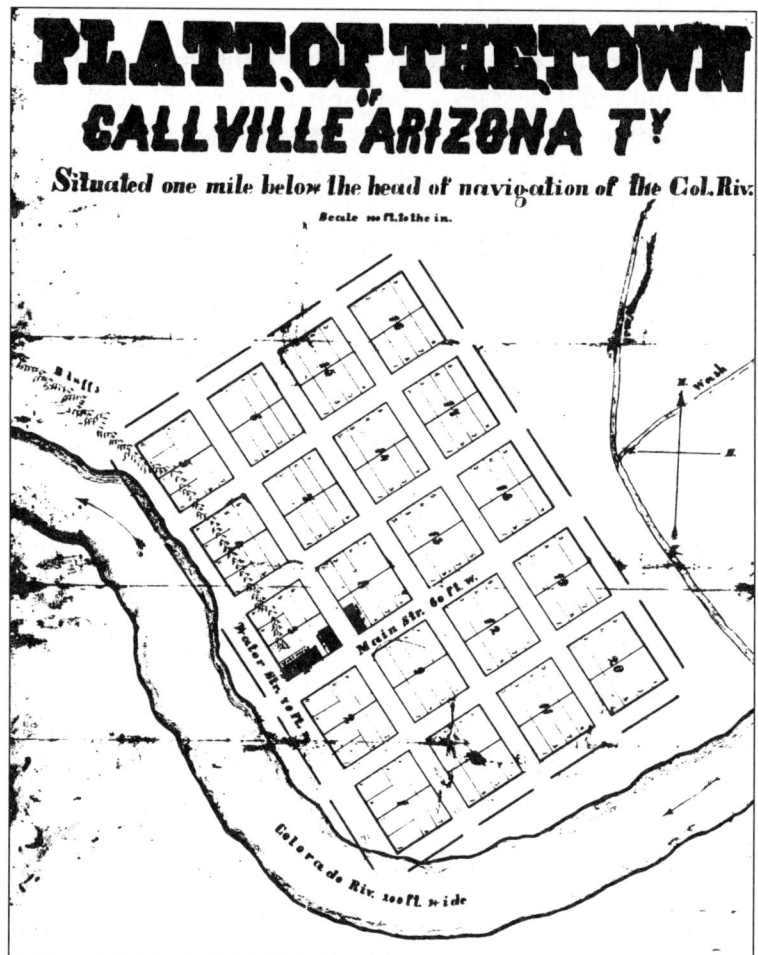

Plat of Callville, Arizona Territory (circa 1866) Source: National Archives

nity on the west and south and also because of erratic water flow in the Virgin and Muddy Rivers. In addition, following the Civil War, it became evident that the transcontinental railroad would be completed, providing a more efficient form of transportation. Furthermore, Callville's isolation in a barren desert made it an extremely inhospitable place to reside.

    Sheath and his company delivered freight to Callville for one more year, but it was soon obvious that further commercial development was unwise and, except for a small U.S. military detachment, the community was shortly deserted. It was totally abandoned in 1868 except for Indians who sometimes took shelter there. For years it remained a site of historic interest, frequently visited by those seeking to view pioneer relics. It was in the spring of 1935 when the warehouse, corrals, and remains of the ghost town were inundated by the waters of Lake Mead. No visible remains are evident today although Callville Bay serves as a popular recreation site.

Problems developed between Anson and Mariah during the latter stages of his stay in Callville. At the time she was thirty-two and he was fifty-six. In most of his sojourns to Callville, he did not take any of his wives, although, as noted, Mary went for six weeks during the spring and summer of 1865. Mariah had a baby daughter (Harriet Louisa) April 8, 1866, after which relations with her husband broke down. The cause of their separation is uncertain. A daughter of Anson's fourth wife, Emma, claimed it was because Mariah did not want to share Anson with the other wives when she moved back from Call's Fort. The more frequent story is that Anson became enraged upon returning from Callville when he heard rumors about Mariah's lack of faithfulness.

Anson's stubbornness and forceful nature served him well as a frontiersman, but these traits ultimately resulted in a total break with his favorite wife. He forced her to leave, accompanied by only her five-month-old baby. Written reports are not in agreement, but apparently she lived briefly with Anson's first wife Mary. As ever, Mary was sympathetic to family members, even those who were competing wives. Then Mariah took the unusual step, even in those days, of riding by horseback carrying her infant child to southern Utah where her mother had taken up residence. Meanwhile, Anson had distributed their other three children among his wives, although Mary ended up with most of the duty. The two older children were accustomed to living with her. She had often cared for them during the winter so they could attend school while Mariah accompanied Anson on his colonizing ventures. Thus for these siblings it was a relatively easy adjustment.

In 1868, Anson got Brigham Young to issue formal papers approving a divorce. After teaching school for a year or so, Mariah married William "Billie" Lloyd. They moved to the Downey-Lava Hot Springs area of Idaho. In 1871, Harriet (then five) returned to live with the Calls in Bountiful. At the time, Mariah was in the late stages of pregnancy with a daughter that ultimately was stillborn. Mariah gave birth to another girl three years later. This daughter died at eighteen, just before her pending marriage. After her second husband passed away, Mariah returned to Bountiful, living out her life next door to her oldest son, Israel, who had married in 1874 and had a large family. Mariah died at age ninety on July 24, 1924.

Including Mariah, Anson eventually had six wives and twenty-three children. His sixth wife, Ann Clark, was an older sister of his second wife, Margaretta. They married in 1870 when Anson was sixty and Ann was fifty-two.

Anson Call family home in Bountiful, Utah

After the marriage, Ann continued to live in Salt Lake rather than at the Bountiful complex. Many wonder how Anson evaded arrest by federal marshals after the strong anti-polygamy laws were passed in the early 1880s. Using his building knowledge, when remodeling Mary's home he added a secret passage leading to a small room in a roof gable where he hid bedding and supplies to last for several days. The marshals made many visits but never found him.

After establishing Callville, Anson spent more time at home looking after his own affairs. Besides his store and farms in Bountiful, he had a farm in Tooele County, and one house and two lots in Salt Lake City. In 1867 he was president of a company that formed the Centerville Rock Mill. When Brigham Young pushed leaders to make their communities independent under his cooperative mercantile program, Anson was appointed president of the Co-operative Silk Producing Society in 1868 and became active in growing mulberry trees. Later that year he was appointed president of the Co-operative Agriculture and Manufacturing Society. In 1868-69, he contracted to provide rails to Union Pacific for a stretch of the transcontinental railroad bed in upper Weber Canyon. He employed forty to fifty men, many of whom were his children and other relatives. In 1874 he was made president of the local branch of the United Order. Also, he was instrumental in establishing the Davis and Weber County Canal Company, and he was vice president of the Davis County Co-operative Stock-head.

Anson was a frequent companion and guardian of President Brigham Young on his annual trips throughout Utah Territory. He accompanied him several times to various communities in southern Utah and to Cache Valley in the north. In 1872 Anson was part of an official church delegation headed for Palestine, but, instead, he spent five months in Great Britain, primarily surveying the stock-raising districts. The party included Apostles Lorenzo Snow, George A. Smith, and other Church leaders.

Anson had many fine qualities besides his well-chronicled colonizing attributes. As noted earlier, he was widely known for his ability to peacefully negotiate with Indian tribes, following Brigham Young's admonition that "it is better to feed them than to fight them." His friendship with one band near Fillmore resulted in his paying a sack of flour for an Indian girl taken captive by a hostile tribe. She went by the name of Ruth Piede. (Piede was a name derived from her Indian tribe but some claim she was a Paiute.) Mary and Anson adopted the girl and she moved in with Mary. Later, with Anson's approval, Ruth married one of Anson's work hands when she was fourteen. Anson also acquired another Indian child, this one a four-year-old boy he named Dan. Dan lived with them until he was fifteen when (according to one report) he ran away with a circus.

The practice of buying Indian children was not unusual at the time. When Anson and others were settling Parowan, Brigham Young's advice was to "buy up the Lamanite children," especially under conditions when they were to be traded or sold to unfriendly tribes or other people who would not care for them. In the long run, Anson's willingness to befriend and negotiate with the Indians rather than do combat with them saved many lives.

A story that demonstrates Anson's strong will and leadership comes from when he was part of the company going to colonize Parowan. Near Nephi in central Utah, they stopped one Sunday for religious services. During his sermon, the party leader, Apostle George A. Smith, noted that it was unfortunate they lacked time to place a bridge across the nearby stream since this road would be the main thoroughfare to the south. Without knowledge of those leading the group, Anson gathered several men in the party that evening and got them to agree to arise after the Sabbath at 1:00 A.M. to con-

Exhibit II

ANSON CALL FAMILY

ANSON CALL
Born May 13, 1810   Died August 31, 1890

FATHER	MOTHER
CYRIL CALL	SARAH (SALLY) TIFFANY
June 29, 1785–May 23, 1873	November 27, 1790–March 15, 1856
Married April 6, 1806	Married April 6, 1806
Died age 87	Died age 65

WIVES and CHILDREN

WIFE	BORN	DIED	MARRIED	CHILDREN	COMMENT
Mary Flint	March 27, 1812	October 8, 1901	October 3, 1833	six (three died in childhood)	First wife. Married in Ohio.
Ann Mariah Bowen	January 3, 1834	July 24, 1924	April 15, 1851	six (two died in childhood)	Brigham Young arranged marriage
Margaretta Clark	May 26, 1828	December 27, 1908	February 7, 1857	six	Martin handcart company
Emma Summers	August 5, 1828	September 18, 1912	February 27, 1857	five	Willie handcart company
Henrietta Caroline Williams	Sept. 26, 1826	December 2, 1890	April 9, 1861	six (all by Josiah)	Wife of Josiah, Anson's brother killed in 1858
Ann Clark	March 4, 1817	April 1, 1893	January 24, 1870	none	Margaretta's sister

Anson had twenty-three children. However he and his wives (primarily Mary) raised two Indian children, Ruth Piede and Dan. They also raised several of Anson Vasco (oldest son of Anson and Mary) Call's children when he died August 14, 1867, at age thirty-three. Anson did not live with either Henrietta Williams Call or Ann Clark Call.

Anson and Mary Flint Call
(circa 1885)

struct the bridge. An astonished Apostle Smith awoke the next morning to find the bridge in place. This "get it done now" work ethic is one frequently found in Anson's descendants.

Anson's reputation was not restricted to his skill as a frontiersman. In a two-page obituary comprising the lead article of the September 13, 1890, *Deseret News Weekly*, the writer concluded, "We had the pleasure of being acquainted with him, and if there ever was a man of sounder integrity than he, we do not know it." In another review of his life, the historian George A. Lambert commends Anson for his "honesty, charity, self-denial, and unfeigned love." He also stated that Anson was known for his "do it now" motto, boundless energy, and instant decision making. He had a reputation for never betraying a trust and for being unpretentious, especially as it related to piety. His fourth wife, Emma, was reported to have said that "his wives thought he was about the grandest man alive," although she acknowledged his need to always be in control, noting, "Whatever he said it was that way and there was no other way. It was the right way."

In 1870, one year after the completion of the transcontinental railroad,

Anson took Mary to visit relatives and friends in Ohio and Vermont. What a contrast from the conditions they had experienced just twenty-two years earlier! The frontier was rapidly fading away, and the West was becoming more settled and civilized. These results were not due just to technical advances such as the railroad, but because of the spirit, daring, commitment, organization skills, and vision of pioneers such as Anson Call.

Anson spent most of his remaining years in Bountiful, serving again as a ward bishop from 1873 to 1877. Then the Davis Stake was created, and he was called as a counselor in the stake presidency. He functioned in that capacity until his death thirteen years later, August 31, 1890, at the age of eighty. Probably his most notable accomplishments were as a leader in establishing outposts that at the time were on the extreme perimeter of Mormon expansion in the three directions it proceeded from Salt Lake City—Parowan on the south, Carson County on the west, and Call's Fort on the north. He stands alongside such men as Lorenzo Snow, Charles C. Rich, George A. Smith, Orson Hyde, Ezra T. Benson, Erastus Snow, Amasa M. Lyman, and Marriner W. Merrill as one of the most effective colonizers under Brigham Young. He is richly deserving of the tribute paid by the historian Juanita Brooks: "Anson Call was one of the great frontiersmen of Mormondom."

CHAPTER 3

STARTING ANEW: ANSON VASCO CALL AND ANSON VASCO CALL II

The next Call in the direct family line between the Calls who came to America in 1636 and the Calls of today was the eldest son of Anson and Mary Flint—Anson Vasco Call Senior (or the first). This designation became necessary because he named his first son Anson Vasco. In turn, Anson Vasco II gave his eldest son the same name so there were three successive generations of Anson Vasco Calls. For simplicity, Anson Vasco I from now on will be referred to as Anson Vasco and Anson Vasco II as "A.V.," an abbreviation used by his close friends and relatives.

Anson Vasco was born in Ohio the year after Anson and Mary were married in 1833. Thus as a small child he suffered the hardships of moving to Missouri, being forced back to Illinois, and finally making the long trek to the Salt Lake Valley at fourteen. At age ten, he knew the early Church leaders and viewed the martyred bodies of Joseph Smith and his brother Hyrum. As a youth, he did farm work but later became skilled in business.

He married Charlotte Holbrook on June 3, 1854, and soon after started a farm in Willard not far from Call's Fort. Charlotte gave birth to A.V. one year later in Willard. The next year Anson Vasco took a second wife, Eliza Catherine Kent. Between the two wives, Anson Vasco had ten children, seven with Charlotte and three by Eliza.

Anson Vasco Call

The year following, 1857, Anson Vasco left on a Church proselyting mission to the Sandwich Islands (now called the Hawaiian Islands). He left in May but never got beyond San Francisco, returning in November when all missionaries were ordered home in case it became necessary to do battle with Johnston's Army. Immediately upon his return, he went with his father to build the Echo Canyon fortifications. He was active for several months in the Mormon militia, serving as a scout to track the U.S. military encampment on the Green River in Wyoming. On one occasion, he was a member of a small group that burned several government supply wagons.

With Anson Vasco frequently away, Charlotte, as many women of the day, took control of the family and operated the farm, becoming the breadwinner. She spun wool, wove cloth, and made their clothing. She used straw to create hats, mattresses, and ornaments. In a November 12, 1864, letter to Anson Vasco when he was serving on a mission in England, she wrote: "You must excuse my writing for I am much more used to turning the spinning wheel than I am writing. We have made about 70 yards of cloth and have 30 more to weave."

As those on the frontier soon learned, the capability to reduce waste and maximize use of every available resource was often the key to survival. On one occasion as Charlotte was picking up wheat kernels that had fallen on the ground, a neighbor observing the activity made fun of her. Charlotte looked up and said, "Never you mind. Before spring you will come to me for bread," and her contrite neighbor was forced to do just that some months later. Frugality was an important trait of early settlers, a trait that characterized many of the Call descendants.

Polygamy offered a high potential for conflict due to the complex relationships associated with husbands having multiple wives and offspring. The problem was frequently compounded when (as with the Calls) the husbands were often away for long periods on proselyting or colonizing missions. Even though some difficulties surfaced—such as those with Mariah—the other wives, especially Mary, were extremely accommodating. When the husbands were gone, wives and families would often move into the Bountiful Call complex. Even when one wife dominated the association with a husband, such as when Anson took Mariah to Parowan, Fillmore, Call's Fort, and Carson Valley, the spirit of accommodation remained strong.

Sometimes, of course, the resentment was not contained and a serious fallout occurred. Lamoni, the youngest son of Anson Vasco and Charlotte (therefore A.V.'s brother), was a printer and writer. In 1892 he started Davis County's first newspaper, *The Davis County Clipper*. In time he turned against his religious background. In 1899 he started a series of publications wherein he challenged the authenticity of the Book of Mormon and referred to Joseph Smith as a fraud. Lamoni issued his publications in various forms at "intervals to suit the publisher." The first series, started in 1899, was entitled *The AntiMormon*. A series in 1926 came out under the title of *Vest Pocket Mormonism*. Although Lamoni disavowed the Church, he was never known to challenge the integrity of his father or grandfather (Anson), calling them honest men.

Earlier in 1864, Anson Vasco was called as a missionary to England. He served in the areas around Newcastle and Bristol. While he was there, his wife Charlotte (A.V.'s mother), contacted typhoid fever and died on July 9, 1866, at age thirty-two. Later when Anson Vasco's health became precarious, he was released from his mission, only to die in his prime at age thirty-three on his return trip home just outside Rock Creek, Wyoming. With his father's death on August 4, 1867, A.V. became an orphan while still a young lad of twelve. This was a traumatic period for the Call family in several respects since Anson's separation from Mariah occurred during the same period.

With both parents deceased, A.V. went to live with his grandmother, Mary Flint Call. Mary was a remarkable woman and undoubtedly a major factor in Anson's success. Even with her poor health she cared for many of

Anson's relatives and also helped oversee their large, successful farm in Bountiful when Anson was away for long periods, sometimes amounting to years. Although only three of her children grew to maturity, Mary's living quarters were always filled with Anson's descendants, mainly children (and/or their spouses) and grandchildren of the other wives. In addition, she raised the Indian girl, Ruth Piede. Many of these responsibilities continued after Anson's death since Mary's life extended for eleven years beyond his, or until 1901.

Everyone spoke highly of Mary—an understanding, attractive woman with small features who would never turn down a call for help. They also admired her enormous energy despite her health problems. In speaking of Mary, Lucina Sessions (daughter of Anson and Emma) said "She was gold—just pure gold." Lucina also recalled a peculiarity of Mary's that caught everyone's attention even though it occurred before Mormon leaders emphasized strict adherence to the "Word of Wisdom," the doctrine that prohibits use of coffee, tea, tobacco, and alcoholic beverages. Lucina stated, "Mary had a little pipe which she used to smoke. It was the cutest little thing and she used it so daintily."

As noted earlier, Mary was well educated, and she quickly took A.V. under her wing and developed his unusual ability to read, write, and spell. He was also strong in athletics, excelling in wrestling, running, and baseball. When he was seventeen, he went to the University of Deseret (now the University of Utah). In 1875 he was a member of the first graduating class. At the time the school boasted of a faculty of four full-time professors. He was one of the top three scholars, displaying unusual skill in mathematics and astronomy. After graduation, his grandfather considered sending A.V. east to school, but Brigham Young advised against it, fearing that A.V. would lose his commitment to Mormonism. (A.V. later did the same thing with some of his sons.)

Accordingly, A.V. took up carpentry, a trade he had learned from Joseph Holbrook, his grandfather. He married Alice J. Farnham on May 17, 1876, after meeting her on a train while riding between Salt Lake and Bountiful. Alice's father had died when she was just five, and she and her mother went to live with her mother's sister, Mary Marrett, who owned the first brick house in Bountiful. Alice graduated from the University of Deseret and was a school teacher. A.V. began teaching school in Centerville while constructing his own home, often beginning work at 3:30 in the morning. In the four years required to complete the structure, they lived with Grandma Marrett. During this time, their first two sons were born. While still in his twenties, A.V. was made superintendent of Davis County schools, became the first president of the Mormon MIA (Mutual Improvement Association) in Davis County, and was appointed superintendent of the cooperative store that his grandfather had established twenty years earlier.

December 28, 1882, A.V. took a second wife, Lucy E. King. Lucy was from a prominent family in Farmington. She was the eldest of nine children. Her mother had died when she was sixteen, and she was responsible for the housekeeping and watching over the family until her father remarried shortly after that. A.V. met Lucy when he was school superintendent and visited the King home to do business with her father who was a school trustee. Soon after their marriage, she moved into the Bountiful home with A.V. and Alice where she had her first child, a son the parents named Franklin.

From early childhood A.V. recalled his parents and grandparents teaching him that it was necessary to have four wives to reach the Celestial Kingdom. Accordingly, he courted Rosa Emily Stayner (known as Emily) and married her October 1, 1883, less than a year after his marriage to Lucy. Emily's mother had passed away when she was a baby of eleven months, leaving her as the only surviving child since her younger brother had died earlier. She then went to live with the sister of her grandmother, Mary Marrett, who had no children of her own. Since Alice and Emily were living together with Grandma Marrett and were also second cousins, this, of course, is where A.V. and Emily became acquainted. (A.V. had courted Emily before Lucy, but Emily initially rejected his marriage proposal because of her relationship with Alice.) Emily was also a school teacher, but she was best known for being a

Marrett home in Bountiful where A.V. II and Alice Farnham lived after their marriage.

Anson V. Call II

talented musician. She played the piano and organ, gave music lessons, and was in demand as a singer. The year after their marriage, Emily gave birth to Thomas, the father of Reuel and Osborne.

In 1862 a federal statute had been passed making plural marriage a criminal offense in all territories, but enforcement was ineffective for the next two decades or until 1882 when the national congress approved the Edmunds Act. This act disfranchised polygamists, redefined polygamy as a crime, and provided for legal action against unlawful cohabitation. The latter phrase now became important in enforcement since no male was allowed to cohabit with more than one wife even if he had several. Also, under the Edmunds Act, federal marshals were permitted (when adjudicating cases involving polygamy) to have jurors drawn from a panel that excluded Mormons. In a test case in November 1884, Rudger Clawson was sentenced to four years in the territorial penitentiary for practicing polygamy. From that date forward U.S. deputy marshals intensified their "polyg hunts" from one end of the territory to the other and in surrounding territories when appropriate.

Mormons engaged in polygamy responded in a variety of ways such as hiding, moving to Canada or Mexico, or going on foreign missions. A.V. took the latter course. In February 1885 he left for a mission to England, leaving Alice with four children and Lucy and Emily with one each. Alice remained in the Bountiful home with her offspring. The grandmas again came to the rescue. Lucy went to live with Grandma Mary Flint Call, and Emily returned to live with Grandma Mary Marrett.

A.V. made the decision to become a missionary in such haste that it was difficult to sell his belongings to raise money for travel. In his clandestine departure, he hid in a wagon in the tithing yard in Salt Lake City (the site of the former Hotel Utah building) while waiting to be set apart by a Church apostle.

The ocean crossing was difficult, and the ship nearly sank in a severe storm. He served in the area around Bristol, the same district where his father had labored. Twenty-one months later he returned to the United States to discover that the U.S. marshals had not backed off from their unrelenting pursuit of polygamists, and he had to go into hiding. This was the start of a long series of events that took him outside Utah Territory to Idaho and ultimately to Star Valley, Wyoming.

CHAPTER 4

ANSON VASCO CALL II: A BRIEF STOP IN CHESTERFIELD

When A.V. returned from his mission in November 1886, he found it impossible to remain in Bountiful for even a short time because of the vigilance of the U.S. deputy marshals. He briefly saw his wives, Lucy and Emily, but Alice was in Logan for a month doing temple work. A.V. obtained a horse and rode 170 miles north to Chesterfield in Idaho Territory where many of his relatives were located. There he could find assistance from his kin and hopefully resume his life with his three wives.

Chesterfield lies thirty miles due east of present-day Pocatello across the high peaks of the Putnam Mountains. It is in a long valley extending north and south that was once heavily traversed as part of the Oregon Trail. The Oregon Trail south of Chesterfield leaves the Bear River and winds north up through the gentle rise of the Portneuf Valley until it reaches Fort Hall where it then turns west, intersecting with the Snake River. No permanent communities were established between Fort Connor (Soda Springs) and Fort Hall on the Oregon Trail, a distance of seventy-five miles, until 1879. Then two of A.V.'s relatives, Chester Call and Christian Nelson, drove a herd of horses through the area and became intrigued with its agricultural potential. Strange as it may seem, the better agricultural land in Utah was being rapidly taken up, and Chester and Christian were feeling hemmed in or at least constrained from expanding their farms in Bountiful. Accordingly, they established a 320-acre ranch along the Portneuf River and made plans to bring their families north.

Eventually, as we shall see, Chesterfield did not prove to be a wise choice either for agriculture or avoiding the law. Agriculture was restricted due to two problems—marginal land (especially that above the more fertile fields along the river), and limited rainfall, making dry farming a risky proposition. Furthermore, the growing season is short, winds are commonplace, and winters are normally accompanied by extreme, sometimes unbearable cold reaching 50 degrees below zero. Thus the region could support a few large farms but was not adequate to underpin a sizeable community. Eventually the land was used primarily for raising cattle and sheep. Chesterfield's economic future was doomed when in 1881 the decision was made to run the railroad through Bancroft (ten miles to the south) rather than directly north following the Oregon Trail past Chesterfield. Another barrier restricting development of the community was the Fort Hall Indian Reservation. It blocked the valley opening to the northwest, thus prohibiting expansion in that direction.

It is natural to assume that a primary motive for establishing a Mormon community in such a remote region just over the territorial border from Utah was for polygamists to escape harassment by federal authorities. This was likely a factor, but it was definitely secondary since Chesterfield was established before the more rigid anti-polygamy laws were passed, and most Chesterfield settlers went there for other reasons. The remoteness of Chesterfield was an advantage to polygamists since the surrounding area for miles around was essentially uninhabited. However, Idaho residents were not receptive to immigration from what they considered the religious fanatics in Utah. Again, as the Saints had experienced in the Midwest, the biggest concern of the citizenry regarding Mormons was their political power. Although a minority, the Mormons—voting as a block—were a major factor in deciding every significant Idaho territorial election from 1872 until 1884. Candidates who lost blamed it on the Mormons, and those who won were reluctant to be identified with them.

To weaken this political muscle, anti-Mormon strategists searched for a way to disenfranchise LDS church members and prevent them from actively participating in politics. In 1884, several years after Chesterfield was founded but before A.V.'s arrival, the Idaho legislature passed a law prohibiting those who belonged to any organization advocating plural marriage from serving on juries, holding political office, or even having the right to vote. This law was vigorously enforced for eight years or until after LDS President Wilford

Chester Call

Woodruff issued his 1890 Manifesto abandoning the "practice" of polygamy. During these eight years, federal marshals were as active hunting down polygamists in southern Idaho as they were in Utah. However prosecution was more difficult if the husband and/or his spouses were in different territories since they were not under one criminal jurisdiction, and parties under indictment had to be joined through common legal action by authorities in each political entity.

Getting back to the two founders of Chesterfield (Chester Call and Christian Nelson), Chester was a son of Anson and Mary Flint, the younger brother of Anson Vasco, and hence A.V.'s uncle. Christian Nelson married Charlotte Vienna Call, the eldest child of Anson Vasco Call and Charlotte Holbrook. Thus she was A.V.'s sister, older by eighteen months. Chester had been a bishop in Bountiful. He had four wives but one died before he relocated to Chesterfield. His last wife he met and married while residing in this small, isolated community. Thus, when he first came to Idaho he had but two living wives. He built a home for each to get around the cohabitation feature of the anti-polygamy law.

Christian Nelson was never a polygamist. His only wife was Charlotte Vienna. The couple had no offspring, although they adopted one and raised three foster children.

A.V. Call II with eight of his nine brothers and sisters, seven of whom were at one time Chesterfield residents. Back row, left to right: Sidney (half brother); Ira (brother); Hannah (sister); Lamoni (brother); Chester Vinson (half-brother); Joseph Holbrook (brother). Front row: Charlotte Vienna (sister); A.V. II; Mary Vashti (sister).

Once Chester and Christian settled in the Portneuf Valley, they attracted several other Mormon families from Utah, primarily relatives. Thus the settlement was not created as a deliberate Mormon colony by Church leaders, but resulted from a group comprised mainly of relatives who decided to relocate. It was natural for A.V. to go to Chesterfield since six of his seven full brothers and sisters resided there. The only exception was Lamoni, the one who wrote the anti-Mormon literature. Also, two of A.V.'s three half brothers and sisters lived in Chesterfield, making a total of eight out of the ten children of Anson Vasco being residents. (See Exhibit III, page 52.)

As other examples of relatives who settled there, two of Chester Loveland's children brought their families. As you will recall, Chester married Anson's sister, Fanny, and subsequently headed the Carson Valley colony. Later they bought Anson's large ranch in Box Elder County, Utah.

Another extremely prominent family in the community was Ruth Piede Call Davids (the Piede Indian girl Anson adopted) and her husband, James

Henry Davids, with their six children. When James was working on Anson's farm in Bountiful, he met Ruth and they were married on Christmas evening in 1863 when Ruth was just fourteen.[1] Anson consented to the marriage based on the promise that James would keep her close by. One year after the marriage, James was part of Anson's party that established Callville on the Colorado River. James died in Chesterfield in 1908. Ruth died there in 1919. They left a strong posterity, both in numbers and prominence. By 1950 the Davids had nearly 200 living descendants, all proud of their heritage and actively engaged in occupations such as ranching, nursing, military service, and teaching.

Chesterfield never passed the stage of being more than a small village. The community did not end up on the Portneuf River where Chester, Christian, and the other early settlers had their ranches. Church leaders advised them to join and form a town on a bluff two miles east near the mountains. (Incidentally, it is not known for sure how Chesterfield received its name. A visiting church authority from Cache Valley claimed the new town site reminded him of his home in Chesterfield, England, but apparently the name was also selected to honor Chester Call.)

The town was laid out in typical Mormon fashion. It contained thirty-five ten-acre blocks divided into four equal lots of two-and-one-half acres each. A count in 1884 revealed twenty-four families and 136 members in Chesterfield Ward. The non-Mormon families in the immediate valley could be counted on both hands. By the time A.V. arrived in 1887, the ward had approximately doubled in size. Ten years later it reached a peak of seventy-nine families and 444 members. After that, the population gradually dwindled for the reasons given previously, becoming essentially a ghost town.

In 1979, Craig Call, Jay's younger brother and Osborne's son, started a movement to have the community placed on the National Register of Historic

Ruth Piede Call Davids

---

1. They were never sure of Ruth's age since Anson purchased her from Indians who had forcefully taken her from another tribe.

Exhibit III

CHILDREN OF ANSON VASCO CALL I WHO RESIDED IN CHESTERFIELD, IDAHO

(Listed sequentially by wife and by child based on age)

CHILDREN OF ANSON VASCO CALL I AND CHARLOTTE HOLBROOK:

CHARLOTTE VIENNA CALL NELSON: Born November 7, 1853. Married Christian Nelson. One of the founders of Chesterfield in 1879. Long-time Chesterfield residents. Died November 21, 1934.

ANSON VASCO CALL II: Born May 23, 1855. Resided in Chesterfield only in 1886–87. Then moved to Afton, Wyoming. Died October 12, 1944

JOSEPH HOLBROOK CALL: Born February 23, 1857. Two wives, Sarah Isabel Barlow and Martha Ester Williams. Went to Chesterfield in 1883 before moving to Afton, Wyoming, in 1888. Died January 15, 1935.

MARY VASHTI CALL MUIR: Born January 29, 1859. Married Moses Muir. Went to Chesterfield in 1881–82. Permanent residents. Died November 5, 1942.

IRA CALL: Born March 23, 1861. Two wives: Emma Jane Barlow and Fanny Loveland. Settled in Chesterfield in 1881–82. Lived in the area the balance of his life. Died January 19, 1928.

HANNAH CALL HATCH: Born January 26, 1863. Married William Ansel Hatch. Went to Chesterfield in 1882. Ultimately settled in Hatch, Idaho, just a few miles away. Later moved to Rigby, Idaho. Died February 22, 1940.

CHILDREN OF ANSON VASCO CALL I AND ELIZA CATHERINE KENT:

CHESTER VINSON CALL: Born October 6, 1859. Early resident, presumably 1881. Resided for many years in Chesterfield. Married two wives who were also sisters, Annis Janett Barlow and Minnerette Barlow. Died January 16, 1943.

SIDNEY BENAJAH CALL: Born December 27, 1861. Early resident, presumably 1881. Lived there until his death in 1906. Married Henrietta Columbia Loveland. Died September 21, 1906.

Places. He viewed the largely intact settlement with its crumbling buildings as a unique preservation opportunity. Here was an abandoned township that had all the appearances of a turn-of-the-century western farm community. The church, school, and store were still basically intact as were many of the homes. Craig took the lead to create the Chesterfield Foundation that is currently in the process of buying back the property, restoring many structures, and adding a museum. The Foundation has been fortunate in that the Davids and their family owned a significant portion of the ground since their descendants have been cooperative in the restoration. This was token repayment for Anson's generosity over a century earlier when he gave a sack of flour to acquire Ruth.

As indicated, Chesterfield was not a haven for polygamists seeking obscurity. Although its primary founder, Chester Call, had several wives, the number of Chesterfield males involved in plural marriage was no higher than the church average of 15 to 20 percent. However, beginning with the new anti-polygamy law in 1884, prosecution by deputy marshals in Idaho became more vigorous. Apparently the first Chesterfield resident to be incarcerated for unlawful cohabitation was Andrew P. Anderson who was arrested in January 1887, just two months after A.V.'s arrival. After a trial, Anderson was sentenced to six months in the territorial penitentiary at Boise. He was fortunate in receiving a light sentence. Shortly thereafter the penalties for plural marriage and cohabitation were increased substantially. After Anderson returned, his message to his Mormon Chesterfield neighbors was noted in the Chesterfield Ward Priesthood minutes for June 11, 1888: "Elder A. P. Anderson was called upon to address the Saints. Having been incarcerated in Boise Pen for practicing the Celestial law of marriage, having been in Six months [he] narrated his experience and life while in the Pen." At the same meeting Neils Graham of Mink Creek, Idaho, spoke of his experiences in the Detroit House of Corrections. He had been sent to Detroit with seventeen other polygamists because Idaho's prison had overflowed with Mormons.

Thus in 1887 Chesterfield residents who engaged in plural marriage took greater steps to be on the watch for U.S. marshals. An example is Joseph Holbrook Call, A.V.'s younger brother by twenty-one months. He moved to Chesterfield with his only wife in 1883. In June of 1886 he took a second wife who at the time resided close by in the Portneuf Valley. At this point, even though he or one of his wives was constantly in hiding, deputy marshals trapped and arrested him five times in less than two years. However, the polygamy charges could never be substantiated and he avoided a prison term.

Thus, A.V. did not arrive in a hospitable environment for someone on the run seeking to find refuge from federal agents. He moved in with his Uncle Chester and immediately began working as a carpenter. Soon he obtained the contract to build the new Chesterfield meeting house, an activity that consumed most of his time during the summer and fall of that year. The only wife A.V. brought to Chesterfield early in his stay was his third wife, Emily, who, with her only child, Thomas, moved in with the Nelsons. Emily was especially welcome because of her much-needed musical talents. Earlier when A.V. served as a missionary and she was living in Bountiful with Grandma Marrett, Emily supported herself and Thomas by giving music lessons.

Besides his struggle to raise enough money to relocate his families, A.V. was becoming increasingly apprehensive over his security in Chesterfield. However, he did bring his second wife, Lucy, and their young son, Franklin, for a brief visit in the late summer. By then both Lucy and Emily were pregnant, and they returned to Bountiful for their deliveries. A.V., at the advice of Chester, decided that it was too risky to stay in the area, and he again starting looking for a sanctuary safe from the federal marshals.

After counseling with Chester, A.V. decided to move to an even more remote and less settled valley on the Salt River across the border due east in Wyoming. The distance is little over fifty miles as the crow flies, but then the land route involved a perilous seventy-mile journey through rugged terrain. The valley, with narrows half way down its length, is shaped like a figure-eight and surrounded by mountain ridges on all four sides. In addition, the north end is blocked by the Snake River which runs through deep canyons prohibiting traffic east and west. (In the late 1940s, the Palisades Dam was built and the associated reservoir now fills the river channel.)

At the time, few remaining unsettled, high-mountain valleys in the region could be found that were deemed suitable for agriculture. In addition, politicians in Wyoming territory were encouraging Mormons to emigrate. In all, it offered A.V. the protection he sought and the potential guarantee that he would never be forced to pull up stakes and be on the move again. It was the same feeling Brigham Young had when he entered the Great Salt Lake Valley forty years earlier.

CHAPTER 5

ANSON VASCO CALL II: SETTLEMENT OF STAR VALLEY

Anyone raised on the frontier was accustomed to hard work, lack of tools, difficult travel, severe weather, and inadequate food and housing, but A.V. and his families were still unprepared for the first years in their new homeland along the Salt River. Local Indian tradition held that no one could live through the winter in this beautiful, high mountain valley that at its depths had a stream flowing the length of the lowlands from south to north until it poured into the south fork of the Snake River. The slightly sloped valley floor drops from 6,500 feet on the south to 5,500 feet at the north, barricaded by the 10,000-foot peaks of the Salt River range to the east and the 8,000-foot crest of the Caribou and Webster ranges on the west.

With nine significant mountain streams and abundant wildlife, Star Valley was a favorite summer haunt for Indians and early fur trappers. Hudson's Bay trappers were in the locality as early as 1818, and for the next sixty years beaver pelts were collected regionally by groups such as the Rocky Mountain Fur Company, Robidoux's Brigade, and Dripps' Brigade. The first developed road crossing the valley was completed in 1858 when the Lander Cut-off portion of the Oregon Trail was constructed. The Oregon Trail, the first permanent road to the Northwest, was blazed in 1843. Because of heavy traffic, by the mid-1850s some sections of the trail through Wyoming were several miles wide, and even then the passageway was crowded with settlers heading for the Northwest, California, and the Mormon Mecca in Salt Lake City. This led to a search for alternate courses that were not as overgrazed, offered a fresh, ample water supply, and were free of the dust and human and animal debris created by thousands of migrants clogging the main route each year. (Over 350,000 travelers traversed the Oregon Trail in the twenty-five years of its primary usage.) The Salt River Valley with its many streams and lush meadows provided an ideal solution to these problems, assuming a road suitable for wagons could be chiseled through the rocky mountain passes.

The Oregon Trail evolved from a variety of trailblazers pushing ahead with no direct government support. Government military detachments, surveyors, and other groups traveled through the region, but their primary assignment was not road construction. Those who broke and developed the trail were primarily adventurers, miners, pioneers, and others lured by the prospects of moving West. The only trail segment built with government funds was the Lander Cut-off. After passing through Casper, Wyoming (then Fort Casper), the Oregon Trail dips south to Fort Bridger and then proceeds north along the Soda Springs–Chesterfield–Fort Hall route before turning south again to follow the Snake River. The government's plan was to cut directly west from South Pass to Fort Hall, thus making the route one hundred miles shorter with the added advantages of improved water and forage. The 256-mile trail was surveyed in 1857. Under the direction of Frederick West Lander, an engineer with the Department of Interior, the road was roughed in during the summer of 1858. Forty-seven needy Mormon laborers from Utah, eager to find employment, helped complete the roadway ahead of schedule.

The cut-off enters the south end of Star Valley from the east. After crossing the Wyoming and Salt River Ranges, it winds down Lander's Canyon into the area south of present-day Smoot. The trail then goes along the Salt River north past Afton to Auburn, turns up along Stump Creek through the Webster Mountains, and heads directly west to Fort Hall. This route never became popular with travelers because of the hard climbs and descents, slippery surfaces, and washouts from flooding streams. It is unclear why the engineers did not originally design the cut-off to continue north down through the valley to Freedom and then over the more gentle passes along Tincup Creek, a much more feasible course.

In any event, pioneers taking the Salt River Valley (as it was then known) portion of the Lander Cut-off were not sufficiently attracted by the local environs to stay for more than a few days. The first colonists intent on settling

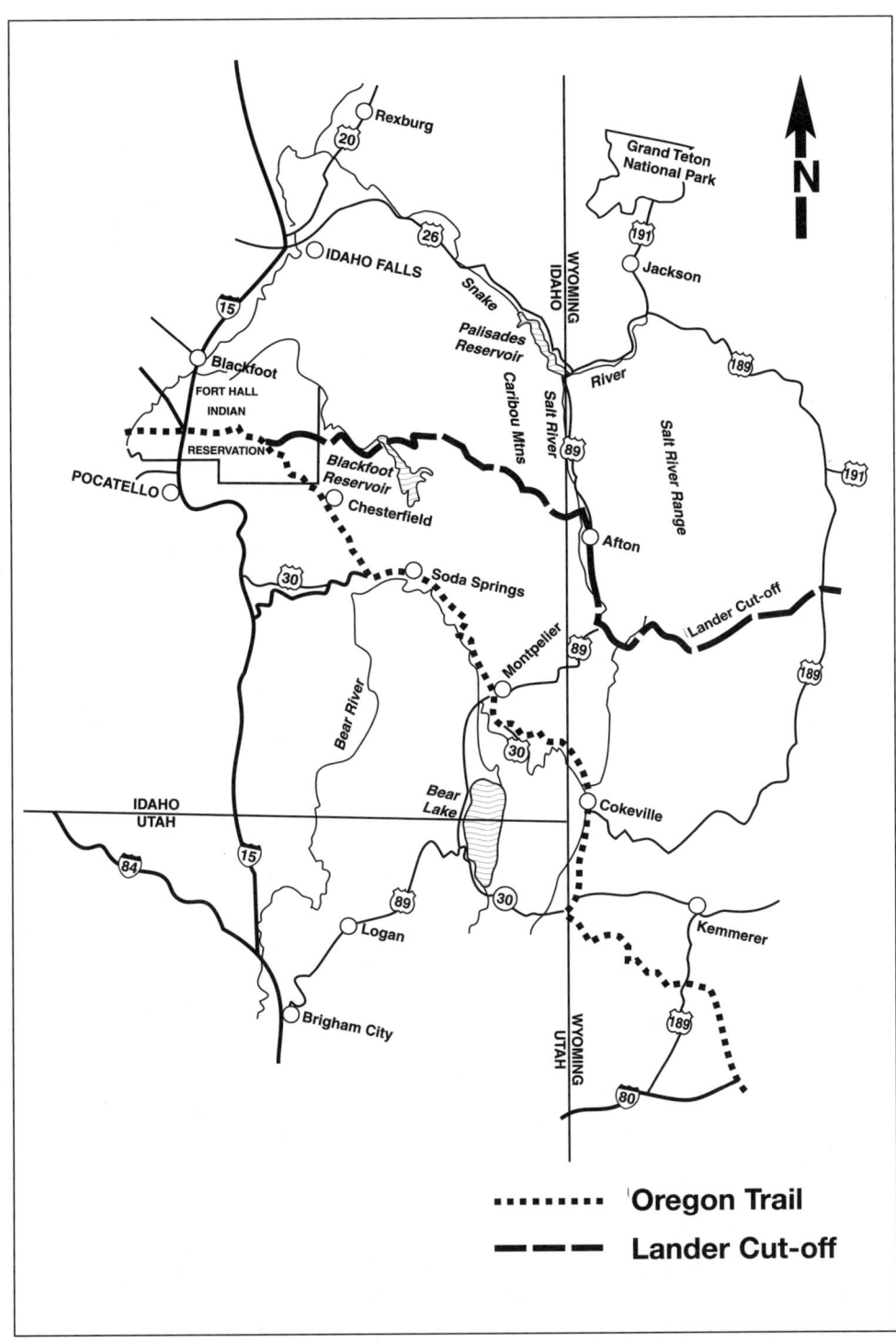

did not come until 1876, seven years after the transcontinental railroad was completed when the Oregon Trail was fast becoming a relic of the past. The earliest permanent settlements within a sixty-mile radius of the valley were those by Mormons who in 1863–64 established communities in the area surrounding the north shore of Bear Lake, southwest of Afton. In 1877, a Mormon delegation led by Moses B. Thatcher and William B. Preston left the Bear Lake settlements to explore northeast into Wyoming. Once in the Salt River Valley, they found no permanent settlers, noticing only several abandoned Shoshoni wickiups. The next year when Brigham Young, Jr. dedicated the Salt River drainage as a gathering place for the Saints, two abandoned trappers' cabins were discovered.

In 1879, colonization of the valley began in earnest when Apostles Charles C. Rich and Moses Thatcher were appointed by church authorities to supervise the undertaking. Nine families (twenty-seven persons) became squatters, although some left the next year following a severe winter that killed many cattle and forced the pioneers to travel on foot to the Bear Lake communities for food. In 1880 the Afton townsite was selected, and the name of the valley was changed to Star Valley after Apostle Thatcher, who, noting its beauty, called it the "star of all valleys." However, the hardship of attempting to maintain year-round residence kept the population to a minimum. Afton was not settled until five years later. The first grain harvest occurred in 1886, just one year before A.V. decided to call it home.

In many respects the valley was to A.V.'s liking. Previously he had expressed his desire to reside in an area where timber was plentiful and nearby, a feature common to the entire forty-five mile length and ten-to-fifteen-mile breadth of the figure-eight-shaped depression. With an average rainfall of twenty-two inches, the climate was also less arid than the environs near his former home in Bountiful. A.V. liked to hunt, and western Wyoming was a sportsman's paradise with ample numbers of elk, deer, sage hens, grouse, geese, and ducks, plus an occasional bear. Furthermore, Wyoming officials were eager to attract settlers to this region.

In 1880, Uinta County stretched across the entire western end of Wyoming from Yellowstone on the north to the Uinta Mountains on the south, and yet the county's total population was a meager 2,879. The Wyoming governor was quick to overlook any issue such as polygamy if he could attract settlers. When officers from Utah Territory volunteered to help their counterparts in Wyoming round up polygamists, the Wyoming governor turned them down. Various versions of his statements remain as part of the legend since the story has been likely embellished through frequent retelling. In effect, he proclaimed, "If we want to prosecute the Mormons we have officers of our own," and to "Leave them alone. They are good colonists." Years later in acknowledging his appreciation, A.V. sent the governor a fine hand-carved mahogany walking cane

The region's only major drawback compared to A.V.'s former domiciles was the long, cold winters resulting in a growing season of just fifty days. This restricts the variety of vegetables and other crops that can be cultivated, leaving farmers few options except to grow certain grains or hay to feed horses and cattle. Otherwise, the primary usage is for pasture. As a result, early settlers were forced to rely more on game, fish, and beef for sustenance. Dairying eventually became the primary industry and, when combined with the attractive mountainous scenery, comparisons with Switzerland were inevitable. Accordingly, the valley soon picked up the title "Little Switzerland of America." As far as A.V. was concerned, dim prospects for agriculture did not deter him since he intended to continue as a carpenter and pursue related business interests.

This was the world A.V. moved into when he left Chesterfield in November of 1887. Afton comprised a mere dozen or so families, and the only store was mobile since it was entirely contained within a covered wagon. Thus new settlers had to be totally self-reliant, although they looked to their few neighbors for assistance, especially advice on prime sources for timber, water, and game. A.V. was fortunate in that the year before his arrival a water-driven sawmill was established on Swift Creek, a stream that flows through Afton.

The first wife to join A.V. in Star Valley was Alice. Lucy and Emily, both in late stages of pregnancy, preferred to have their deliveries in the safer confines of the Great Salt Lake Valley. Emily had her second child, Charles, on December 16, 1887, while in Bountiful living with Grandma Marrett. Lucy bore her second child, Stella, one month later on January 21, 1888, while under the care of Grandma Mary Call in Bountiful. A.V. became a father three times in less than four months when Alice gave birth to her sixth child, Caroline Charlotte, on April 22, 1888, five months after homesteading in Afton. (For a list of A.V.'s wives and their children see Exhibit IV, page 76.) A.V.'s biggest challenge once he relocated was to construct adequate housing for his three wives and their newborn children.

Prior to heading for Star Valley, A.V. left Chesterfield to visit Bountiful in September 1887. He took Emily and their son Thomas, returning with Alice and her four children. Still wary of apprehension by federal marshals, they slipped out of Bountiful under cover of darkness in a wagon loaded with their belongings—a small cook stove, rocking chair, dishes, clothing, and bedding. They left behind the comfort of their brick home and the convenience of a forty-year-old community with numerous stores, commercial services, and cultural events. A.V. was taking a step back to the frontier, giving up the comfort of the city life that his father and grandfather had helped establish.

A.V. went by way of Chesterfield to obtain flour, potatoes, bacon, dried beef, and other provisions from Uncle Chester. He was also going to meet Chester's younger brother, Anson Bowen Call (hereafter referred to as Bowen), who was taking his family to start a new life in this high mountain valley in Wyoming. At the time, Bowen was not a polygamist. A.V. and Bowen decided to leave their wives and younger children in Chesterfield while they hastily constructed temporary housing in Afton, after which Uncle Chester would bring the spouses and families. On October 7, 1887, with three heavily loaded wagons, A.V. and his two boys (Anson Vasco III, age ten, and Adolphus, age eight) and Bowen with two nephews from his wife's side of the family (Thompson) headed north to pick up the Lander Cut-off before turning east to Star Valley. They were fortunate in that the winter of 1887–88 was one of the mildest in years. Nonetheless, the trip was arduous. The Lander Cut-off was now used primarily for driving herds of cattle and sheep to the summer range. In sections the road was so steep, rutted, and slippery with red mud that all three teams had to be hitched together to pull one wagon over the grade.

After three days they entered the valley and camped on the east side. Their first task was to stake claims as homesteaders north of Afton in an area surveyed the prior year. Then they acquired lots in the Afton townsite, paying $1.50 for each two-and-one-half acre lot. A.V. purchased lot 3, block 7, located on the current streets of Main and Third Avenue. Bowen selected a lot one block north on the east side of Main Street. There, with the help of the Thompson boys, they hauled logs and built two cabins. A.V.'s was a 16-by-14 foot room with a log exterior. The interior was of rough lumber obtained from the sawmill. The only source of outside light was a double-sash window. The roof was composed of poles covered by dirt, straw, and sod. It proved to be a favorite nesting place for mice that frequently fell into the interior. Sheets were spread on the ceiling above the bed to prevent the mice from dropping on their covers during the night. A water bucket was kept on a bench near the door. One day when one of the children went to get a drink, she found several baby mice that had fallen into the bucket and drowned.

On November 16, just five weeks after A.V. and her two sons departed

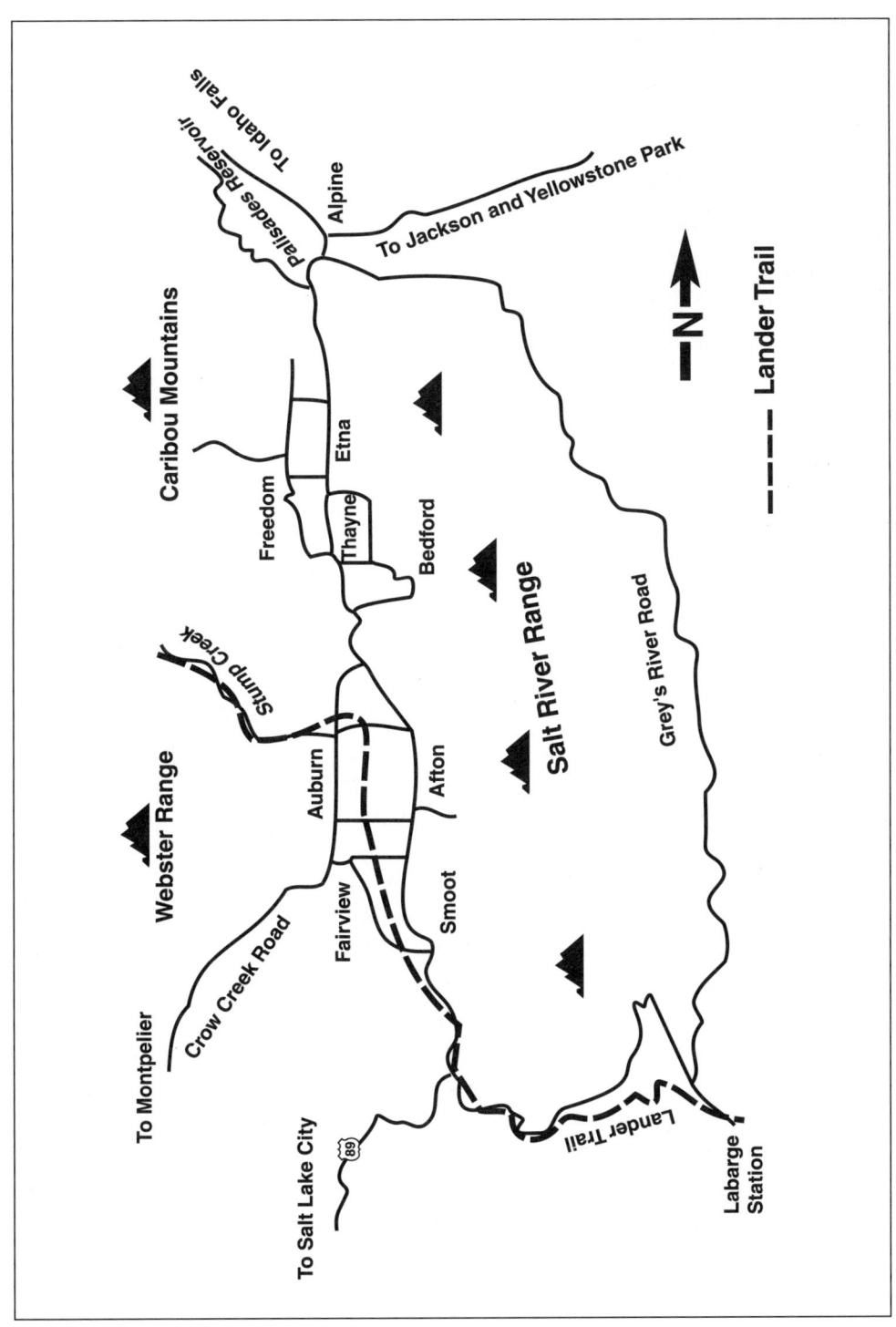

Alice Jeanette Farnham, first wife of A.V. Call II.

Chesterfield, Alice arrived with the two daughters in a wagon driven by Uncle Chester that also contained Bowen's wife, daughter, and mother-in-law. As the team pulled up in front of A.V.'s cabin, Chester jokingly remarked to Alice, "Here is your mansion." The immediate landscape surrounding the cabin appeared desolate, almost totally void of buildings, fences, or trees. Only a few small cabins could be seen on the horizon. As she opened the door and peered into the small room, she recognized her rocking chair, bedding, and cooking utensils. She was elated to see the floor was of rough lumber rather than dirt. The winter supply of food was piled in one corner straddled by a temporary bed for the children. In the northwest corner, a bunk bed extended from the wall. A trunk under the window held all the family clothing. Several shelves loaded with pots, pans, and other items were on the opposite wall. At one side was a crude table A.V. had roughed out using his carpenter's bench and tools. These occupied the room's entire south end. The interior was crowded but cozy in the cold winters when temperatures occasionally dropped to 40 or 50 degrees below zero.

Once settled, A.V. immediately set to work using his carpentry skills. He fabricated a turning lathe made entirely of wood, powered by a foot treadle. Using this and his other tools, he made a variety of furniture and most of the early coffins in the valley. He became skilled in making chairs, tables, bedsteads, flour bins, and rolling pins. In time he gained a reputation as the valley's most skilled carpenter. He traded his services for food, clothing, and other necessities since little money was available as a medium of exchange. Later he often remarked that "he never saw a dime of money that winter."

Though the winter was mild, on occasion the snow piled almost as high as the cabin. According to early colonists, snow on the valley floor was often two to three feet deep, although records for the current century show the average snow level to be less than half that. In the more severe winter of 1889–90, standing in the doorway A.V. could not see over the snow. Steps of ice with boards on top led to the exterior. As a child in his father's home, Thomas recalls seeing badgers on top of the snow peering in at eye level through the window. Under these conditions, the only travel was by skis or snowshoes. During the long winters before coal oil was widely available, indoor lighting came from burning a rag in a dish of grease, or torches made of pitch pine.

On June 4, 1888, when travel conditions became appropriate, A.V. set out for Bountiful to pick up Lucy and her two children. Stella was not yet five months old. Being snowbound during the winter, A.V. was unaware of Stella's birth until April when Christmas presents arrived by mail from Grandma Farnham. A.V. made the round trip in just over a month, returning on July 7. Lucy and her two children moved in with Alice and her five. The combined household of ten living in space where it would be difficult for all of them to lie down at once was giving new meaning to the term "cabin fever!"

Lucy King,
second wife of A.V. Call II.

Rosa Emily Stayner,
third wife of A.V. Call II.

These crowded quarters quickly intensified A.V.'s efforts to construct a temporary enclosed lean-to on one end of the cabin for Lucy and her children. Soon after, he moved her into more permanent housing by completing a one-room, 16-by-16-foot structure on the lot to the west. After finishing this in early August, he pushed to get Alice and her family of five into more expanded quarters by completing a new two-room home just east of the log cabin. These latter two structures were one step up from a log cabin. The frame construction consisted of walls composed of two boards with paper in between and a shingle roof.

Even after completing a lean-to and two other houses, A.V.'s construction projects for the summer were not over. He erected another residence across the street on the southwest corner of block number 8, lot 3; this one was for Emily. He rushed to Bountiful in October to transport her back with their two children—Thomas (four) and Charles (ten months). Emily was reluctant to leave her native home where she enjoyed high social status, was in demand because of her musical skills, and could choose from a host of local cultural events. Her introduction to the valley did little to raise her spirits. With four inches of snow on the ground, the wagon containing Emily tipped over in a mountain pass and rolled down the hill. Fortunately no bones were broken, but she was lame until the end of the summer. The major damage was a weakening of her commitment to reside again on the frontier. After she became pregnant that winter, she insisted on returning to Bountiful for the delivery. Anson made the trip with the family during the summer, and a daughter, Charlotte, was born October 12, 1889. Emily remained with her children in Bountiful for nearly a year, returning to Afton the next fall.

Thomas, the eldest of her two sons, recalled their sparse furnishings in their first one-room home. An old organ box served as a table. The only finished seat was a rocking chair that A.V. made after Emily arrived. A toilet table with a curtain surrounding it was in one side of the room. When the family returned in 1890, Anson had finished a two-room home, but she bore five more children before moving into a more attractive eight-room house a decade later. By then the two oldest sons—Thomas, now fifteen, and Charles, twelve—were skilled enough to do much of the work. Adjusting to Star Valley was not easy for Emily. She was a refined lady who had the means and desire to enjoy a comfortable existence in Bountiful. Struggling to survive under the harsh conditions then prevalent in this mountain region did not provide her the challenge or feeling of achievement that it did for many others.

In reviewing the Calls' first two years in Star Valley, one has to admire the longsuffering, tolerance, and understanding displayed by pioneers at the time, especially those who were members of the multi-family polygamous units headed by one male. It is easy to rationalize that their amazing capacity to endure came from circumstances beyond their control. Certainly they had few other short-term alternatives, but even so, one has to marvel at their ability to adapt and their will to survive.

By the fall of 1888, A.V.'s original log cabin was being used only for his workshop and to store goods. Joseph, his younger brother, had remained in Chesterfield with his two wives, but now he wanted to reach the safety of Wyoming. Accordingly, A.V. offered him the cabin, although he kept the workshop in one end. Joe arrived October 28, 1888, after another harrowing trip when a wagon dropped into a stream bed, spilling the children and many of their precious possessions under the wheels. However, no one was seriously harmed. Joe and eight family members lived in the cabin for nine months before he finished a three-room home. Joe was a valuable companion for A.V. Later he became his business partner and together they constructed many of the early homes and major buildings in the valley.

In time, A.V. augmented the housing for each wife. Within a dozen years they all lived in some of the valley's finest structures. The first improvement was to Lucy's domicile. Two rooms were added on the ground floor, giving the home a T shape with bedrooms in the loft or attic. This expansion proved to be extremely important since Lucy became the mother of four more children between 1889 and 1896. Her next child, born in 1898, survived for just over a month, but she had three more after that, making a total of nine offspring living at home by 1904.

Alice's residence was expanded next with a four-room addition. Again the timing was appropriate. In 1890 when the renovation was over, she moved in with her five children. Then she gave birth to another boy in August and one more two years later. The next son was stillborn in 1895. Her last child, Lorna Louise, was born August of 1899.

Continuing their hardships, the winter of 1889–90 was as severe as the winter of 1887–88 was mild. Food supplies in the valley became dangerously low, and occasionally the snow drifted over cabin roofs. After a court trial, A.V. was ordered to give his neighbors a cow for reportedly shooting their dog. During that winter, most of the livestock in the valley died due to weather and lack of feed. A.V. kept most of his animals alive, but it required taking the straw from every bed in his household to feed them. After the winter was over, he concluded that even if he had kept the cow, it would have died from hunger.

Star Valley experienced limited growth during the decade from 1890 to 1900. In 1891 there were 174 families and 1,041 residents. By 1900 these figures more than doubled to 414 families and 2,219 residents, but population density was still small for an area covering 450 square miles. Travel to and from the valley remained difficult although roads were improved, and a passable wagon trail up Crow Creek Canyon and south to Cokeville was established in 1890. Railroad lines were never extended into the valley, so goods had to be transported by teams and wagons until motorized vehicles became available.

A testament to the region's remoteness was that several outlaws wintered there between 1890 and 1894 with little fear of being captured. Outlaw stories are some of the favorite tales of this period. Well-known desperados such as Butch Cassidy, Tom McCarty, and Matt Warner each spent at least two winters in the valley. McCarty and Warner (both originally from La Sal, Utah), posing as Montana ranchers, bought land and opened the valley's first saloon just north of Afton. Their exploits as outlaws are difficult to document, but they were reputed to have made several bank robberies late in the fall in locations such as Denver and Telluride, Colorado. Then, often with a posse on their tail, they rode into Star Valley just before snowfall closed the passes, thus making if difficult for lawmen to follow. McCarty and Warner were on friendly terms with the locals. No one in Star Valley had enough money to make robbery worthwhile, and they openly fraternized with the settlers, eventually marrying two of the local maidens.

One reason McCarty and Warner became accepted was their reputation for "Robin Hood" generosity derived primarily from the aid they gave settlers during the dreadful winter of 1889–90. The most well-known incident is one Warner related, although the accuracy is difficult to document. (However, residents at the time did acknowledge that the outlaws provided much needed clothing and other provisions.) According to Warner, W. W. Burton, the owner of the valley's only store, had some food available but would not sell it to customers on credit. This angered the two outlaws, and they forced their way onto his premises where many locals were gathered. The outlaws demanded that those present be given all the supplies they wanted. In turn, the outlaws would pay Burton half what he intended to charge, an offer they assumed was reasonable because of his inflated prices. Burton showed some hesitancy, but the strong-arm tactics of the outlaws soon convinced him otherwise, and he accepted their proposal of $1,150 after those in attendance had emptied his shelves.

Star Valley also proved to be a safe haven for polygamists. Knowing their journeys were futile, federal marshals rarely came to the valley. Even when they did, a system was developed to forewarn those in jeopardy. A lookout was established on a low bench-like knoll that overlooks Crow Creek Canyon, the route via Montpelier that the marshals would generally use. The knoll, just southwest of present-day Fairview, became known as Signal Hill. From this mound, smoke signals would be sent skyward warning those in the upper end of the valley who had cause to be concerned (polygamists, fugitives, etc.) when unrecognized parties were approaching. Seeing the billow of smoke, those who had reason to be wary would quickly scatter. If the newcomers were friendly, a second smoke column would arise indicating there was nothing to fear. Other places in the valley also received their names from polygamist ties, notably the city of Freedom in the lower valley.

On occasion settlers had unfriendly encounters with Indians, but most contacts were peaceful, generally tribes coming each summer to enjoy one of their favorite hunting grounds. They traded goods with the farmers, or, as was more common, begged for food. The Indians were even known to use A.V.'s workshop to sharpen knives and tomahawks on his grinding stone. When a group of white men from Jackson Hole tried to stop the Indians from hunting between April and September in accordance with the recently passed Wyoming state law (Wyoming became a state in 1890), the "Indian Scare of 1895" developed. Several Indian chiefs were arrested near the Hoback River, twenty-five miles up the Snake River from the north end of Star Valley. Following the arrests, a scuffle occurred and one Indian was killed. When a band of approximately one hundred Indians was sighted near Star Valley, the word rapidly spread for the settlers to prepare for attack. Local residents cut loose their livestock and gathered into the communities, setting up barricades to defend themselves. As it turned out, the Indians were led by police officers from the Fort Hall reservation. Rather than being on the warpath, they were out trying to prevent further hostilities.

During his first year in Star Valley, A.V. was asked to teach school to the fifteen youths in the area. However, he deferred to Bowen who was in more need of a steady occupation and income. Like A.V., Bowen had attended the University of Deseret and taught for several years in Davis County. He instructed two years in Afton before he left for Colonia Juarez, Mexico, located southwest across the border 150 miles from El Paso, Texas. In Star Valley, Bowen met Harriet Cazier and she agreed to enter into plural marriage. However, this was in December of 1890 after Wilford Woodruff's Manifesto. Mormons at the time who insisted on taking more plural wives were advised by church authorities to go to Mexico, the course Bowen pursued. He lived the remainder of his life in that country, eventually having four wives and twenty-five children. Frequent visitors from the United States included his mother, Mariah Bowen Call, Anson's second wife. He died January 2, 1958, at ninety-four.

After A.V. and Joe formed their partnership, they started building frame houses and barns. A.V.'s two oldest sons, A.V. III and Adolpus, now ten and twelve, spent most of their spare time working for their father. The partnership quickly gained recognition for producing quality work, leading to contracts for the design and construction of mills, stores, and churches. Their first major project was the Afton Ward chapel. It was a one-story frame building dedicated August 13, 1892. A.V.'s design featured a high octagonal tower on the front above the chapel, topped by a pointed cone roof. The weather vane at the peak extended over one hundred feet above ground level.

Soon after, Joe and A.V. borrowed $1,500 to build and operate the valley's first furniture and hardware store, becoming agents for the Co-operative Wagon and Machine Company of Montpelier, Idaho. The one-and-one-half story frame building had leans (rooms with a more flat roof angle) on both ends. One served as a carpentry shop and the other as a shed for wagons and machinery. They operated the business for twelve years. It was only modestly successful because money was scarce in the region as few people had more than just enough to survive.

Both Joe and A.V. became engaged in a variety of ventures, some as partners and others alone. A.V. turned his 160-acre homestead one-fourth mile south of Afton into a farm where he raised grain and hay to feed horses and cows. He also constructed an octagon barn sixty feet in diameter that could be recognized several miles away. Later, he acquired forty acres one mile north of the city. Much of the farm work was handled by his wives and children. In addition, for seven consecutive winters, A.V. taught students of high school age. The classes were offered in A.V.'s home since there was no school building.

Joe was the fun-loving member of the family. He and A.V. built Afton's first dance hall, a two-story building with the hall on top and a harness repair shop and furniture store below. It was located where Colters Lodge (formerly the Valleon Hotel) now stands. Joe operated the dance hall, the most popular place in the valley on Saturday night, for nearly twenty years. Residents rode horses from miles in all directions to attend the dances. Many would stay overnight, attend church the next day, and return home Sunday evening. The hall, also called the opera house, was used to stage the area's first dramas. Occasionally, a play would be presented after which the blocks of wood and benches were moved to the walls, and musicians would strike up the music for the lively dancing that followed. For five years, Thomas, A.V.'s son, played the cornet in the band.

In 1909, Joe's dance hall, furniture store, notion counter, and carpentry shop burned down. He reconstructed a larger, more modern dance hall and kept the notion shop. In 1910, in conjunction with the dance hall, Joe opened the first movie theater. It used limelight to flash pictures on the screen. Joe was inventive in many ways including his reported ability to thwart prohibition laws. Also, without a dentist in town, he became the acknowledged expert in pulling teeth, often performing the extractions in a special chair situated in a window of the furniture store.

As their sons matured and became involved in the businesses, Joe and A.V. decided to break up their partnership. Joe kept the dance hall and associated shops. A.V. had another hardware-type store and received property and other forms of compensation.

A.V. organized the initial acting company that produced dramas and provided a variety of entertainment in the opera house and local chapel. The valley's first drama, "The Charcoal Burner," featuring A.V. as one of the leads, was staged in the winter of 1888–89. He liked to act and frequently got family members involved in the two or more plays presented each year, normally in the winter. Seventeen years later after A.V. had married for the fourth time, his last wife, Margaret, had her music students present the operetta "Elenora" in the opera house. The plays drew large enthusiastic crowds and were the highlights of the long winters. Those who had witnessed the live plays considered them far more entertaining than either motion pictures or television that came later.

After A.V. and Joe ended the partnership, A.V. continued to obtain contracts for most of the major buildings in Afton and surrounding areas. In June 1900 he contracted to erect a school house in Afton. It contained six classrooms, recitation rooms, and offices at a cost of $3,000. In the summers of 1905–06 with two sons, Charles and Christian, he built a school in Bancroft, Idaho, ten miles from Chesterfield where less than two decades earlier he had gone to escape federal marshals.

His crowning achievement as an architect and builder was the Star Valley Stake Tabernacle. On July 2, 1904, he was appointed chairman of the building committee. Work began following the laying of the cornerstone in August. It required five years to complete the large structure, dedicated by LDS Church President Joseph F. Smith on August 15, 1909. A.V. was paid $5,000 for designing the building and coordinating the volunteer labor that did most of the manual work. It was a valley-wide effort by all Mormon families who, besides their time, contributed money and handicraft or baked goods to be sold. With limited local resources, many of the faithful had assumed that such a grand building was beyond their means.

The structure is of middle-English design with two main levels. The tower in front consists of six small, square stories topped by a four-sided peak that stretches 140 feet above the ground. Before remodeling, the tabernacle featured spires on all four corners of the second story and also by the main entrance. The exterior was of sandstone from a quarry on Poison Creek in the Greys River drainage. In the chapel behind the choir was an imposing, elaborate, hand-pumped organ. (A fake front gave it the appearance of a pipe organ.) A pipe organ was placed in the new chapel in 1987 following a major remodeling. The tabernacle was a unique building that deserved, but did not receive, recognition similar to other early Mormon tabernacles, such as the ones in Paris, Idaho, and Brigham City, Utah. Two reasons account for this lack of comparable acclaim. First, it is not on the main street going through Afton, being two blocks to the east. Therefore, it is not obvious to those traveling along Highway 89. Second, renovations or modifications both to the exterior and interior, especially a major addition in 1943, gave it a more modern appearance resulting in a strange blend of the old and the new. In the process of making these extensive changes, the former chapel was converted into classrooms, and a new chapel was added to the rear of the building.

As A.V. approached fifty, he devoted more of his time to civic affairs. When Afton was incorporated in 1902, he was elected as the first mayor for a one-year term. He was reelected in 1903 and 1904, and then again in 1912, 1913, 1914, and in 1924, 1925, and 1927, a total of nine terms. As

Buildings in Afton designed and constructed by A.V. Call II.

mayor in 1912 and 1913 he oversaw the installation of the city's first water system. In addition he was the valley's first notary public, a land appraiser of a three-county area for the Federal Land Bank, and a government weather observer, a responsibility he held for twenty-five years.

His most important religious assignment was as a counselor in the Star Valley Stake Presidency for twelve years. On August 13, 1892, the Star Valley Stake was created by dividing Bear Lake Stake headquartered in Paris, Idaho. LDS Church President Joseph F. Smith presided at the meeting when George Osmond was installed as stake president with William W. Burton as first counselor and A.V. as second. The stake initially had seven wards. Two of A.V.'s wives were also given appointments. Alice became first counselor in the stake primary, and Lucy was chosen as secretary in the stake relief society. For years, A.V. performed an important role in the presidency, especially planning new facilities such as the stake tabernacle. However, the circumstances leading to his stepping down from the presidency in 1904 turned out to be the most bitter experience of his life.

The tragedy leading to his resignation was the death of his second wife, Lucy, then the mother of nine living children. The oldest at twenty-one, Franklin, had left home. The rest were under sixteen. The youngest was not

Star Valley Stake House soon after completion in 1909.

A.V. Call II when he was second counselor in the Star Valley Stake presidency.

yet a year old, born February 1, 1904. Lucy died unexpectedly one month later on March 4. A.V. struggled over what to do with his young family of eight, three of whom were under the age of four. His first wife Alice took them in for a short time, but later they returned to their home under the care of the two oldest sisters, one sixteen and one thirteen.

The nature and sequence of the events that followed are unclear because little documentation is available. Apparently A.V. decided again to enter polygamy, take a fourth wife, and in the process provide someone to care for his seven motherless children. This was fourteen years after President Woodruff's Manifesto, but the vestiges of polygamy were all around. Plural marriages, such as those to his three previous wives, were not annulled and cohabitation was common. The other two members of the stake presidency were also polygamists. In addition, for some time after 1890, plural marriages continued to be performed, although on a far lesser scale than before the Manifesto, except among the Mormon community in Mexico. One reliable study revealed that as many as 250 post-manifesto marriages were sealed through LDS ceremonies.

According to A.V., he discussed his plan to take another wife with President Osmond. (Osmond and his wife, Georgina, had worked on Anson's farm in Bountiful in 1855–56, the first two years after their arrival from England.) Osmond apparently did not object, even recommending that he select someone younger who could handle the rigors of raising a family of seven. A.V. then began courting Margaret Ann Hepworth, a daughter of a local farmer who was the stake patriarch. A.V. was forty-nine and Margaret was nineteen.

At this point the documentation becomes confusing. The following is the version reported by Thomas (A.V.'s son) in a taped recording he made before his death: During the period A.V. was courting Margaret, a stake president's meeting was held in the home of First Counselor W. W. Burton prior to the upcoming stake conference. Apostle Francis M. Lyman was the visiting authority. He told the group that he was aware A.V. was courting a female member of the congregation, and he warned A.V. that he would have to step down from the presidency if this continued or if he again entered plural marriage. A.V. looked for support from President Osmond, but apparently received none. A.V., a determined individual who was not known to back down, said he was going to go ahead with the marriage and resigned.

The following related information is contained in the *George Osmond and Family Pioneers* book published by the Osmond family in 1985:

> In the Conference report from Star Valley is the following: At a Conference held at Afton June 4, 1904 attended by Apostle Francis M. Lyman, the resignation of second Counselor Anson V. Call was received and accepted. At another Conference held June 4, 1905, Wilford A. Hyde was sustained as Second Counselor to President George Osmond.

A third account and the one most difficult to dispute is taken from page 7 of the *Journal History of the Church* for Thursday November 17, 1904: (The *Journal History* is an official document of the LDS Church maintained by various church scribes.)

> The meeting of the First Presidency and Apostles was held as usual. A letter was read from George Osmond and William W. Burton to the affect [*sic*] that it was common report that Brother Anson V. Call, a counselor in the Stake Presidency, had married a plural wife recently and they ask that some of the apostles attend the conference and investigate the affair. Letter referred to Brother Lyman.

Earlier on October 12, 1904, A.V. and Margaret were married in a ceremony performed (according to one report) by her father who was the stake patriarch. This date is consistent with the information contained in the *Jour-*

*Margaret Ann Hepworth,
fourth wife of A.V. Call II.*

nal History and lends credence to the accuracy of this version.

From the information contained in the *Journal History*, one would have to conclude that A.V. resigned at the December 4, 1904, stake conference, not the June 4, 1904, conference, and his resignation occurred after the marriage, not before. Several facts support this view. First, December 4, 1904, falls on a Sunday and June 4 does not. Second, it is unlikely the stake would take one year to appoint a replacement for A.V. after he resigned. Third, he was appointed chairman of the building committee for the tabernacle on July 2, 1904, when he was still considered to be a member of the presidency. Fourth, he had no trouble being re-elected mayor of Afton in 1904 but after this date he was not elected for another eight years.

In any event, it was A.V.'s misfortune that Apostle Francis M. Lyman, president of the Council of the Twelve, was assigned to resolve the matter. At the time, Mormon officials were attempting to demonstrate complete compliance with federal laws prohibiting polygamy since Reed Smoot's election to the Senate was being challenged by other senators in Washington based on their contention that the Church continued to support not only polygamous cohabitation but also polygamy itself. A.V. was also unfortunate because Lyman was the apostle noted for interpreting the Manifesto as *completely* banning all new plural marriages. A.V. was a stubborn man of extreme pride, who stood by his convictions, even when confronted by a man of Apostle Lyman's stature. (The belief is common among many of A.V.'s relatives that Apostle Lyman was later excommunicated from the Church for adultery. This is incorrect. However, he did later have some difficulties with A.V. when he was Afton's mayor, and a company Apostle Lyman was associated with was putting in the city's water system.)

Margaret was a capable homemaker who accepted Lucy's children as her own. Margaret's first child was stillborn on July 11, 1906. She had nine more within fifteen years, making A.V. the father of thirty-seven children by four wives. (See Exhibit IV, page 76.) Lucy's three oldest were married or left home shortly after the marriage. The youngest four, all sons, were so thoroughly integrated into the family that Margaret's oldest living daughter (also named Lucy) never realized they were half brothers until she was eight years old. Margaret was an excellent cook and seamstress, always keeping the children well dressed. In 1908–09, A.V. built the family a large home on Fifth Avenue between Washington and Adams streets. It was one of the first in the valley to have electricity, an indoor modern bathroom, and cement sidewalks.

As President Osmond wrote in his diary, "A.V. Call was a fellow who would never settle for less than the best. He owned the finest carriage, finest team, and finest home." Long after his death, residents would recall how he

Afton home of A.V. and Margaret Call.

Exhibit IV

ANSON VASCO CALL II FAMILY

ANSON VASCO CALL II (A.V.)
May 23, 1855 - October 12, 1944
Died age 89

WIVES:

ALICE JEANNETTE FARNHAM
August 5, 1859 - May 21, 1939
Died age 79
m. May 17, 1876

LUCY ENGLESBY KING
Sept. 21, 1865 - March 4, 1904
Died age 38
m. December 28, 1882

ROSA EMILY STAYNER
Dec. 11, 1856 - June 12, 1950
Died age 93
m. October 1, 1883

MARGARET ANN HEPWORTH
June 11, 1885 - Feb. 13, 1922
Died age 36
m. October 12, 1904

CHILDREN:

ANSON VASCO III
May 18, 1877 - April 26, 1975

FRANKLIN
Dec. 24, 1883 - Sept. 2, 1952

THOMAS JOHN
Aug, 20, 1884 - June 11, 1976

ANN
July 11, 1906 - July 11, 1906

ADOLPHUS ALVIN
Feb. 28, 1879 - June 4, 1952

STELLA (KENNINGTON)
Jan. 21, 1888 - May 24, 1979

CHARLES STAYNER
Dec. 16, 1887 - April 29, 1970

LUCY MARGARET (NIELD)
June 6, 1907 - July 29, 1993

ALICE MAUD (BURTON)
July 12, 1881- Jan. 16, 1973

CHRISTIAN JOSEPH
Nov. 21, 1889 - Jan. 11, 1958

CHARLOTTE V. (ROBERTS)
Oct. 12, 1889 - Feb. 12, 1980

IVAN LEON
March 30, 1909 - March 29, 1979

CLAUDE
Aug. 8, 1883 - Aug. 8, 1883

MARY VASHTI (LOW)
Oct. 20, 1891 - Oct. 14, 1966

HORACE AUTHUR
July 28, 1892 - Oct. 11, 1982

RAOUL
Sept. 30, 1910 - March 12, 1988

ELLA (COOK)
July 14, 1884 - Sept. 30, 1980

FREDERICK WILLIAM
Jan. 27, 1894 - Oct. 7, 1957

ROSA MAY (SPACKMAN)
Sept. 18, 1894 - March 22, 1982

MARIUS ANSON
March 22, 1912 - February 1987

CAROLINE C. (BURTON)
April 22, 1888 - Sept. 8, 1979

WALTER LEROY
May 9, 1896 - April 5, 1956

CYRIL ALFRED
April 28, 1896 - April 19, 1984

CECIL EDMUND
January 19, 1914- May 5, 1986

FARNHAM LAMONI
Aug, 16, 1890 - Aug. 3, 1982

LAURA ANN
March 7, 1898 - April 18, 1898

MARY EDITH
March 12, 1898 - Nov. 3, 1899

WALDO
Feb. 26, 1916 - March 16, 1916

CHESTER ALFRED
Dec. 18, 1892 - April 18, 1983

IRA EDWARD
March 22, 1899 - Aug. 5, 1941

ROSSEAU (ROSSO)
Sept. 1, 1917 - June 4, 1988

ALFRED
April 3, 1895 - April 3, 1895

GEORGE ALBERT
July 6, 1901 - Jan. 1, 1980

RUTH MARY
Nov. 26, 1919 - Dec. 2, 1921

LORNA LOUISE (SCHOLTE)
Aug. 21, 1899 - April 23, 1987

EDGAR ALLEN
Feb. 1, 1904 - May 8, 1973

REVA CHARLOTTE (CLARK) (TODD)
February 10, 1922-

liked to wear woolen shirts rather than coats during the winter and drive his white-top or black-top buggy with a well-bred matched team. Osmond describes one pair as follows: "They were fitted out with a well trimmed harness, lots of red, white and blue rings and keepers. Brass knobbed hames, polished and all the leather well shined."

A.V. and Margaret were extremely compatible, and A.V. was devastated at her unfortunate death from kidney poisoning February 13, 1922, three days after the birth of her last child. She was just thirty-six. A.V. being thirty years older was sixty-six.

After A.V. married Margaret, his other two wives continued to live in Afton for several years. In 1898 his first wife, Alice, lived in the large twelve-room house A.V. had built on speculation but was unable to sell. Of her nine children, one had died and two were married or had left home. Her last child was born August 21, 1899. With such a large home she took in boarders, and her residence became known as "The Call House." In the spring of 1905, she moved into a smaller home on the corner of Madison Street and Third Avenue. A few years later, at age fifty, she took out a claim on a 160-acre homestead in Etna and, with the aid of her children, cleared and cultivated the land. Years later she spent long periods in Utah with her family before passing away in Afton May 21, 1939, at seventy-nine.

In 1898, Emily (A.V.'s third wife and the mother of Thomas), lived in her eight-room house with seven children, the youngest four all under age six. The girl born in 1898 died the next year, reducing her family to six. A.V.'s arrangement with both Emily and Alice was that after their children were older and could be of assistance, he would furnish each family a home but the wives and children were to provide whatever else they needed to live on. For a time Emily continued with her music—singing, teaching, and accompanying—although hearing difficulties later forced her to drop such activities. After her older children left home, the eight-room house was sold and a smaller one was built in Afton.

Emily never became reconciled to the rigors of living in Star Valley, having a part-time husband, and being a polygamist wife. In her latter years, she was essentially estranged from A.V., refusing on one occasion to have her picture taken with him. In 1925 at age sixty-nine she moved to Logan, Utah, near some of her children. Although almost totally deaf, she lived by herself until her death June 12, 1950, at ninety-three.

As years went on, A.V. dropped out of his businesses, turning most over to his sons under long-term loans. He sold the hardware store on the corner of Main and Fifth Avenue to his son Christian J. who used it as a springboard

A.V.'s 80th birthday party, Afton South Ward Chapel, May 23, 1935. Relatives prominent in this history include A.V. (center of first row); Joe Call's widow is to the right of A.V. (neither of A.V.'s two surviving wives attended); Thomas (second row, first person starting on left); Osborne and Evan (two individuals directly in front of the second pillar from the left); Verna, Renel's wife (directly in front of Osborne); Ethel, Thomas' wife (lady directly in front of the open door); Renel (second person to the left from the right pillar, one row down).

to a notable business career. After Margaret died, A.V., now sixty-six, spent most of his time raising the remaining seven children (three had died as infants). Lucy, the oldest living child, was fourteen. She took the lead in helping Anson bring up her younger brothers and sisters until she married six years later when A.V. was seventy-two. Fortunately his responsibility for child-rearing had diminished since the three older boys were all sixteen to nineteen, leaving the remaining three at ages fourteen, ten, and six. The fourteen-year-old, Cecil, was deaf and never married. He lived with his father and gave much needed support. Assistance was also provided by the other children still at home and those married, especially Lucy and her husband, and Ivan and his wife Beulah. Ivan and Beulah were especially important in raising Reva, the child born just before Margaret died, who was only six when the her oldest sister, Lucy, married.

All of A.V.'s children by Margaret had a high regard for their father. He displayed many of the traits of his Call ancestors—extremely proud, stubborn, highly skilled as a builder, intelligent, a disciplinarian, frugal, extremely honest, quick to get to the point, and unwilling to back down from any challenge. Some outsiders were hesitant to associate with him because of what they interpreted as his gruff exterior, but his family adored him, and he was a man who commanded respect. He was not only independent but he expected the same of his children. When the boys were old enough to work and fend for themselves, they knew they were to be on their own.

Margaret and A.V.'s second living child, Ivan, recounted how A.V. would oversee the distribution of food during meals. He would bake bread every other day, often eight loaves at a time. At meal time he would slice the bread and hand a piece to each child along with cheese or the other items to be consumed. He would never cut off more than was necessary, but he never denied them a second helping. His specialty being bread, the children soon longed for other food, but this was not a major sacrifice for a family without a mother in the home. Scarce, more expensive food was kept under lock and key.

The extent of A.V.'s church involvement after resigning from the stake presidency is unclear. According to his son Thomas, A.V. never took the sacrament after that and was rarely involved in church affairs. As of this writing, A.V.'s only living child (Margaret's youngest daughter)—Reva Todd—stated that A.V. always sent his children to church, saw that they were baptized, and had family prayer. However, he normally did not accompany the children on Sunday morning. He also performed most of the ordinances for his children, including the blessing and naming of Marius, Ivan, Cecil,

Waldo, and Rosseau. However, it is apparent A.V. could not put behind him the circumstances surrounding his resignation. At age eighty-nine, just prior to his death on October 12, 1944, after falling while doing some construction, he expressed his feelings in a statement to his son Thomas: "I don't know whether there is a hereafter or not. I think there is but I am not sure. My mother and father have gone, my brothers and sisters are all dead, and I am the only one left, and none of them has come back and told me about the hereafter."

Following in the Anson Call tradition, A.V. was a remarkable colonist. In the struggle to provide for his families and settle one of the most remote areas of the West, he was willing to endure hardships that today challenge the imagination. He was a man of high standards and strong resolve who constantly strived to improve his condition. He had the versatile skills necessary to survive and prosper in one of the West's most difficult regions to settle.

CHAPTER
6

THOMAS CALL: CONTINUING THE BUILDING TRADITION

The next generation in the A.V. Call family faced a world far different from their ancestors'. The United States was starting the major shift from an agrarian to an industrial society, the frontier was almost nonexistent, the Mormons were no longer on the run, and the Church's position on polygamy switched from tolerance in certain situations to outright rejection—even cause for excommunication.

Thomas Call's generation was caught in this transitional phase. Members were striving to overcome the insecurity and nomadic existence of their ancestors. This generation wanted to secure the toehold their parents had made in the various regions of the West and start accumulating assets in the form of better homes and mechanized farm implements to increase output and reduce the enormous demands on their physical energy. They saved to purchase conveniences such as indoor plumbing, ice boxes and refrigerators, metal stoves and ovens, and other inventions that would take some of the drudgery out of their existence. If fortunate, they could even have enough extra for vacations and other forms of leisure provided they could squeeze in the time.

These were not the pioneers whose journeys were worth tracking because of their historical significance—actions that would dictate the place their offspring would be reared, the church they would belong to, and the likely nature of their occupations. Rather, this generation consolidated the gains of their ancestors, provided stability in community and family life, and concentrated on improving their standard of living. Thus, as we move from the earlier Calls to Thomas and his peers, we switch from religious activists and colonists constantly on the go as part of the most significant migration in the history of the U.S. west to the those caught in the more mundane existence of staying put and making the most out of their current circumstances.

Another major change occurring in Thomas's time was the role of those who were now to be the "builders" in society. As Joseph Smith had predicted, Anson was a great "builder" in colonizing the West. However, by 1900 the major western communities were established, and industries were sprouting on their periphery. Accordingly, the new "builders" were the entrepreneurs spawning the enterprises that would be the driving force in raising the national standard of living, providing employment for the rapidly expanding populace, and introducing inventions that offered comforts and conveniences far beyond their ancestors' dreams.

The former community builders and the new captains of industry had many traits in common. Both were trailblazers excited by opportunity for adventure, willing to take risks, and not afraid to lead the way. They were driven not by greed but by the desire to create something important not only to them but to their associates.

Being A.V. and Emily's eldest son, Thomas was sure to learn the carpentry trade from his father. Thomas recalled that at age six he declared his intention of following in his father's footsteps. Not many years after gaining access to A.V.'s tools, he started making toy wagons, comb cases, hand sleds, and clock shelves. His career as a full-time carpenter was delayed until he graduated from high school, but on many evenings and Saturdays he worked alongside A.V. and was involved in major projects such as building his mother's home and that of "Aunt" Alice's. He recalls long twelve-hour days with only Sundays off for church and rest.

In his early teens he enjoyed traveling with his father to pick up freight at the Montpelier railroad depot. Normally snow in Crow Creek Canyon would not completely melt until June. These conditions made it a five-day, one-way trip in regular freight wagons, but A.V. and Thomas would take two smaller ones (generally white-top buggies), cutting the time to two days if they left at 4:00 in the morning. Thirty miles into the journey they stayed at a location known as halfway house. It consisted of little more than a series of shed shelters and an area for camping, and was generally crowded with a variety of travelers and mail carriers. Once forty-five males (mostly freighters) were counted surrounding a huge evening bonfire. The difficult leg of the trip was down Montpelier Canyon. Before bridges were constructed, in one six-mile stretch the wagoners had to ford the stream twenty-six times. Years later when an improved road was established, the shipping point was switched from Montpelier to Cokeville.

As a youngster seeking recreation, Thomas liked to ride the family's blue-roan mare down along Swift Creek to the Salt River where he would hunt ducks or snare fish. However, he never became an avid outdoorsman like his father and gave up hunting as a youngster. During the winter he would climb a side hill with friends and coast down the crusted snow on homemade sleds. With his father's large families, he had numerous playmates for indoors games or his outdoor adventures.

In 1900 when sixteen, Thomas and a cousin (Joe's son) became caretakers of Joe's dance hall and opera house. This allowed them to attend the theater productions and dances free. As earlier noted, he later played cornet in the band and assisted his father when dramas were presented. He also played the violin and was a member of the brass band organized by Thomas F. Burton.

After graduating from high school, Thomas continued to work in his father's hardware and machinery business. In addition, he would often go from farmhouse to farmhouse seeking small jobs as a painter or carpenter. Three years later at a church meeting he met a young woman who within a few months would be his bride. Ethel Grace Papworth moved with her family from Crescent, Utah, (South Salt Lake City) to Afton in 1905. Her father, Osborne T. Papworth, ran a large herd of sheep on the Wyoming range, and when the laws changed it became necessary for him to become a state resident to maintain his grazing rights. Thomas was immediately taken by Osborne's dark-haired daughter who had an eighteen-inch waist. At the dance the next Saturday, he excused himself from the band for one tune and asked her to be his partner for one waltz around the floor. When walking her home that night, she refused his offer for a date, stating that she intended to marry a beau she had in Utah. Thomas responded that the young man was very lucky and he would honor her wishes. However, they continued to see each other, and after Ethel returned to Crescent that summer, she decided Thomas was the right choice.

During the winter Thomas obtained sufficient lumber to build a house. He had it roughed in by the time they were married on September 19, 1906,

Thomas and Ethel Papworth Call at the time of their marriage.

in the Logan Temple. He was following the first cardinal rule of a frugal person—never pay rent. The home had six rooms, three on each floor, and was located on the northeast corner of lot 3, block 7, in Afton.

Thomas and Ethel eventually had ten children, all living to maturity. (See Exhibit V, page 85.) Within six months of their marriage, Ethel became pregnant with Reuel, their eldest son. She bore four more children in the six years following. Work was hard to come by, forcing Thomas to take a variety of jobs such as building sheds, repairing furniture, hanging wallpaper, shingling roofs, painting barns, and playing in the orchestra for $2 a night. By 1916 he had mastered most of the building trades and could finish an entire dwelling on his own. From that point on he specialized in residential construction. The next year he completed a seven-room bungalow at 204 Washington Avenue for his expanding family. The last five children of Thomas and Ethel were born there, and it remained as the couple's Afton residence for the balance of their lives. Neither home originally had central heating. It was the responsibility of the oldest boys to cut seven to ten cords of aspen one year in advance for fuel.

By his own count, Thomas built (sometimes with a partner) over fifty homes. Initially all were in Star Valley, but later his work took him to Utah,

Exhibit V

THOMAS JOHN CALL FAMILY

FATHER
THOMAS JOHN CALL
August 20, 1884 - June 11, 1976
Married September 19, 1906
Died age 91

MOTHER
ETHEL GRACE PAPWORTH
April 27, 1887 - October 29, 1971
Married September 19, 1906
Died age 84

CHILDREN:

	BORN	DIED	SPOUSE	MARRIED	CHILDREN
Reuel Thomas Businessman	January 29, 1908		Lillie Bell Stock (Divorced Sept. 10, 1932) Verna Anson	June 22, 1927 January 9, 1933	one four
Eileen Ethel	July 28, 1909	November 27, 1987			
Evan Papworth Carpenter/builder	February 1, 1911	June 5, 1989	Bessie Warren	July 11, 1935	fourteen
Rosa Vivian Homemaker	August 29, 1912	February 26, 1985	Floyd S. Bagley	May 22, 1934	seven
Gerald Papworth Painter/builder	Sept. 16, 1914	Sept. 13, 1934	Wanda F. Haderlie	June 7, 1933	one
Osborne Papworth Businessman	June 22, 1917	Sept. 7, 1964	Janice Miller	August 4, 1936	five
Spencer Papworth Engineer	Sept. 22, 1919	January 2, 1993	Marie Pead	October 8, 1940	five
Thelma Ree Clerical/homemaker	August 17, 1922		Bernard Gusse (Divorced January 1955) Ronald Enfield	April 10, 1945 Sept. 18, 1959	three one
Robert Papworth Oil/gas business	Sept. 20, 1926		Emma Jean Moore	July 17, 1946	four
Venna Maxine Banking/homemaker	October 10, 1927		Doyle E. Veigel	August 15, 1946	three

Idaho, and Montana. Many of the houses were for his children and grandchildren. He also contracted for banks, seminary buildings, gasoline stations, stores, and various state and federal buildings. The biggest project he worked on was the Valleon Hotel in Afton, a four-story, thirty-five room structure built in 1939 by his sons, Evan and Reuel. At the time this hotel featured the largest ballroom in western Wyoming and some of the finest accommodations for travelers. He also worked on other projects for his enterprising sons such as Bob's home and service station in Rexburg, Idaho, Osborne's thirty-two unit motel in Soda Springs, Idaho, and Reuel's large airport hangar and aircraft factory in Afton, Wyoming.

Thomas was especially fond of Reuel's three oldest boys—Larry, Val, and Bill—probably because they were the offspring of his eldest son. Also, each had worked for him doing carpentry chores, and Reuel was often away on business. An added factor was that Reuel did not share Thomas's religious fervor. Thomas's special interest in helping raise the boys carried over until after they were married. In one ten-year period, Thomas helped Val build five homes for his family, one every other summer in Afton. For Val's first home, Thomas put up the money based on the provision that he it be paid back with interest. As for the price, Thomas stated "It will be the cost of the materials plus 10 percent. If 10 percent is good enough for the Lord, it is good enough for me." After the home was finished, Val and his family occupied it for a year or two, sold it, and then started building again. Val was trying to make ends meet while teaching school, and his real estate transactions bolstered his income. With each home priced in the $12,000 range, he could make several thousand dollars per transaction.

In the late 1960s when Larry was in Great Falls, Montana, operating a blending plant (a simplified form of a refinery) and other family businesses, Thomas assisted him as he had Val. Thomas came during the summer and worked through Thanksgiving helping Larry build a family residence, no small undertaking for Thomas since he was then eighty-four. He also financed the $12,000 to cover construction costs. Not to show favoritism, Thomas built two homes for Bill in Afton.

In the early 1960s, Thomas became involved in home construction in Logan, Utah, building one for his sister, Rosa Spackman, and one for his sister-in-law, Wilda Papworth. Thomas and Ethel liked Logan's milder winter climate, and they found it convenient to be near the Logan Temple. Thomas became a committed temple worker, often performing endowments seven hours a day, five days a week. Ethel started on the same schedule but could not maintain it due to hearing problems that had bothered her since childhood, and also she did not experience Thomas's overall good health. In 1964 Thomas and Evan bought several lots in the island area of Logan within walking distance of the temple. Thomas built four homes, including one for himself. (The island is the flat gorge created by Logan River as it flows from the mountains to the east. Foothills parallel it on both sides.) From 1964 until Thomas's death in 1976, winters were spent in Logan and summers in Afton, although Thomas was often in locations such as Great Falls building dwellings for relatives. In the year or two before Ethel's death, when her health was failing, they resided in Logan year round.

Evan's first major construction project was erecting the Valleon Hotel in Afton as Reuel's partner. Evan then managed it for ten years. Earlier he had worked with his father and became highly skilled in the building trades. Later, he sold building materials in Afton and started a ready-mix concrete plant. (Thomas bought building materials from Evan but some resentment developed because Thomas expected to receive them at cost.) Evan was involved in other major projects such as Strawberry Dam in Bedford, Wyoming. After selling the Valleon Hotel, he purchased a 400-acre farm two miles north of Afton where he and Bessie raised their fourteen children. In 1970 after most of their children had graduated from high school, they moved to Logan near Thomas. Evan became a major builder in the area, constructing and managing seventeen apartment houses and many single-family dwellings. Evan at this time operated mostly on his own. He enjoyed working with Thomas, but they often had disagreements over the size and quality of materials for a project.

At age eighty-four, Ethel died October 29, 1971. Thomas lived nearly five more years, passing away June 11, 1976, at ninety-one. He continued to do carpentry work almost until the time of his death. This was difficult because Thomas was small, being only five-feet-four-inches tall. In his latter years, due to an arthritic shoulder, he could not raise a hammer over his head. He always yearned to be taller so that he would not be as dependent on ladders or for someone to help hoist plasterboard and larger pieces of lumber. Yet Larry recalls when working on his Great Falls home, how Thomas, then over eighty, would scurry around on the second-floor rafters aiding in the construction. His agility was clearly that of a man much younger. When he was ninety, Thomas had one complaint about going to the temple. He didn't like being around "all those old men."

Following in the paths of their parents and grandparents, all of Thomas's brothers and sons mastered at least one of the building trades, even his brothers, Horace and Cyril, both of whom later became chiropractors. As

Janice, Jay's mother, proclaimed, "All of the Calls are builders—they all know how to put up a structure." Vivian, Thomas's daughter, put it another way: "The Calls all have sawdust flowing in their blood." Robert, Thomas's youngest son, recalls, "As soon as I was old enough to handle a paint brush and swing a hammer my father had me working. I am grateful for that although I didn't like it at the time."

Due to their austere circumstances, Thomas and Ethel did not push their children to go on church missions or attend college. Evan was the only child to fulfill a mission, and, although several briefly attended college, Spencer was the only one who finished more than three years. (Three children did go on church missions with their spouses after their children were raised.) However, Thomas and Ethel were always devoted churchgoers. At that time when it was common for members to hold more than one position, Thomas was appointed ward clerk on his twentieth birthday, serving for thirty-five years. He simultaneously held various Sunday school and priesthood positions and was on the High Council for eleven years beginning in 1933. Church work was a little more difficult for Ethel with her hearing difficulties, but she served as secretary and librarian, and, in spite of her disability, sang in various church choirs.

Ethel was an immaculate housekeeper who managed to keep the premises tidy despite raising ten children. This emphasis on keeping things orderly and clean was passed on to many of the children and is evident in how the grandchildren operate their businesses today. Thomas was a strict father who "took his children to the woodshed" whenever he deemed it necessary. This trait of being a taskmaster was common to his father and grandfather and later to many of his children. Anson the colonizer had a reputation for being stubborn and a firm disciplinarian. In his latter years when Mary would read to him in the evening, his son Bowen recalls how he "was required to sit quietly on a stool or get tapped on the head with Grandfather's cane." A.V. was no less demanding. Although it was certainly the tenor of the times, many in-laws consider Thomas and the Calls to be more strict than were their own parents or grandparents.

The demands Thomas placed on his children were two-pronged. He held high standards for their behavior, and he had limited tolerance when they deviated too far from these expectations. The result was that at an early age most of his children—notably Reuel, Osborne, and Evan—wanted to get out from under his control as soon as possible. In the end, it probably benefited Reuel and Osborne since the construction trades became only a sideline for them. Interestingly enough, Reuel and Osborne experienced the same difficult relationship with their boys. In Osborne's case it was primarily with Jay, his eldest offspring.

Some of the paradoxes inherent in human behavior are evident in Thomas's ties with his children. Though he was strict and demanding, at the same time he dearly loved each one. It grieved him if they did something wrong, but he was convinced that dropping his standards would only be to their detriment. While Thomas's harsh discipline alienated his sons, at the same time he was seeking their support. Like many individuals, Thomas had a strong front, but he personally required continual reinforcement. As his grandson Larry stated, "He was head of the household but he needed encouragement more than his children knew."

Another peculiar, almost contradictory, Call trait, (shared by A.V., Thomas, several of Thomas's sons, and many of their descendants) relates to how they direct individuals who work for them. The tendency is to have high performance standards for employees (many of them being their children), but to give them little direction in how each task is to be performed. Larry recalled talking with Thomas about his relationship with A.V. Thomas said that when he was young, A.V. would tell him to do something but he would never show him how—just give him the order to "get it done." While Thomas was figuring out how to proceed, A.V. would get impatient, grab the hammer, and pound away until the task was finished. Then, Larry added, "It is so funny because this is exactly what Thomas did with me when I was thirty-five. He would tell me to do something on the house and then come back and let me know I was not doing it the right way." Evan, highly skilled as a builder, had a similar relationship with some of his children who continued in the building trade. Interestingly enough, with all of their business success, Reuel and Jay display the same trait of hiring employees and then giving them little instruction regarding their duties. As managers, they assume the best way to develop initiative and get employees to learn is to let them struggle on their own.

Another common Call family characteristic, as noted earlier with Anson, was a strict code of honesty. Suppliers had such a trust in Thomas that he had open access to their facilities. When he would send a worker to the local lumberyard to replenish his supply, the yardman would take the list and tell the individual to pick out what he needed. The owner of the sawmill on Swift Creek in the canyon east of Afton told Thomas he could come and get lumber any time whether he was there or not. Reuel and Jay have the same reputation for honesty. In most cases, neither prefers contracts or signed agreements. A handshake is sufficient. Marvin Sessions, who leased Reuel's first station in Afton for seventeen years, said, "In all those years we never had one signing with a pen. Reuel always carried through on any verbal agreement. His word was as good as a bond."

Thomas's values, including his acceptance of work as a moral good, were steeped in his pioneer heritage. The Mormons had long ago learned they could overcome their trials only through hard work, resulting in the hallmark work ethic that has given them recognition ever since. The insecurity of their early days on the frontier is reflected in the advice from Mormon headquarters to keep a two-year food supply, avoid personal debt, and abstain from frivolous activities. "Waste not, want not" was a familiar Mormon theme much more common then than it is today. In addition, they expected their children to be obedient and show respect for the sacrifices of their ancestors. Outsiders (Gentiles) were to be treated with kindness, but children should be cautious about fraternizing with them, especially if it might result in marrying outside the Church.

Without question the one trait characterizing Thomas that is the most widely known to all of his descendants was his frugality. Every child and grandchild who knew him has several tales. The extent to which he deplored waste and scrimped to save are almost incomprehensible to our current throwaway society. Before relating some of these anecdotes, a clear distinction needs to be made between someone considered a "cheapskate" versus a person who is "frugal." Being cheap raises an ethical issue. A cheapskate is someone who avoids paying his or her fair share. Such individuals attempt to push their expenses off on to others, and scheme to take advantage of their associates. However, with Thomas, frugality was a virtue like honesty or helping others. Since all resources are limited, waste is an unnecessary diminishing of assets, and, in the long run, is damaging to the individual and to the ultimate good of society. Above all, extravagance is to be avoided since it is motivated by self-aggrandizement rather than need.

Thomas was never a cheapskate, but he was the epitome of frugality. This was quite natural since frugality is often driven by financial insecurity. Accordingly, Mormon pioneers were known for being self-denying. Many, such as Anson, had lost their homes and farmlands on several occasions and thus had to start over from scratch. Furthermore, many pioneers for years lived on the edge of starvation. Thomas was also influenced by what is referred to as the "Great Depression mentality." Those who lived through the economic depression of the late 1920s and the early 1930s observed neighbors lose everything, even their land when mortgages were foreclosed. Although not often witnessed in Afton, residents were aware of the nationwide

Thomas and Ethel Call's 50th wedding anniversary in 1956. Surrounded by their children and their childrens' spouses. Left to right: Verna (Reuel's wife), Reuel, Maxine, Janice (Osborne's wife), Doyle Veigel (Maxine's husband), Thelma, Spencer, Emily, Bessie (Evan's wife), Osborne, Thomas, Evan, Bob, Emma Jean (Bob's wife), Floyd Bagley (Vivian's husband), Marie (Spencer's wife), and Vivian.

breadlines resulting from 25 percent unemployment. From such experiences, people like Thomas scraped to save every cent, preparing for the rainy day that was sure to follow.

As part of frugality, placing family limitations on food consumption has a long Call connection. Anson's fourth wife, Emma, recounted the restrictions on the four families in the Bountiful compound. During the winter, sides of beef would be hung from the barn rafters. On Saturday a carcass would be lowered and a chunk cut off for each family. The wives all knew they were not to expect more until the following weekend. Thomas would give a similar directive each fall to Ethel. Thomas would fill her flour bin and declare that it would have to last until spring. His instructions to the children were to never cut off butter by the chunk but to always slice it thin. He delighted in tutoring his children and grandchildren on the proper way to eat an ice-cream cone. As he told Larry when he was fourteen, "You don't bite it, you lick it."

An amusing related tale involves Thomas when he was in Great Falls building Larry's home. Hazen Spackman, a brother-in-law of Thomas who was almost twice his weight, was helping them. Larry's wife would prepare a lunch each day that typically included homemade bread, vegetables, and fruit. Just before noon, Thomas would stop work and lay out the lunch. On each plate he would place a slice of bread, two halves of peaches, and a few vegetables. Then he would put the leftovers away. After Hazen had finished the meager helping, especially small for a man his size, he would ask Thomas for more. Thomas proceeded to take out the bread, cut off one slice, and quickly put the remainder back. This was followed by Hazen asking for more peaches, and again the food was rationed out one portion at a time. Later,

Thomas and Ethel's children on the occasion of Thomas's funeral, June 1976. Front row, left to right: Bob, Evan, Spencer, and Reuel, Back row: Vivian, Maxine, and Thelma.

Thomas would remark to Larry, "Hazen eats lunch like he's trying to get rid of it." Larry, knowing his grandfather, enjoyed watching the daily give-and-take.

Thomas's frugality represented itself in many ways. When working away from home, he slept in the unfinished basement or in the construction storage shed. No work was to be hired out if you could do it yourself, and there were few construction tasks Thomas could not handle. He was quick to tell others if he thought they were building a home too large for their needs and to chastise his daughters and daughters-in-law if they bought bread rather than made it. He cut the ribbons off floral pieces after a funeral, and used a pencil until the stub was too short to be grasped. When his son Osborne married Janice Miller, Thomas insisted that he purchase a wedding ring one size too large for her finger, stating "In a few years she will gain weight and the ring won't fit." Now, nearly sixty years later, the ring still slips off of Janice's finger. His frugality was extended even to his own medical care. When his health started to fail, he refused to go to Salt Lake City for better medical assistance because it was too expensive.

Most tales of Thomas's frugality relate to his work as a carpenter. Every material that could be reused he salvaged. Waste was almost unknown. Val recounts that when he was a child Thomas paid him 50 cents a day to pull nails from boards and then straighten and sort them by size in cans. Thomas reused old boards by cutting them off at both ends, just short of the nail holes. When Thomas tore down an old home, he would frequently take out the staircase, rework it, and set it aside for his next construction job. Although Thomas saved by recycling materials, he never scrimped in workmanship. Locals who had difficulty removing boards because of their many nails knew the work probably had been done by Thomas.

Thomas never bought new tools except to replace those few lost or completely worn out. People would smile at the comment that Thomas was the only carpenter anyone knew who could wear out a hammer. His grandson, Gerald Bagley, proudly has on his wall one of Thomas's hammers with a blunted head from continual pounding. He was so careful and protective of his tools that when an acquaintance asked to borrow a paint brush he measured the length of the bristles before lending it and upon its return.

Mixed in with this frugality was a willingness to be generous if the situation warranted. As noted, he would lend relatives money to build their own homes. When Reuel was old enough to drive, he borrowed money from his father to purchase a car, but Thomas would not give him a dollar for gas or the Saturday dance since these were not as essential and hence Reuel's responsibility. Yet when Reuel started showing his entrepreneurial spirit by wanting to build a gasoline station on a prime piece of property at the north end of Afton but lacked funds for the purchase, Thomas agreed to build the owner a home next door if he would trade the property to Reuel.

What benefits besides financial security did Thomas derive from ninety-one years of prudent living? It gave him great pleasure to will his real estate to his children and $2,000 to each of his fifty-four grandchildren. ($2,000 in

Janice Call and her children at the time of Thomas's funeral. Left to right: Jay, Candace, Craig, Janice, Lance, and Sharon.

1976 was the equivalent of $7,000 today.) He instructed his grandchildren to use the money for education, genealogical work, starting a home, or getting out of debt.

Before moving to the entrepreneurial activities of the next generation, two other relatives of Thomas's era who experienced business success deserve to be noted. The first example documents the logical assumption that the family's entrepreneurial genes came from more than just the Call line. Ethel's parents were Osborne Tavener Papworth and Grace Christy Covey. In 1886 Grace's grandfather, Enoch Covey, formed a company with his sons to raise sheep on Utah and Wyoming ranges. At Enoch's death sixteen years later their herd exceeded 24,000. Because of the size of the enterprise, the sons then split the company into several businesses. One son, Stephen, took part of his share and formed a joint venture with his brother-in-law, Osborne T. Papworth, creating the Afton Livestock Company. They eventually controlled a herd of 60,000 sheep, primarily on the Wyoming range. Cokeville, Wyoming, was the main headquarters for the various Covey sheep operations.

When the federal government started to restrict rangeland usage a decade later, Stephen switched his attention to other business interests, although he did not totally divest himself of sheep. When the family divided their joint holdings in 1902, Stephen and several brothers formed the Covey Investment Company. In the following years they built numerous cottages, large apartment houses, and major business buildings in Salt Lake City, including the popular Coconut Grove Ballroom. At one time the investment company had 364 apartments, making the Coveys the largest landlords in the area.

Then in 1933, Stephen joined with other family members to organize the Covey Gas and Oil Company. They opened at least twenty retail stations in Utah, Idaho, Wyoming, and Nevada. They also built a refinery in Casper. Their Mobile service stations featured a sign with the Mormon Meteor race car on top, the car Ab Jenkins used to set world speed records on the Utah salt flats. These stations became direct competitors of those later established by Osborne and Reuel. Eventually Stephen's company expanded by opening a series of Little America motor lodges and hotels, making him one of the most successful businessmen in Utah. Stephen's advice to his children just before he died carried a familiar Mormon pioneer ring: Keep out of debt, avoid get-rich-quick schemes, and pull together as a family.

Unfortunately, after separating from Stephen, Ethel's father—Osborne T. Papworth—did not fare as well. Besides sheep, Osborne had a 320-acre ranch just south of Afton (part of which is now Call property), another ranch in Cokeville, and a meat market and grocery store in Afton. In addition, he served one term as mayor and held other city offices. Later he invested in cattle. One winter a group of ranchers drove their cattle to Nebraska to escape the severe weather, and Osborne lost most of his herd. This setback was compounded by a fall in sheep prices, and he was forced to sell most of his property before he died in 1932.

Another notable Call entrepreneur, although not a descendant of Thomas, was Christian Joseph Call, the second son of A.V. and Lucy (A.V.'s second wife). Christian was fourteen when his mother died in 1904. He lived with A.V. and Margaret, his stepmother, until 1911 when he married. Soon after, he bought the hardware store from his father and operated it until 1926. He also built and developed the Star Valley Power and Light Company. In the next few years he engaged in a variety of enterprises in Ogden and Salt Lake City before returning to the hardware business by opening a store in Idaho Falls. He followed this with the purchase of several O.P. Skaggs grocery stores, eventually moving to Salt Lake City and becoming president of the chain. Then, at age fifty-five, he sold his share in Skaggs, moved to California, and invested in the Sav-On Drug Company. As president, he expanded the business into a chain of one hundred stores, all but one in California. Sav-On was one of the first chains to offer a broad line of goods in addition to drugs and notions. A multimillion dollar annual business, the chain became one of the largest in California, all the more remarkable because Christian pushed the company to those heights in just over a decade before dying January 11, 1958.

CHAPTER
7

EARLY ENTREPRENEURS: REUEL AND OSBORNE CALL

*T*he following is a record the author made after his initial acquaintance with Reuel Call, eldest son of Thomas and Ethel Call:

Saturday morning around 8:00 A.M. while having breakfast, I received a telephone call. The party on the line said, "This is Reuel Call. I'll land in the Logan airport in forty-five minutes and I have another forty-five minutes for an interview." I hurriedly dressed, traveled across town to the airport, and soon saw a twin-engine Cheyenne I land. Out stepped the pilot and only occupant, a sprightly man who appeared much younger than his eighty-six years. He said, "Let's climb back in the airplane and chat for a while." He pulled down a folding table top, and I listened while he told one interesting story after another of his many business dealings with Osborne, Jay, and others who were petroleum pioneers in the Intermountain region.

It was quickly apparent that I was dealing with a genuine old-style entrepreneur; someone who was an authentic trailblazer in creating the first businesses to sprout out of the recently settled lands of the West. Born in 1908 in Afton, he had no close business role models, no ready source of capital, no significant local support services, and no concept of how to start and operate a business. Yet within thirty-five years after graduating from high school he was recognized as "probably the most knowledgeable gasoline salesman in the West," and owned businesses that posted annual sales in the millions. I was fortunate to have the chance to interview some of this original stock—someone who in his day faced enormous obstacles to starting a business, although at the time the changing economy created numerous opportunities.

Like all of A.V. Call's sons and grandsons, as a small child Reuel learned the various building trades. One winter during high school he constructed fox kennels for his father. In striving to be on his own, he soon obtained part-time work as an attendant in Dixon Burton's service station, one of the first in Afton. There he gained an early awareness of the petroleum industry, but his initial major business success was not in oil but in entertainment. Starting in high school and for several years thereafter he rented large halls (such as his Uncle Joe's dance hall in Afton) and turned them into temporary roller rinks. Those interested in trying the sport could rent skates for 25 cents an hour. After success in Star Valley's small communities, he branched out to towns over one hundred miles away such as Lewiston, Utah, and Blackfoot, Idaho. His enterprise became so profitable that in 1928 he sold it to a party in Blackfoot for $4,500 (approximately $30,000 in 1995 dollars). This provided him the initial capital to follow other business pursuits and to support his new wife, Lillie Bell Stock, a young lady he had courted in high school.

While pursuing his roller-skating venture, Reuel searched for a more long-term opportunity and was attracted by automobiles, airplanes, and related contemporary businesses evolving out of the race to mechanize transportation. Retailing gasoline seemed within his reach, and after searching for a prime location in Afton, he settled on the northeast corner of Washington and Fourth Avenue. However, a cabin was on the lot, and the owner—Sheriff Roen (Roe) Hale—was not eager to sell. Finally Hale agreed to trade the property if Thomas would build him a home valued at $1,800 to the east of the station. After relocating the log cabin to the city of Fairview, Thomas built the home and the station in 1928, thus giving Reuel a start on his petroleum career. The lot was also large enough for him to add a home for his new bride. The first gallon of gas Reuel sold from this small corner station was in May 1928. The station consisted of a salesroom, canopy, two pumps, and a car lift with a grease pit below.

Reuel operated the facility until October of 1933 when he hired Marvin Sessions as an attendant and truck driver. Gasoline sold for 25 cents a gallon, higher in Star Valley than many areas because of transportation costs. Sales were brisk in the summer but dwindled to almost nothing in winter. A decade earlier on wintry occasions when drifts closed the roads for weeks at time, barrels of gasoline were transported by horse from Logan, Utah, a distance of over 120 miles. However, soon gasoline was available throughout the year at the railroad terminal in Montpelier. When Sessions was employed, Reuel obtained fuel from the Sinclair terminal in Kemmerer. It required a full day for the driver to traverse 200 miles of winding dirt roads in a ton-and-a-half truck with a 1,000-gallon tank on the back and four fifty-five gallon barrels hanging sidesaddle. Four years later Reuel upgraded his delivery service by purchasing a two-ton Chevrolet truck with a 4,500-gallon semitrailer. The semi could haul four times the load, but time was often lost because the increased weight caused it to frequently sink up to its axles if the soft roadbeds were muddy.

The Star Valley station site selected by Reuel demonstrated his unusual skill in picking ideal retail locations. For years after it was highly profitable and near the top in company sales, even when his retail outlets numbered fifty. However, competition was always intense since gasoline was considered the business of the future, and stations were popping up like dandelions in the spring on every major intersection. At one time the Washington and Fourth Avenue intersection had stations on all four corners. One was branded Mobile and owned by his Covey relatives.

In 1937, Thomas completely rebuilt Reuel's Afton station in a major expansion that added bays for washing and greasing. At this point, Marvin Sessions agreed to lease the facility. Marvin had qualms about giving up his $90 monthly salary to assume the lease. However, Reuel, wanting more freedom, made it easy for him to purchase the inventory by adding 1 cent to the price of the wholesale gasoline until the debt was paid off. In 1949, Marvin and his brother-in-law built an addition to house a complete line of sporting goods. Marvin remained as the lessee until 1952 when he opened his own competing business.

In 1977, Reuel's station was demolished and replaced by the Maverik Country Store format with its western-style exterior. Reflecting the changing times, the two full-service pumps were replaced by six featuring self-service. The full-line service station was superseded by a 1,500 square foot store offering groceries and other goods besides gasoline. The attendants became essentially cashiers rather than personnel trained to change tires, replace antifreeze, and do basic automotive troubleshooting.

After completing the station in Afton, Reuel built or purchased others in nearby communities such as Cokeville, Thayne, and Jackson, Wyoming, and Randolph, Utah. In those days cars had small gas tanks, obtained low mileage per gallon, and were unreliable. Therefore, filling stations could be found in every community of any size. Often the facilities were minimal, consisting of little more than two pumps stuck in front of an existing country store. Sometimes the pumps were so close to the roadway that cars filling up on the outside lane blocked traffic. In some locations the general stores dispensed fuel from a fifty-five-gallon drum with a hand pump.

With a mind ever alert to new business opportunities, Reuel soon concluded that his company would grow faster if he distributed fuel to these small stations and also to farmers who were rapidly substituting tractors for horses to pull their farm machinery. Thus he started wholesaling under the name of Reuel T. Call Petroleum Products. Initially he obtained his supply from the Independent Gas and Oil Company owned by a group of businessmen. The only other bulk plant in the valley was controlled by a major national petroleum company, Conoco. (Bulk plants are large storage tanks for the wholesale distribution of fuel.) Independent Gas and Oil expanded its operations and later became part of PARCO (Producers and Refiners Company). Reuel arranged to become one of its agents, and his wholesale business was on the increase. Later PARCO was purchased by Harry Sinclair who made it part of the nationally branded Sinclair Oil Company with its major refineries and headquarters near Rawlins, Wyoming. All stations and distributors serviced by the new owner were required to carry the branded name, thus forcing Reuel to place his various operations under the Sinclair umbrella.

A distributor (also called a jobber) differs from an agent in that the distributor owns the inventory, bulk plant, and associated equipment. In time Reuel bought the Sinclair bulk plants in Afton, Montpelier (the closest rail head), and Georgetown, Idaho, and captured the Sinclair distributorship from Yellowstone Park in the northwest corner of Wyoming to the Four Corners area of Utah, Colorado, New Mexico, and Arizona—a distance of over 600 miles. In width, his region covered a narrow strip encompassing Lincoln and Unita counties in Wyoming and areas on both sides of the state lines through Utah and Colorado. Since no pipelines serviced the region, Reuel was forced to pick up fuel at the refinery near Rawlins and truck it over 300 miles to his bulk plants and major dealers. (One of Reuel's drivers, LaViel Hildreth, for six years following World War II received $30 each time he completed the 600-mile circuit.)

Reuel's two decades as a Sinclair distributor turned out to be highly lucrative; but, as is common with entrepreneurs, he was never content with his

Afton, Wyoming (Washington and Fourth Avenue), Christmas of 1938. Reuel's Sinclair station is lower left. Covey Gas & Oil Co. owned by Reuel's uncle is upper left. Service stations were on all four corners.

current success and constantly sought new opportunities. He tried to improve his situation by pushing Sinclair to give him better rates at the refinery, "at least equal to his uncle Steve Covey who had the Mobile stations and Little America," and he actively sought new customers wherever he could find them. He looked for ways to get involved in oil wells, refineries, trucking, or any other investment that would test his business skills. In the typical Call "building" tradition, the challenge and thrill came from undertaking a project and seeing it evolve into a praiseworthy structure or a successful enterprise, much like devoted gardeners eagerly await the first blossoms on their prize plants in the spring. With successful entrepreneurs, the satisfaction must come in the "doing," not just in the financial rewards. If financial gain is the dominant or only goal, such misguided motives are sure to lead such a person astray. Too often money changes people, especially when the initial quest for comfort and security turns into greed.

As the local Sinclair distributor, Reuel aggressively marketed the company's products. However, being a branded distributor proved far too confining. In his desire to grow, he looked for cheaper fuel sources and became involved in wholesaling and trucking on a broader scale, an action that placed him at odds with Sinclair. In effect he was operating both as a Sinclair distributor and as an independent through Reuel T. Call Petroleum Products. He greatly expanded the independent arm of his business by arranging not only to purchase and distribute finished products from independent refiners, but to truck them crude oil from wells or terminals. Reuel developed strained relationships with Sinclair not only because of his growing non-Sinclair sales but his difficulty in keeping the two businesses separate. Eventually Sinclair forced him to drop his account, just prior to its selling out to another company.

Reuel's success is reflected in the gallons he pumped and delivered. In 1935 his total annual wholesale operations accounted for 293,000 gallons. This amount rapidly increased until 1954. Then Conoco and Sinclair built a pipeline (Pioneer) extending from the Sinclair refineries near Rawlins to Salt Lake City, thus placing terminals much closer to dealers in locations where Call Petroleum had been doing most of its business. Even with this more ready access of fuel, Reuel continued to expand his independent trucking and wholesale operations to the point that by 1968 the gallons sold exceeded one hundred million annually, eventually reaching a peak of over 231 million in 1973.

In the late 1950s after parting ways with Sinclair, Reuel searched for a new name to identify his stations. He stopped at his small Moab, Utah, outlet managed by a "live-in" couple, Brad and Barbara Hulen. She came out from watching the western television show "Maverick," and suggested the Maverick name. Reuel inquired what it meant, and she responded that it was "something offbeat. Like a critter you can't catch and brand." After his recent "renegade" experience with Sinclair, Reuel decided the name was appropriate, although he insisted it be misspelled as "Maverik," consistent with his reputation for being unconventional.

Reuel did not confine his interests to oil. In 1935, still early in his career, he decided to undertake another major project that if not unconventional was at least extremely challenging—the construction of a large ballroom and hotel in Afton named the Valleon. Along with his brother Evan, an excellent builder, they started by opening an outdoor dance floor, a 70-foot-square concrete slab that would accommodate 150 couples. Four years later in August of 1938, they began construction on a $75,000 four-story (five with the basement), white-stucco hotel. When completed the fashionable facility featured thirty-five rooms with baths, a coffee shop, a sizable swimming pool in the basement, and one of the largest ballrooms in the Intermountain area. The ballroom, attached on the back of the hotel to the east, had a combination indoor-outdoor dance floor divided by sliding doors.

Evan supervised the construction and Reuel arranged for financing. Thomas (Evan's father), Marius (a half-uncle to Evan although the same age and eventually his building partner), Osborne (Reuel's brother), and other relatives worked on the project. Essentially all of Reuel's early business operations involved relatives, many of whom were well-trained carpenters. At the time jobs were difficult to find, and Reuel wanted to be of assistance. Later he attempted to provide them opportunities in occupations other than carpentry since the valley was overrun with Call builders.

In the late 1930s, construction of a four-story concrete building in Afton was extremely difficult. Cement had to be pushed up ramps in wheelbarrows or hoisted up in buckets. However, the hotel was finished on schedule with the grand opening occurring July 7, 1939, within a few days of when the improved road along the Snake River to Yellowstone Park was finished. This was the Wyoming stretch from Alpine to the Hoback River, known as the Grand Canyon of the Snake. Reuel and Evan had assumed that with the improved road Afton would become a major stop for those going to Yellowstone, and thus the community would benefit from a big boost in summer tourism. Otherwise constructing a large hotel during the Great Depression in a small settlement of approximately 1,500 (with fewer than 5,000 residents in the entire valley) was considered by many to be foolhardy. Reuel's

Reuel's Afton station with the Valleon Hotel to the rear, November 1939.

petroleum business was prospering thus giving him enough collateral to arrange for a loan, but the burden of making major monthly payments proved difficult, especially for Evan and his family.

Once the hotel was complete, Evan served as manager until it was sold to Ralph Flygare in April 1945 for $100,000. In November 1947, Ralph resold it to Osborne Call (Ralph's brother-in-law, Reuel's brother, and Jay's father) and John Wallace, a banker in Soda Springs. Osborne and John then arranged for Bob Call (a younger brother of Osborne and Reuel) to manage it for the next four years. After that, Osborne and John leased the hotel to two different parties until they eventually sold out in May 1958. It has been resold and remodeled several times since and is now known as Colters Lodge.

For years, dances at the Valleon were the valley's main Saturday-night attraction. Admission in the 1940s was 40 cents for gents, 10 cents for ladies. Rooms were $2 for a single and $3 for a double. In this big-band era, several orchestras with national reputations such as those of Guy Lombardo, Floyd Ray, T. Texas Tyler, and Tommy Dorsey were featured. Because of its size, the large ballroom was also used to host various civic and social functions.

Another of Reuel's early interests was flying. After taking lessons, he soloed in 1932 and from that date he has continuously owned or rented an airplane and, as noted, remains an active pilot at eighty-eight. He has flown a variety of aircraft, and each year spends more than one hundred hours as a pilot; his lifetime total is now estimated at over 20,000. At various times he has had hangars in New Mexico, California, Arizona, and Woods Cross, just north of Salt Lake City. His retail operations stretched over ten western states, not including Alaska where he currently owns a Trailside General Store. Developing and managing such a far-flung empire would have been difficult if not impossible without his flying expertise and a landing strip close to his Afton home.

His love of flying eventually led him to develop and manufacture aircraft. By the 1940s he had owned ten different airplanes designed to take off and land at sea level. Such planes were often difficult to navigate in the thin air and land on the short strips common in the Rocky Mountains. Never one to pass up an opportunity, he began contemplating how he could develop and fabricate a plane specifically designed for mountain flying. Such a thought would have been quickly written off as pure fantasy by anyone else in a valley that had no aeronautical engineers, metallurgists, manufacturing engineers, or support services of any type. Furthermore, Salt Lake City, the nearest metropolitan area, was 200 miles away. However, Reuel was not to be denied.

In 1937 he contacted his uncle, Ivan Call (a son of Margaret and A.V. but one year younger than Reuel). Ivan had completed a master's degree in civil engineering and was currently teaching physics at Star Valley High School (later to become principal). When Reuel asked him if he could design an airplane, Ivan was obviously taken aback by such a request. However all of Reuel's relatives had witnessed what he had accomplished in the petroleum industry, and Ivan was not ready to write his nephew off as eccentric. After Ivan smiled and said, "Why not?" Reuel told him he had already ordered parts and was ready to develop a prototype under his new company—Call Aircraft.

Next Reuel had Thomas build a 100-by-60-foot hangar with an engineering room and office in one end. Then Ivan set to work designing the trusses for the new craft. Reuel was fortunate to find Gaylord Swartz, an aircraft mechanic and an experienced welder on chrome steel tubing. Gaylord taught Reuel the special welding techniques for this metal, and together they fabricated the fuselage. Within a few weeks the prototype was in the air with Reuel as the test pilot. The plane's performance met their expectations, so Reuel applied for a certificate from the Civil Aeronautics Administration (CAA) to manufacture and market the aircraft and moved to get his $250,000 project past the engineering stage.

After two years of testing and the tightening of specifications, Reuel arranged for the CAA to inspect the plant as a final step in awarding the company a certificate to produce the aircraft. The team arrived on a day etched in American history—December 7, 1941, the day of the attack on Pearl Harbor. Now materials to build the aircraft were impossible to obtain, so Reuel, in an attempt to keep his work force busy, obtained contracts to repair planes damaged by military pilots training for combat at Pocatello, Idaho, and Laramie, Wyoming.

Reuel in his CallAir office. (circa 1940)

After the war, market conditions to introduce a new commercial plane were far more difficult. Manufacturers of military aircraft were converting to civilian production, and every potential commercial buyer was swamped with offers. As soon as materials were available, Reuel and his advisors agreed on a standard design for the plane, naming it CallAir. Four models were offered for sale, each with slightly different features. The standard model capable of handling two or three passengers is a low-wing, cabin monoplane with a cruising speed of 110 miles per hour and a range of 650 miles. It is known for its high horsepower-to-weight ratio, broad wings, and sharp turns.

Reuel had managed to retain most of his work force, primarily Call family relatives, through the war. Earlier in 1940, Spencer Call, Reuel's brother, was working to finish a degree in civil engineering at the University of Wyoming. He had signed on as project manager, taking the lead in doing the detailed design necessary to get the prototype ready to manufacture. He continued through the war years, but Ivan was called into the military, and his loss was permanent since he chose not to return at the end of hostilities. Other Calls prominent in the company included Lamoni (Reuel's half cousin), in charge of building the fuselage; Dora, Lamoni's wife, who placed fabric on the wings and fuselage, and chrome on the metal tubing; Carwin, Lamoni's brother, responsible for all wing components; Marius, supervisor of welding; and Barlow Call, a more distant relative, the test pilot. Barlow later became president when the company incorporated in 1959.

Some "outsiders" held important positions, especially Carl J. Peterson who was employed an 1939 because of his expertise in aeronautics. He became the main test pilot, and eventually vice president for sales. The work force after 1946 averaged ten employees, reaching a high of twenty-five when production peaked ten years later.

In 1949 the typical plane carried a price tag of $4,545. Demand was sufficient to sustain production of several per year (approximately fifty in total), but never adequate to keep the company financially in the black. As a result, Reuel started devoting more effort to his petroleum interests, and the company lost additional key personnel. Spencer's departure was the most significant. He stepped down in 1947 because of his "passion for the outdoors" and started a sand-and-gravel business in Star Valley with his brother Bob.

In November of 1953, new life was pumped into the company when Herbert Anderson asked to convert the CallAir to agricultural usage by removing the turtle-back and one passenger seat to make room for a hopper tank for spraying. This model A-4 duster and spray plane was an instant success, and the factory upped production to one per week. In 1957 this aircraft sold for approximately $10,000 fully equipped versus the standard CallAir now priced at $7,000. Production grew steadily for the next two years, but was still insufficient to bring an attractive return. In 1959 the company was incorporated for $1 million, with Reuel holding most of the stock. The business was sold the next year to Jeff Magnum from Texas. It changed hands on two more occasions in the following seven years before operations were transferred to Florida under the ownership of Aero Commander, a division of North American Rockwell. In later years other companies used the Afton location to produce light utility aircraft and aerobatic or stunt planes. In total over 2,000 aircraft have been built in the Afton facilities.

In conjunction with the development of the CallAir, Reuel came up with several unique inventions, some of which involved using an airplane engine for non-flying purposes. First Reuel designed an attachable ski allowing the

CallAir factory, Afton, Wyoming. (circa 1950)

CallAir to take off and land on snow without removing the wheels. This proved useful for ranchers in remote locations such as the Youngs in the Greys River basin. This was followed by developing a propeller-driven snow car, a forerunner of the snowmobile.

The impetus for development of the SnowCar occurred out of need. A person with a contract to deliver mail between Ashton, Idaho, and Yellowstone Park came to Reuel seeking a means of transportation to get over roads closed by snow. The CallAir engineers designed a vehicle with two skis on the back and one on the front, driven by an 85-horsepower aircraft engine with a special three-blade "pusher" propeller, much like the air boats currently used for duck hunting. Two passengers could ride in tandem in a heated enclosure. The patented SnowCar has a water-bug appearance with its three legs propping up an oblong cab. These cars became popular with fish and game employees, ranchers, and others traveling long distances over the snow, but demand at the time was never sufficient to warrant mass production. In the mid-1950s, with an average price of nearly $3,000, the SnowCar was in the same price range as a new automobile.

As a takeoff of the SnowCar, the company later developed a powerful three-wheel motor scooter that met with only limited success. Though the SnowCar was ingenious, like most of Reuel's inventions, it was ahead of its time. This same problem later plagued Jay in some of his ventures.

During the CallAir era, Reuel continued with his petroleum distributorships, added stations to his retail chain, and rapidly expanded his petroleum wholesale trucking operations. CallAir proved to be a drain on his oil interests, often requiring a cash infusion to keep his pet project alive.

Meanwhile, Reuel was instrumental in getting several brothers started in the petroleum industry. Two years after Bob and Spencer formed the sand-and-gravel business, Reuel told Bob that he had two Sinclair distributorships available, one in New Mexico and another in Rexburg, Idaho. Bob chose the latter. Backed by financial assistance from Reuel and Osborne, Bob opened a station and bulk plant on the highway south of Rexburg. Thomas, with Bob's help in his free time, built the station and a residence to the rear. The Sinclair station and bulk plant, although remodeled and expanded several times, continues to operate at the same site with a still-growing business now managed by Bob's two sons.

Reuel's involvement with Osborne was much more extensive, eventually resulting in a merger of their petroleum interests. Osborne, born in 1917, was nine years younger. By the time Osborne graduated from high school, Reuel was already one of Star Valley's most successful businessmen with his

Janice Miller and Osborne Call, Star Valley High School winter carnival, February 1935.

significant petroleum holdings, and he had plans under way for constructing the Valleon Hotel. Osborne had Reuel's drive and interest in converting any reasonable opportunity into a business venture. In this respect, Reuel served as a significant, perhaps indispensable, role model. In time they became each other's most important advisors, supporters, and companions (both on the job and after hours.) As Reuel states, "Osborne was the best friend I ever had. He was such an outgoing person. I had more fun with him than anyone I have ever known."

Like the other children, Osborne learned the various building trades from his father, helping him on many projects. In high school he was president of his senior class, active in sports, and respected by his peers. He dated an attractive girl, Janice Miller, one year younger. Janice's parents, George and Louisa Miller, raised registered Herefords on a ranch one mile east of Thayne on the Thayne-Bedford road. The year Janice graduated from high school, the two were married during the austere conditions of the Great Depression. In the first year after their marriage, Osborne worked for Reuel and Evan in constructing the Valleon Hotel, and he helped fabricate struts for the first CallAir planes. Their first child, Sharon, was born just short of a year after their marriage. To provide for his family, Osborne took various odd jobs

Osborne (light shirt) in front of the Alpine, Wyoming, station he built for Reuel. (July 1939)

as a painter and carpenter. On occasions, Janice assisted him with wallpapering while their new baby slept in a basket close by. Osborne managed (with Thomas's support) to build a small four-room frame home, adequate for the young couple, but with plumbing limited to cold-water lines. The "bathroom" was a misnomer in their case. It contained only a toilet and wash basin with no bath or shower facilities.

Reuel liked the skills and spirit of his younger brother, and for the next two years he kept Osborne busy constructing gas stations in Jackson Hole, Alpine, and Cokeville, Wyoming. In the winter of 1939–40, through a friend of Reuel's, Osborne built an addition to a motel in Ashton, Idaho, 135 miles from Afton. In the spring, Reuel had Osborne on the go again starting a station in Soda Springs, Idaho, on the community's busiest commercial intersection where Second South (U.S. Highway 30 and 34) intersects with Main Street. The tenants on the corner possessed a ninety-nine-year lease. Their building contained a mortuary on the first floor and an Odd Fellows hall on top. Reuel and Osborne had the difficult task of moving the two-story structure two blocks northwest, near the cemetery, before they could acquire the property.

In the summer of 1940 when the station was under construction, Janice gave birth to Jay, their second child. Sharon, the older sister, was then three. Reuel asked Osborne if he wanted to stay and manage the station. At first he declined. However, Janice, tired of being on the run, persuaded Osborne to remain in Soda Springs. Within a short time they arranged to purchase the station although Reuel kept ownership of the land.

Osborne was a deal-maker with few equals. The first major hurdle for a budding entrepreneur is to acquire backing or capital. Osborne's uncanny ability to envision and negotiate barter arrangements with suppliers and property owners eliminated his need to put cash up front on many of his business endeavors. As soon as the ground was broken for the station, he was exchanging construction materials and services for the future delivery of gas. Using this approach, he cut down on required capital and locked in customers. Later when he owned an automobile agency, for five years in succession, he swapped an associate a new car in exchange for a local building. As owner of a motel, he arranged a similar fuel barter agreement with the company providing laundry service. And, as was quite often his practice, he purchased choice property in Rupert, Idaho, with a new pickup as a down payment.

Another of Osborne's winning characteristics was the length he would go to acquire and please customers. When a lumber truck was driving

Osborne (holding Jay), Janice, and Sharon. August 1940 in Afton just prior to their moving to Soda Springs.

through town, he jumped into his pickup with a tank on back, followed the driver to his camp fifteen miles into the mountains, and promptly sold him the load of fuel. He would often get up at night to fuel trucks under a contract he had with a company in Chicago that delivered to the West Coast. When Osborne heard that Irv Norcross was planning to bid a construction project for a bowling alley, he called and arranged to build and finance it under a lease-back arrangement with his friend. More than once when Janice was shopping she returned to the parking lot only to find that Osborne had sold her car, and she had to wait for a ride or walk home. He was often at his dealership at 6:00 A.M. trying to catch farmers before they went to their fields. One of his associates claims that Osborne made most of his car sales before 9:00 in the morning. To Osborne, people were customers, customers were the source of business, and hence the source of business opportunities. He would leave few stones unturned to expand his rapidly growing holdings. As he told one of his mechanics, "The difference between you and me is that if you were running this and sold a new car and made a good profit, you'd think of taking the day off. Not me. If there is a guy down the road a few miles with a flat tire, I'd go down and fix it, even if it only involved making 50 cents."

The third characteristic contributing to Osborne's success was his congenial, friendly personality. Jolly, gregarious, and fun-loving, he was liked by everyone. He had a loud voice, hearty laugh, and handsome appearance. Although always on the go, he was never very efficient at delivering fuel to farmers because he could rarely pull himself away without talking to each for half an hour. When he ate at a restaurant, every patron nearby had met him before he finished his meal. His relatives agree that he was the most outgoing of Thomas's and Ethel's ten children, with the possible exception of Gerald who died of a ruptured appendix just three days before he was twenty.

These characteristics made Osborne a super salesman, according to Reuel "the best one I ever knew." More than once after delivering a car to Salt Lake and arranging for a ride home, he would sell his host a new automobile by the time they reached Soda Springs. Customers came back year after year, enchanted by Osborne's personality even if they still questioned whether he had given them a "good deal" on their purchases.

Because of his wheeling-dealing nature and reputation as a "shrewd operator," some were cautious in doing business with Osborne. The lengths he would go to save a nickel and his "Call frugality" were well known, and he could be a tough negotiator. However, as Clem Walker, a mechanic in his employ for several years, stated, "Oz was the best guy I ever worked for. He really treated me good. He was not above making a few dollars on a car deal, but if he said he would do something, his word was good as gold." He could also be generous. He once told a nephew that if he couldn't find a better car than the one he was driving, he would give him one and he did. On another occasion, he put four new tires on the car of a person he knew to be in financial distress.

With these attributes, little could prevent Osborne from eventually reaching his financial goals; but, as in most instances when someone starts from scratch, the first few years were never easy. As one of his former employees said, "Oz came right up out of the dirt." The family's initial home in Soda Springs (70 West Third South, a block from the station) was a duplicate of the one in Afton—four rooms and only a basin with a cold tap and toilet for a bathroom. Bathing took place in a portable galvanized tub filled with water heated over a metal stove. In January 1941, six months after Jay was born, Janice moved with her two children to Soda Springs even though the home was unfinished. During World War II, Janice tended the station while Osborne was out delivering gas, and she kept the books for years after that. On such occasions, Sharon, while still quite small, was left to tend Jay or to take him to the neighbors.

At the time, Soda Springs provided the same barriers to starting a business as did Afton. It was a rural, low-income community with a population of under 2,000, hardly an attractive market for someone raring to go and intent on being a major retailer. However, like Reuel, Osborne found many ways to supplement his income besides operating a filling station.

After opening the station in the fall of 1940, Osborne set up a bulk plant and arranged through Reuel to become a Sinclair jobber. He then started delivering fuel and heating oil to farmers in a radius of forty miles. His prospects

Osborne's Soda Springs station and dealership. Second South and Main. (March 1947)

looked favorable until World War II broke out, gasoline became limited, and rationing followed. Osborne's business initially benefited from significant tire sales, but with rubber being in even more short supply than gasoline, tires were subject to stringent rationing. However, Osborne was fortunate in that many of his clients were farmers who needed fuel to operate their farm machinery and thus were given special priority in the government's rationing scheme.

With gasoline sales decreasing, Osborne searched for other ways to supplement his income. Fortunately his capacity to find new opportunities resembled a hunting dog's ability to smell a pheasant. He first arranged to deliver freight in the area for the railroad and then for Garrett Truck Lines. As automobile production stopped when factories became engaged in the war effort, cars became scarce and extremely valuable. Osborne seized on the situation to eagerly plunge into the used-car business. He would buy old taxi cabs and other well-worn vehicles in Salt Lake City, take them to Soda Springs for refurbishing, and sell them on his lot next to the station.

His success with used cars provided the incentive at the war's end to acquire a Plymouth-DeSoto dealership and also one for Diamond T trucks. A short time later he got the rights to sell Studebaker trucks and then GMCs. To house his dealerships, Osborne expanded his service station, erected a small repair shop, and added a showroom for two cars. Besides new and used cars and trucks, for several years he sold Westinghouse appliances. He kept the Plymouth agency until 1954 when the Chevrolet-Oldsmobile dealership (including Chevrolet trucks) became available, a coveted prize since Chevrolet was the largest selling car in America. Recognizing its value, Osborne expanded and updated his showroom and service area, making it one of the most upscale in the region. He typically had twenty or more vehicles for sale on his outdoor lot and four in the showroom. The repair and maintenance areas had the capacity for fifteen vehicles. The mechanics were especially pleased with the new shop because hot water pipes heated the floor during the winter.

In 1955, Chevrolet came out with a major technical advance in car engines with their valve-in-head V-8 motor. With eight employees and Osborne's charm and willingness to make a deal, he became the major dealer in the region and sold a large number of cars for a medium-sized agency. As his most profitable single venture, it rapidly pushed him along the track toward reaching his goal of being a millionaire. However, owning such a business in a small town is not without its problems. Most residents know the owners and therefore the condition of cars turned in on a trade. If Osborne made

Call Motor Company truck in front of Soda Springs station. (circa 1950) (courtesy of LaViel Hildreth)

someone a special deal on a new model, the word soon spread to others. Also, he was burdened because customers sometimes would not buy a car unless he financed the balance. Some never totally paid off their vehicles, especially if they got a new model every other year.

Osborne enjoyed the status associated with owning the agency and liked being a salesman. However, for someone with "building" in his blood, who was most content when engaged in a new enterprise, being tied to a showroom every day proved too confining. Osborne also never adjusted to handling dissatisfied customers who found fault with their cars or with his perceived unwillingness to give them a good deal. Only his family was aware of his sensitivity to customer complaints.

Another factor leading Osborne to sell the agency was that he knew how well Reuel was doing with his retail petroleum operations, and he wanted more of the action, especially since he now had the capital to move aggressively ahead. When an attractive offer surfaced in 1958, he sold the dealership, but kept the Sinclair station and buildings.

Earlier, at the end of World War II, Osborne had gone back to building service stations and pushing his Sinclair distributorship. In 1945, he and a friend from Montpelier, Vernal Peterson, built a station and Studebaker showroom in that city. However, within a short time Osborne traded his half to Reuel for other property. This was followed by a partnership with John Wallace to purchase Afton's Valleon Hotel in 1947. The next year Osborne undertook his first major, independent construction project when he hired Thomas and others to help build what was then Soda Springs' largest motel. In anticipation of the population and trade boom following Monsanto's disclosure of plans to open a phosphate plant just north of town, he constructed the thirty-two-unit Caribou Lodge on his property, one block west on U.S. Highway 30. Six years earlier he had purchased a three-unit apartment house (he later expanded it to five units) and several acres of land at this location. After he bought the land, he moved his family into the apartment house while constructing a large home to the east. Then, in 1948, on property he owned across the street to the west, he buried the bulk plant tanks, put up a warehouse, and in 1949 finished the Caribou Lodge. The motel was an instant success, although within several years others opened and the market became more competitive.

Osborne, constantly active and on the go, initially delivered gas out of a small truck with a 500-gallon drum on the back and only a five-gallon can as a measure. In 1954 he upgraded his delivery service by adding a Sinclair 1,000-gallon delivery truck, giving him two vehicles to keep on the road. Now Jay was fourteen and qualified for an Idaho driver's license. He was soon working summers and on weekends delivering fuel to farmers when still quite small—so small he had difficulty peering over the steering wheel.

At the time, transportation costs were separately identified and added to the price of a car. It was common for dealers to reduce this expenditure by traveling to Detroit and driving vehicles back. Osborne frequently made such trips, especially when he had other business in the Midwest. When friends traveled through Chicago, he would schedule them to return with a car for his dealership, generally with another one hitched on behind.

Once when Osborne was going to Detroit to pick up two Diamond T trucks and return them, one piggyback, Janice assumed she was along just for the ride. However, in Chicago, Osborne arranged for her to drive back two Chevrolet trucks in the same piggyback fashion. The agent at the factory had reservations about her ability to chauffeur such a load, but Osborne assured him it was all right. When the couple stopped in Nebraska to get gas the attendant exclaimed to Janice, "My ____, are you driving those trucks back to Idaho? My wife won't even drive to the grocery store!" Janice just shrugged him off, long ago being accustomed to such unusual duty.

Osborne's reputation "for always having something going" was never more evident than between 1958 and 1963 after he sold his Chevrolet dealership. First he built a larger home on nineteen acres of farmland three blocks west of their residence on U.S. Highway 30. Then, as noted above, he constructed the Soda Springs bowling alley in 1960, followed by the purchase of a major office building in Kemmerer, Wyoming, the next year. This facility at the time was under lease to the U.S. Forest Service. The next two years he obtained contracts with the U.S. government to build and lease back post offices in Soda Springs, Ashton, and Gooding, Idaho. Meanwhile, he was increasing rather than diminishing his efforts to find new retail gas locations, always pressing to augment his growing chain.

This flurry of activity would not be unusual for someone who was sitting back and contracting these projects, but, much like Thomas, his father, Osborne was reluctant to pay others if he could do it himself. He would often get someone to help do the heavy work on a new station, but he generally ended up doing the painting and finishing touches. His children can remember how hard he toiled when building their new home on U.S. Highway 30. He dug the sewer and water lines with a shovel, rather than renting a backhoe, and became exhausted from feverishly finishing the cement in the rain.

Osborne could be blunt and stubborn, but he rarely displayed anger. One of the few times came when a person he disliked backed over his freshly laid cement in front of the Soda Springs post office. Underlying his congenial nature, acquaintances in Soda Springs remember him as muscular ("able to carry a beam on his shoulder up a ladder"), intense, and extremely ambitious. As one speaker at his funeral noted, "I have never known a man who was more industrious than Osborne Call. He had the drive of three or four men."

His strong work ethic might have partially been his downfall. He had a heart attack in 1961 and was told to cut back on physical work and rest three or four hours a day. He was just forty-four at the time and well on his way to reaching his goal of being a millionaire by age fifty. After his heart attack, he decided that one way to cut down on his physical activity was to get back into the automobile business, and he acquired a Rambler dealership from Nash Corporation. Also he made this decision because he missed selling and the prominence of heading an automobile agency. However, he kept his main interests in real estate and in developing his chain of retail gasoline stations. He and Reuel traveled the West searching for property and even flew to Alaska to investigate prospects there.

In the spring of 1964, Osborne had nineteen stations, mostly at other Idaho locations such as Pocatello, Burley, Twin Falls, Boise, Buhl, Caldwell, and Lava. All carried the more recently established Maverik name with Reuel as the primary wholesale fuel provider. The small cut-rate stations that Osborne built required a typical investment of $7,000 to $12,000, although one reached the hefty sum of $15,000. Osborne's success in retailing gasoline followed Reuel's strategy: find locations on major highway arteries on

Osborne Call family when Candace graduated from high school, May 1964. Osborne died four months later. Left to right: Osborne, Janice, Sharon, Lance, Jay, Candace, and Craig.

the outskirts of a community where property is less expensive; make your investment as low as possible; operate as an independent to keep fuel costs down; and always price competitively.

The strategy was effective but not without intense, sometimes cutthroat competition. Both Idaho and Utah have the reputation of being states where a large number of petroleum independents became the pioneers in self service—Pat Griffin of Gasamat, Ferris Lind with his Stinker stations, Sam Bennion of V-1 Oil Company, and Don Pieper to list a few. Some operated in a single region or one community like John Boozer in Idaho Falls. Ownership frequently changed with both the small and large independent chains. The Beeline stations under Sam Bennion before long became Frontier and, later, a part of Husky under Glenn Nielsen in Cody, Wyoming. Realistically, the name of the competitor made little difference. In this highly-competitive, fast-moving industry, all operators realized that if they reaped strong profits at a particular location someone would soon move in to share the harvest. A station could be highly profitable one year and lose money the next if a price war broke out, a competitor opened next door, or the local economy crashed.

Osborne had two traits conducive to creating health problems. The first was his inability to relax. With his go-go mentality, idleness was a sign of waste. Candace, his daughter, recalls that when he came home exhausted late in the evening and sought to unwind by watching television, he generally fell asleep in his chair. Family vacations were brief and involved the most direct route to the destination. The children soon learned they were to pack early in the morning for the return trip home. After a hard day on the road with Reuel (who is not much of a night person), Osborne could not rest in the motel and would press him to go out for the evening. Once when fishing on Blackfoot Reservoir with Roy Brown, Jay's brother-in-law, Osborne grew so anxious from just watching his fishing pole that he insisted on rowing the boat around in circles. A doctor's order that he rest for three or four hours each day was more than he could bear.

The second damaging trait was similar and one that differentiated him from both Reuel and Jay. Osborne not only found it difficult to relax, but at night he would continue to worry about what was going on in his businesses. He was known to pace the floor after midnight when he was thinking of changing automobile dealerships, pondering over the decision. He would tell Janice how he envied Reuel "because at night Reuel could put his head on the pillow and fall off to sleep while I thrash back and forth mulling over business decisions." As Blake Aland, an employee who worked for Osborne and Reuel, stated, "Osborne would work and worry, and then worry and work. Reuel would just go along and take things in stride." Osborne's happy-go-lucky exterior misled those who did not know him well because he was often churning inside.

In April 1964, Reuel and Osborne decided to combine their petroleum interests and form a corporation named Caribou Four Corners. The name was selected representing Osborne's Caribou interests (Caribou Lodge and Caribou County where Soda Springs is located) and Reuel's long standing holdings in the four-corners area of Utah, Colorado, New Mexico, and Arizona. Osborne contributed his nineteen stations, a tanker truck, pickup truck, and some land in Idaho Falls. Reuel put in a variety of property: just under fifty stations and twenty trucks; a refinery under construction at Farmington, New Mexico; and, most important, a complex including a refinery built in 1962 at Redwood Road and Thirteenth South in Woods Cross, Utah, the area where most of the refineries in the Salt Lake Valley are now congregated. On the same site, Reuel had a hangar adjacent to a landing strip and an office building and apartment. Osborne received 19 percent of the stock, Reuel 71 percent and John Wallace, the Soda Springs banker, 10 percent. The Calls still had a $300,000 outstanding note from John, and, in essence he traded it for stock in the corporation.

Maverik refinery at Woods Cross (north of Salt Lake City), spring 1963.

The merger took place for a variety of reasons. Obviously with their combined holdings the company became a significant player in the retail petroleum industry in at least a four-state area. By spreading out geographically, they were less vulnerable to a business turndown in one area or the dominance of a strong local competitor. Osborne was in bad health, and Reuel's three sons were no longer working in his business, so joining added backup for each brother. And, probably most important, they had tremendous respect for each other and assumed synergy would be created through joint ownership.

In reality, it was legally consummating an arrangement that in essence was already in place. Reuel was the wholesaler for Osborne's operations, and many of Osborne's stations were leased by Reuel who was paying him one percent per month based on the facility's value. It seemed much simpler to formally pool their resources and talents. The only question was how they would work together since each was highly independent and liked to run his own show. Several weeks after the merger, Osborne was already talking with Jay about starting some stations. Reuel and Osborne were too similar to benefit from possible complementary skills. Both liked to make deals, eagerly searched for new opportunities, resisted constraints imposed by others, and kept their lives private. Neither was content nor necessarily skillful in sitting back and managing once a new business or series of businesses came into being.

After the heart attack, Osborne took better care of himself and his appearance improved, but medical knowledge at the time was not sufficiently advanced to offer corrective surgery. Occasionally Osborne had chest pains, and relatives and friends repeatedly warned him to cut back, but frequently he was caught painting tanks, laying cement, or engaging in some other demanding physical task. In September 1964, Osborne and Jay were planning to meet in Montana to build a station for Caribou Four Corners. Osborne stopped in Pocatello to do some cement work with one of Caribou's employees. Later the two were in Idaho Falls having supper at a restaurant when Osborne walked to the cash register and keeled over from a fatal heart attack. In some respects it could be considered a fulfillment of his wishes since he had once told Jay's wife that he would rather be dead than not able to work.

8

DEVELOPMENT OF MAVERIK AND RELATED FAMILY ENTERPRISES

At Osborne's death, he left his widow, Janice, and five children. Sharon, the oldest child, was twenty-seven, married to Larry Anderson (a fuels engineering professor at the University of Utah), and the mother of three children. Jay, twenty-four, was married to Teddy Lou Brown, and living in a trailer house next to the Maverik station in Willard, Utah, that he was buying in installments from his father. Jay also operated a small minimum-investment Maverik station under lease from Reuel located less than ten miles away on the north side of Brigham City. Jay and Teddy had two children—Thad, two, and Crystal, only twenty-four days old when Osborne died. Jay's younger sister, Candace, was eighteen and a recent high school graduate. The two younger boys, Craig and Lance, were sixteen and eleven. With three children at home and a variety of business interests to look after, Janice's problems were more than coping with the emotional loss of a spouse.

Reuel, Osborne's partner in the Caribou Four Corners joint venture, had a similar though older family. Reuel and his first wife, Lillie Bell Stock, divorced after five years. They had one child, Cherie. Reuel then met Verna Anson when she was visiting relatives in Star Valley, and they married on January 9, 1933. They are parents of three boys and one girl. Larry, the oldest, was thirty when Osborne died. After completing a bachelor's degree in mechanical engineering from the University of Wyoming, he briefly worked for

Reuel, Verna, and their children. Left to right: Val, Verna, Reuel, Larry, Tommie, and Bill. (circa 1957)

Maverik. In 1964 he was teaching in the LDS Seminary program in Utah. Earlier he married Kathleen Winters and they were parents of two children. Val, twenty-seven, had completed a degree in business and accounting from Utah State University followed by a year of employment with Maverik. After teaching four years at Star Valley High School, he became an instructor in the Afton LDS Seminary program. At the time, he and his spouse, LaBerta Wolfley, had three children. Bill, twenty-five, was working on a master's degree in music at Brigham Young University prior to completing a doctor of Music Arts at the University of Illinois. He married Helen Fields and they had two children. Reuel and Verna's youngest child, a girl named Tommie Loy, was twenty and attending Brigham Young University working toward an arts degree. The following year she married Lawrence (Larry) Schreiber who later came to work for the company.

The fledgling Caribou Four Corners corporation was left in a management crisis with Osborne's death. The company had been in existence only six months, and the retail end of the business was still being consolidated. With two refineries coming on stream, an expanding trucking and wholesaling operation, and over sixty retail outlets, the firm was rapidly moving toward being a fully integrated petroleum enterprise. Reuel's sons were attending college or teaching, and Jay was just twenty-four with limited experience. Even more awkward, the employees providing key administrative support were adequate for a small business, but lacked the background and depth to accommodate Caribou's growing, diverse operations.

When Osborne died, Reuel wanted to keep the company intact, and he immediately suggested to Janice that Jay take Osborne's place as a vice president. Although Reuel and Jay had limited prior contact, Reuel saw Jay's potential as a talented entrepreneur. He considered his nephew to be confident, aggressive, inquisitive, and a quick learner. Of more importance, he was a self-starter and willing to make the personal sacrifices necessary to tenaciously ramrod new projects into being.

The uncle and nephew have similar characteristics that contributed to their instant bonding. They share a love of flying, both enjoy initiating projects and being deal-makers, and they become easily bored, especially when their time is required to administer an enterprise once it is up and profitable. In addition, they share the Call traits of frugality, stubbornness, and a constant striving for independence, especially the freedom to pursue any project of their liking. One commonality that tied Reuel closer to Jay than to his three sons was that both spurned elements of their Mormon heritage. They had weak identification with the Church and did not conform to some Church standards, primarily those that were health related.

Before examining in detail how Maverik developed, it is important to emphasize the circumstances and traits associated with successful entrepreneurship since Jay and Reuel are classic examples. All studies show that when a person with limited finances starts a new business, it turns into a totally consuming activity requiring unrelenting dedication and enormous energy. The aggressive entrepreneur is constantly searching for funds to bolster his shaky enterprise and cannot afford the luxury of hiring adequate staff support. Yet the business is typically woefully undercapitalized. Without question, the rigor required to obtain the first million dollars is far greater than that needed for the millions that might follow. No one starting a complex new business can expect a mere eight-hour work day or forty-hour week. In fact attention diverted to other matters is considered a drain on time, energy, and resources that might be fatal to the embryonic enterprise.

The dark side of entrepreneurship is that in the start-up phase of a new venture, founders tend to neglect their families, find little time for the arts or community affairs, often read little except in their field of business interest, and are restless if detained very long in other activities. The total commitment, narrow focus, and sacrifice of family, recreation, and other pleasures all typify Reuel, Osborne, and Jay as they built their companies and conformed to the limited but exciting entrepreneurial lifestyle.

When Jay received the offer to join Caribou, he was uncertain in how he should respond. He had turned down an invitation to put his Willard station into the company when it was formed, and he had already looked for other property to acquire. However, he welcomed the prospect of further association with his favorite uncle, and he knew he would benefit from experience in a larger company. When Janice urged him to accept the position and look after the family's interests, he accepted in November 1964.

As was Reuel's practice, he brought Jay aboard with no specific assignment. Osborne had left a station underway in Fallon, Nevada, and minor

Jay standing by his Tripacer airplane, 1962.

construction projects in Craig, Colorado, and elsewhere which drew Jay's initial attention. Later, he spent most of his time in building and overseeing stations, but he also worked on collecting major overdue accounts, helped fabricate highway signs to advertise locations, and actively marketed Caribou fuel to new wholesale customers. He operated with almost complete freedom although he often served as a troubleshooter and point man on an "as required basis."

Reuel was pleased with Jay's performance, and he knew which incentives to dangle in front of his nephew to get maximum effort and help keep him with the company. Reuel offered to provide him a Mooney airplane if he collected $30,000 from a delinquent account in American Falls, Idaho. A Mooney is a popular single-engine, four-passenger aircraft that cruises at 180 mph. Reuel also made the offer because he did not like Jay flying his single-engine Tripacer, a plane with a high fabric-covered wing that he had salvaged out of a farmer's field in Colorado. With the promise of such a reward, Jay was not to be denied, and soon he was flying the Mooney in what he described as "a red-letter day for me."

Jay stayed with Caribou Four Corners for over three years, until February 1968. The primary motive leading to his resignation was one characteristic of Osborne and Reuel: He wanted to run his own show, and, much as he admired Reuel, Jay would not be content until he was his own boss. Osborne would have admired his son's decision. After one of Reuel's boys graduated from college, Osborne, advocating typical Call independence, told him to go out on his own rather than work for the Call Petroleum Company.

Reuel and Jay in front of a Caribou Four Corners's airplane (1966).

For Jay, salary was not a consideration. His pay was adequate though by no means excessive. The desire to run his own company superseded everything else. Individuals associated with Caribou at the time, such as Mel Baird, were not surprised at his decision. Mel knew that "right from the start Jay was going to do it." Reuel was aware of his nephew's desires from previous discussions. On one occasion, Jay had revealed his "all or nothing" attitude by telling Reuel, "I am either going to create a big business or be a clerk in a Holiday Inn." Reuel saw so much of himself in Jay that he made little attempt to deter him, although Jay had to apply pressure for approval to establish his own stations in Ontario (just across the Idaho border in Oregon), and Lewiston, Idaho, before he left the company.

Other factors also influenced Jay's decision. He experienced some disappointment because the company was not more aggressive, especially in using long-term debt to finance expansion. Also, Larry was scheduled to return to Caribou as a vice president in late 1966, and Val and Bill gave indications of likely joining as they did two years later. The company was going to be crowded with Reuel's offspring, and Janice and her family had limited

*Caribou Four Corners Board of Directors, November 1977.
Left to right: Verna, Janice, Val, Reuel, Larry, John Wallace, and Bill.*

power as minority stockholders. Also, some contention was developing between Osborne's heirs and the Caribou Four Corners board of directors, and Jay did not necessarily want to be caught in the middle.

Janice was dissatisfied because of her inability to get an immediate cash return on the Caribou stock owned by her family. In Osborne's brief legal will, he followed the typical practice of leaving half his estate to his wife and the balance split among the children. At the time of his death, only a small distribution was made to the siblings. Approximately half of Osborne's assets were tied up in Caribou Four Corners and the other half in the Caribou Lodge, post offices, a building in Kemmerer, and other property. For a short time Janice attempted to manage the latter enterprises. Operating the motel proved especially burdensome. She sold it twice to different buyers, but on each occasion she got it back because they were unable to fulfill the sales contract. Eventually it was permanently sold, and the other properties were placed in a family partnership that is still in existence based on the guidelines contained in the will.

In the interim, with two of her unmarried children going on LDS missions and all three attending college, Janice experienced significant financial demands. The cash flow from the properties was fairly substantial, but winding up the debts and other loose ends proved exceedingly troublesome and difficult for her to handle, even when Jay attempted to assist. Individual debts owed Osborne totaled over $60,000, and many debtors refused to pay, giving the impression that the obligations were no longer valid. Thus Janice pushed for greater income from Caribou Four Corners. The company, however, was asset rich and cash poor, making if difficult to buy back the stock. Since the corporation was private, not public, the stock had to be purchased internally. It was seven years before payments were made to Osborne's family. Then, instead of dividends or the purchase of stock, a significant salary was paid to certain board members including Janice. However, the Internal Revenue Service said such payments must be classified as dividends rather than salaries, and the practice was stopped.

Eventually, after continual pressure by certain members of Osborne's family, Craig sold his stock to the corporation under an offer the board made in 1976, and the rest of the family followed in 1978. The total buyout involved over $1.5 million with payment staggered over several years; although a large sum, it was less than Janice and other family members had anticipated.

During the 1960s and 1970s, several problems plagued the fast-growing company. Because of Reuel's numerous ventures and loose management style, it was never easy for employees to cover his tracks and proved especially irritating to his sons. Reuel is an eternal optimist who assumes that everything will work out no matter what agreements he makes or the extent of his commitments. He limits his focus to what interests him, is not guided by fixed rules, and is driven to undertake new projects and challenging ventures for the satisfaction of seeing them completed rather than financial reward. In fact, he rarely looks back to see what administrative entanglements or debris he has left in his tracks or to calculate his monetary gain or loss. He is strictly a doer, not a bean counter, and is completely enamored with his work and lifestyle. He operates at a steady, non attention-getting pace that proves deceptive because he wears down most others and is rarely forced to accept failure.

This management style created few serious problems in the early years. In the 1930s, Reuel hired Nora Roberts to handle bookkeeping and run the office. She was one of the most devoted, hard-nosed, totally committed employees of her day and a different breed than is typically found in the current work force. For thirty-three years she rarely took a vacation choosing instead to monitor Call Oil finances like a watchdog guards a manor's treasury. She chastised Reuel when he transferred $30,000 to keep CallAir afloat, and scrutinized expenditures like a miser reviews accounts. Reuel never had to ask her about his financial status. He could tell by looking at her smile or scowl as he walked in the office. As support for someone who does not like to be concerned with details, Nora was invaluable, managing for years to keep the company out of serious financial trouble. However, in the 1960s conditions were rapidly changing with the refineries coming on stream and the company's big expansion in trucking and wholesaling. Also, the nationwide trend was for office functions to become automated, and she found it difficult to keep up, especially with computer applications.

Caribou's major problem in the 1960s was identical to the typical difficulty found in most growth companies. Expertise adequate at one level becomes inadequate as the company expands, resulting in operations getting out of control. From 1967 through 1970, Caribou's sales doubled, going from $18.7 million to $37.6 million, but profits did not increase accordingly. In fact, in 1967 the company experienced a net loss, and in 1969 their net profit was less than .001 percent of sales. Gallons sold also essentially doubled during the period going from 85 to 165 million, partially due to the two refineries in Kirtland and Woods Cross, plus a one-third interest in another in Cowley, Wyoming. In addition, the company opened a profitable blending plant in Great Falls, Montana. (This facility blended high-grade fuel and low-grade fuel with lead to obtain acceptable octane fuels at lower unit cost.) With this increase in activity, plus a government program that subsidized small refineries, obviously something was amiss in Caribou Four Corners when the company was still struggling to keep in the black.

This is the situation that faced Caribou when Reuel's three sons were re-employed. As indicated, each had worked briefly for Call Oil during the summer while attending college or following graduation, but none had remained permanently. When employed in the 1950s, (consistent with Reuel's philosophy), they had no specific responsibilities, the company was not short of help, and those on the payroll felt threatened by the prospect of family members taking their jobs. Several considerations caused the sons to return besides their minimal pay as school teachers. Their father was nearing normal retirement age, and they feared losing their inheritance through the company's dissolution, bad management, or acquisition by Jay or others. Accordingly, they decided to join and put their considerable potential into learning the business and getting it on the right track from their perspective.

Shortly after Larry appeared on the scene, Reuel assigned him to Great Falls, Montana, thus clarifying Larry's role and minimizing the threat to employees in Afton. In Great Falls, Larry was to start up and operate the blending plant, open several retail outlets, and be the regional manager. He handled these responsibilities for six years or until 1972 when the company was reorganized and the brothers, now confident from having tested their skills

Reuel with several employees and close associates. Left to right: Marie Aland, Reuel, Verna, Jenny Baird, Kathleen Call, Larry Call, Mel Baird, and Robin and Charles Starboe. (The Starboes were partners in a business with the Bairds). (circa 1966)

in the business, assumed more responsibility for day-to-day direction. While in Montana, Larry was frequently involved in the corporate office's financial problems. On one occasion he arranged to borrow a half million dollars to keep the company financially liquid.

Val joined Caribou after completing his teaching contract in the summer of 1968. Using the knowledge from his degree in business and accounting, he diligently worked to upgrade his skills so he could straighten out the company's financial difficulties and speed up the processing of accounts through automation. A large revenue stream from a variety of supposedly productive operations was being funneled through Caribou's coffers, and his challenge was to speed up the cash flow and turn more of it into profit. As Val put it, "We had a viable business—lots of money running through it. We just had to figure out how to keep some of it."

The cash difficulties were rooted in several problems. Again, most resulted from facets of Reuel's personality. As Mel Baird, recalled, "Reuel was always more inclined to help somebody than collect the money they owed him." In Reuel's push to make things happen, financial considerations were secondary. Also, as noted, the first rule of a frugal person is to not pay rent. The second is to avoid paying interest. Reuel did not believe in being highly leveraged (high debt in relation to company assets), and he therefore refused to incur debt if payments extended over several years. By attempting to expand using only the cash flow from current operations, he was often forced to rely on float to avoid being overdrawn. (Float is the difference in time between when a check is written and a debit is made to the appropriate bank account.) The problem with their depending on cash flow was that many Caribou customers were either slow in paying their bills or skipped paying them at all. This difficulty was compounded because the company was also billing late.

When Val took over accounting, he was alarmed to discover three weeks of invoices (amounting to $600,000 to $700,000) sitting in baskets awaiting processing because the company "delivered fuel more rapidly than it could type and process invoices." Reuel was fortunate to have Orin Geesey, a close friend and president of the First National Bank of Kemmerer, on Caribou's board. Orin recalls standing at the end of the Kemmerer airport runway several evenings waiting for Reuel or one of his sons to land with $200,000 to $300,000 in checks so he could immediately deposit them to prevent enormous overdrafts. It is difficult to imagine a banker more accommodating!

Besides the financial billing and collection problems, weaknesses also existed in various operational controls. Reuel's philosophy of holding down wages and minimizing investment in fixed assets resulted in opportunities for the dishonest. Dale Larkin, at one time a driver for Reuel, recalls how some truckers delivering crude oil to Caribou's refineries would collect for a load even though they only partially dumped the fuel. This went undetected because the company had neither scales nor a sufficient number of employees to monitor what was taking place.

In the midst of these problems, after completing his doctorate in music, Bill came aboard in 1968. He looked after operations in Banning, California, for a year and then returned home to specialize in the retail side of the company.

In 1972, when all three brothers returned to Afton, their roles were differentiated through being assigned specific responsibilities as vice presidents. Larry was over refining and trucking, Val over finance, and Bill over retailing. At this point, Reuel had expanded wholesaling until 75 percent of the company's revenues came from this source. The company was selling twenty million gallons a month in a ten-state western area, with 20 percent of the deliveries being made in Washington and Oregon. As a jobber of finished petroleum products, Caribou sold to twenty major customers such as Flying J, Cowboy Oil Company, Mars, Kiabab Industries, Autotronics, Bonus International, Rio Vista Oil Ltd., Kar Kwik, and Gasamat. Caribou's fleet of forty-seven trucks would load at refineries or terminals throughout the West and deliver to customers' regional bulk plants or storage facilities, a joint network that required traveling over four million miles a year.

At this wholesale peak, Maverik's refineries provided less than 25 percent of total company needs. The Woods Cross facility had a daily capacity of 7,500 barrels, Kirtland 3,500 barrels, and Sage Creek only 2,000 barrels. The company had also acquired fifteen oil and gas wells, mostly near the Kirtland refinery. Although comparatively small, the refineries made a significant contribution to the company's profits primarily due to the "small refinery bias" policy of the federal government. In fact, national and international events were the primary factors influencing Caribou's profitability in the 1970s and early 1980s as explained in the paragraphs that follow.

Petroleum is the world's most important commodity and constitutes the largest international competitive market. The base product—crude oil—differs little from continent to continent and is traded, priced, and distributed worldwide. Without oil, essentially every major national industry and transportation system would be forced to shut down. Petroleum provides 40 percent of all energy resources consumed in this country, and, when combined with its sister product, natural gas, the two are the source of nearly two-thirds of U.S. energy consumption. From a military standpoint, oil has been essential in determining the victors in every major war during this century. Petroleum comprises 25 percent of all world trade, is the largest single item in the balance of payments between nations, and can give even small, unpopulated countries world power. Little wonder that all governments attempt to control, regulate, and influence its acquisition and use.

Although the petroleum industry is active on every continent, its control and distribution are relatively concentrated. Besides the major world economic powers, the industry is dominated by fewer than a dozen giant companies plus another fifteen or so countries that own petroleum reserves and have nationalized refining, storage, and distribution.

With this concentration, it is not surprising that when the eleven members of the Organization of Petroleum Exporting Countries (OPEC) quadrupled their crude oil prices in 1973, instant upheaval was created in world markets. Initially, every firm that either sold, processed, or was a major consumer of oil was hit by the shock wave, followed by a ripple effect that missed few of the earth's human inhabitants. When the Israeli-Arab war broke out the same year and the United States supported Israel, OPEC cut off supplies to the U.S. creating immediate shortages and long lines at American service stations, many of which closed when their storage tanks reached empty. When a severe jolt occurs in international markets, large firms can generally absorb the blow without its being fatal for the company. However, such a shock can be terminal for small companies short on reserves. On the other hand, if events are favorable, a small firm can reap rapid rewards in an industry such as petroleum where profit margins are uncertain and often meager.

Getting back to how these international events influenced Caribou, when the company opened its refineries in the early 1960s and purchased one-third of the another in Cowley three years later, the national situation for small producers was extremely favorable. In 1959, the Eisenhower administration put quotas on petroleum imports to limit the influx of cheap oil, hoping this protection would encourage local exploration and lessen dependence on foreign sources. This made gaining access to the cheaper imported oil a financial plum. Rather than dividing import quotas among refiners based on their size, the government awarded small refiners a larger portion than their capacity justified, primarily to prevent a few majors from forming an oligopoly. This situation made it possible for Caribou to trade its import quota to a West Coast refinery where foreign crude was delivered for a similar amount of crude from a closer source (a Rocky Mountain supplier), thus avoiding the transportation costs while obtaining crude at about half the national price.

This subsidy provided a significant monetary windfall for small refiners until the international price went above the U.S. price in 1973 following OPEC's joint decision to quadruple prices. This reversed the U.S. situation giving the major integrated petroleum companies the upper hand. They controlled the cheaper crude supply and could starve independents who had no producing wells. To avoid this domination, the government again stepped in and forced U.S. majors to distribute both crude and finished products to their same customers in the exact proportions as before the embargo. At about the same time, as a part of President Nixon's price-control program, petroleum came under the price-setting umbrella. To encourage exploration and production, "new" crude or that produced above the levels in 1972 was not regulated and therefore quickly moved up to the world price. The government issued valuable paper "entitlements" to all refiners as a method to distribute access to the "old" oil (that produced at the 1972 level). In the distribution formula, the government again relied on the "small refinery bias," giving small refiners a larger proportionate share. With old oil being cheaper, it increased the profit margins of refiners who could obtain it. An entitlement had value similar to money. One refiner could sell it to another without receiving delivery of the crude. Caribou on occasion sold these rights to other refiners for as much as $1.50 a barrel—a tremendous windfall of several million dollars through paper transactions. The law was an administrative nightmare, but it kept the small independents competitive.

Thus, from 1960 through 1982, the wholesale side of Caribou rose and fell in response to national and international events. The company's distribution peak of 231 million gallons in 1973 was reduced in the next five years by 42 percent or down to 135 million gallons because of gasoline shortages and other market inequities. Even with this drop Caribou did well financially because government subsidies at the time allowed all but the most inefficient, small refineries to be profitable. The situation became even rosier when the Carter administration started to deregulate oil prices in 1979, just before world prices escalated due to the Shah of Iran's overthrow followed by the Iraqi-Iranian War. These events, plus the universal response of producers and consumers to hoard fuel because of the emergency, caused crude prices to gush from $13 to $34 a barrel. This big price jump again served to push small refinery profits even higher, given their government-imposed advantage. Thus Maverik's net income vaulted to several million per year in 1979 and 1980, even though the annual gallons sold dropped to one hundred million.

Although U.S. refineries briefly benefited from the events of those two years, the impact on the world economy was the opposite. Inflation again heated up forcing a major recession. Interest rates in the United States skyrocketed to over 20 percent. The euphoria from the small refiner's good fortune had hardly started to wear off before the Reagan administration, in one stroke, created their demise. In 1981 the oil industry was deregulated, thus eliminating the small refinery bias. Now economies of scale put the big refiners back in the driver's seat, and their smaller counterparts, no longer able to compete, had to shut down. Maverik essentially closed its refining shop in the spring of 1982. Simultaneously the company attempted to dispose of its oil and gas wells, eventually exchanging them for stock in Greenwood Resources Inc. Maverik's wholesale business carried on for one or two more years but at one-quarter of the 1973 peak. By 1985 all the company's exploration, refining, and wholesale operations had ceased.

The brothers' decision to concentrate Maverik's entire business in retailing became obvious at this point. Events earlier in the 1970s also were favorable for the independent, cut-rate retailers. After OPEC's actions caused fuel prices to rise by 35 percent in 1973 followed by their tripling by the end of the decade, drivers became more price-conscious. In prior years, branded oil companies (referred to as the majors) had a significant advantage over independents. With cars needing frequent repair and maintenance, consumers relied on branded dealers because of their facilities, advertising, and superior reputation for qualified service personnel. As cars became more reliable, maintenance and repair service became less important. Improvements were also made in gasoline quality and consistency resulting from more rigid government standards. As a result, the fuel sold by independents was less suspect. Accordingly, within a little over a decade, the market share of the eight major gasoline marketers dropped by 10 percent to 46.7 percent of retail sales in 1981.

In the 1970s, Maverik executives made several attempts to upgrade retailing. Progress was slow at first. By the mid-1970s, only one-third of company income came from retailing, primarily because surplus capital was directed elsewhere. Maverik outlets were fast becoming outdated with the trend to self-service. Many small food markets and country stores were putting pumps in front to sell fuel, hailing the rise of the convenience store (referred to in the industry as C-store) format. Although the Moab station sold groceries as did a few others, the first conventional Maverik C-store did not open until 1972. By 1977 the company was pumping capital into converting all others to the C-store format. With this financial drain, retail expansion was curtailed and the number of stores remained stable at fifty-five to sixty.

As one would anticipate, the events of the 1970s and early 1980s widened the breach between the sons and their father. Reuel wanted to continue pushing in all directions—wholesale, trucking, and retailing. With his entrepreneurial instincts, Reuel was constantly coming up with new schemes, adding customers, making deals to truck products, taking options on land for new stations, and arranging to expand refinery capacity. He not only had the touch of an entrepreneur, but he had numerous opportunities to demonstrate this skill. He personally knew many major oil industry figures in the Intermountain area and a broad smattering of those on the West Coast. Furthermore, with mobility provided by his airplane, he maintained face-to-face contact with most of these associates on at least a quarterly basis. As Larry states, "I have never met a man like dad who had customers all over the West. He knew everyone."

From their perspective, the brothers' problem with their father was how to corral him. The three sons, rather than being bold risk-takers and promoters, had developed into professional managers eager to efficiently operate the company that was in place. They wanted to narrow the scope of operations, focus on what was profitable, and locate a more limited niche in the market where they could consistently compete on even terms.

Their goals were to "turn an unstructured company in to a structured one," and to concentrate the firm's limited resources on the industry segment offering the greatest profitability, which eventually they decided was retailing.

Reuel's perpetual optimism and "never quit" philosophy clashed with the direction his sons were pushing the company, and they eventually won over a majority of the board of directors. In the early days of Caribou Four Corners, the board consisted of Reuel and four family members (Verna, Larry, Val, and Bill); Jay and his mother; John Wallace, a banker and major stockholder; Orin Geesey, the Kemmerer banker; and Mel Baird, president of Saveway Gas in Billings, Montana, and a frequent companion and aide to both Reuel and Jay. Jay and Janice were dropped from the board when the company purchased their stock. Then Orin resigned when federal laws were passed prohibiting bankers closely connected with a company from being board members. In time, the board's complexion changed giving the three brothers control, primarily due to their stock ownership.

How Reuel's children came to become majority stockholders goes back to events of the early 1970s. At the time, Reuel and Verna set up a trust allocating 25 percent of their stock to their grandchildren and a larger portion to their five children. Some of the grandchildren sold their stock for down payment on a home, schooling, and other purposes, but others remained as shareholders. In 1972 the company established a profit-sharing program followed later by an employee stock ownership plan (ESOP). Under the ESOP, a portion of each year's income is contributed to a fund that is essentially a defined-contribution pension plan for employees. As a result of these actions, Reuel and Verna ended up in the vulnerable position of holding only 25 percent of the voting stock. They owned the largest block, but that controlled by their three sons put them in control.

As the void between Reuel and his sons continued to widen, in 1978 the board of directors voted for Larry to replace Reuel as chief executive officer and president with Val and Bill as the vice presidents. Reuel remained as board chairman although at this point he was carrying on significant competing operations outside of the company.

This change in leadership was consistent with research studies on entrepreneurship. One well-known survey documented that start-up companies on average go through 2.7 chief executive officers before the business is large enough to go public with its stock. Entrepreneurs typically do not make strong professional managers once a company is on its feet. Entrepreneurs like to create and promote rather than monitor processes, allocate resources, organize activities, and administer controls. The reverse is also true. Professional managers rarely are effective entrepreneurs. However, in a company's life-cycle both types of leaders are essential.

Initially the new officers avoided major changes. These were profitable years resulting from conditions in the international petroleum market, and their immediate problem was to better organize refining and wholesaling. On the retail side, they concentrated on upgrading the stores to get them more in line with competitors like 7-Eleven, Circle K, and other strong chains.

The new corporate hierarchy presented a paradox because Reuel had never been subjected to significant restraints imposed by others, and no one expected him to change as he neared seventy. Battle lines within the board formed over his desire to purchase a larger aircraft, expand the refineries, and continue enlarging trucking. The conflict came to a head when Reuel insisted on establishing a station in Homer, Alaska, a project he thoroughly enjoyed pursuing, but obviously one that would be difficult to monitor and service. His sons were especially disturbed because they felt company resources could be better used elsewhere.

Unfortunately, their differences were exacerbated by early father-son relationships, contrary lifestyles, approaches to religion, and certain longstanding moral issues. Reuel had been frequently away when they were growing up, so the children were not particularly close to him. However, this gulf between father and sons was little different from that Thomas experienced with several of his children. Like Thomas, Reuel was strict with his boys, gave them little room for deviation, and expected them to be on their own at an early age. When they were older and it came time to choose a career or perform specific tasks in the company, he reacted the opposite, giving them near total independence. Reuel urged his children to attend college, and he opened the door to their working in the company, but he never pressed them to join. Such decisions were clearly theirs.

Although Reuel has high respect for his offspring, his personality and values are more compatible with Jay's. These two are both classical entrepreneurs who generally choose to put business first. They are often nonconformists, yet have high respect for the opinions of others. They feel that mature individuals should be free to make their own decisions, and, in relation to their own actions, they are willing to "let the chips fall where they may." All are traits that occasionally put them at cross swords with some relatives.

When Reuel and the board of directors disagreed over the handling of certain assets or plans for acquiring new properties, Reuel's response, generally with his sons' concurrence, was to take these out of the company and do them on his own. When the brothers wanted to dispose of company property or stations in Tonopah, Nevada, Palm Springs and Beaumont, California, Bridge, Montana, and Phoenix, Arizona, Reuel acquired them and began to operate independently. Initially he used the Maverik name, but this proved awkward and confusing, and conflicted with the wishes of his sons. In 1982, he formally established his own company, selecting the title of Trailside Country Stores. (This company is controlled by two separate corporations. CallAir handles property acquisition and is responsible for constructing stations. The Wyoming Alaska Leasing Company manages the stations once they are opened.)

With the refineries closed and Reuel functioning more on his own, Bill, Val, and Larry were now free to develop company strategy. Exploration and drilling were out of the question even with their experience of operating fifteen wells. Development and exploration require massive amounts of capital, far beyond Caribou's treasury. The brothers disliked refining and wholesaling because of the severe profit and loss swings and felt their company was too undersized to be exposed to such gyrations. Also, it was clear that the government would not likely institute new programs favoring the small refiner, and, with the limited size and sophistication of the two Maverik refineries, they could not otherwise be competitive. Operating as a jobber had some advantages, but was highly competitive and could be risky without a guaranteed source of supply. In addition, independent trucking became chaotic in the early 1980s following deregulation of this industry. In all, with limited resources and depth of management, the prudent course for Maverik was to concentrate in one narrow retail segment where competition was less threatening, namely the rural areas in and adjacent to the Rocky Mountains in Utah, Idaho, and Wyoming.

In view of this strategy, in 1983 it was natural for Bill with his retailing expertise to become president. Larry moved over as vice president of operations. Some lip service had been given to rotating the presidency among the three brothers, but this did not occur and Bill has remained in this position. In 1983 store numbers at fifty-five were near the low in Caribou's history, partially resulting from several outlets being sold the prior year. Using resources formerly tied up in refining and wholesaling, the brothers undertook an aggressive plan to build thirty stores in the next three years. In February 1987, the company name was formally changed to Maverik Country Stores, Inc., acknowledging the new emphasis and more limited focus. The company went from ninety-three stores in 1988 to 112 in 1991. In seeking to gain greater competitive advantage, Maverik introduced fresh-baked goods in

1992 and a cash-only policy in February 1993. Both changes have been effective. In recognition of the emphasis on baked goods, some store titles have been changed to "Maverik Country Store and Bakery." In 1993–94 after dropping credit cards and lowering fuel prices, the company's same-store gallon sales went up by 18 percent and total gallons sold by 22 percent. The company claims it prices 1 to 7 cents per gallon lower than the competition in 80 percent of the markets that it competes in.

In reality, the retail strategy changed little from Reuel's philosophy sixty years earlier—minimize investment, keep expenses low, avoid debt, price at the bottom of the market, and concentrate on rural areas. The primary difference today is the emphasis on selling a growing variety of merchandise besides fuel because of the higher margins. Care is also taken to make the stores as attractive as possible given the minimal investment strategy.

In the late 1980s with Bill, Val, and Larry firmly in charge and Reuel active in expanding Trailside stores, the three brothers sought to consolidate stock ownership and eliminate some associated distractions. Their sister, Tommie, and her husband, Larry, had shown an interest in getting out, and the company purchased their holdings in 1989. For several years the brothers had attempted to buy their father's interest. Such action was not just touchy emotionally, but was also delicate financially because it would place an enormous financial burden on the company unless handled properly. In 1990 Reuel's 25 percent ownership amounted to over $5 million based on Maverik stockholder's equity of between $22 and $23 million. The only way Reuel could be bought out without enormous financial damage was by spreading the payout over several years.

When John Wallace died in 1990, the Maverik board of directors intensified their efforts to purchase his shares, originally representing 10 percent of the company, as well as Reuel's 25 percent. John left most of his shares to Idaho State University and to a cancer research center in Boise. Their boards both preferred cash to these securities, and they agreed to participate with Reuel in the buy-back negotiations. The bargaining broke down several times because an agreement could not be reached on the share price. This came about because the stock's appraised value was higher than book value. After several years of rather contentious negotiations, Jay was brought in as a third party to resolve the impasse. With his help, in 1993 the company agreed to acquire the stock of all three parties, paying over $7 million. Of this total, 78 percent is being paid in ten yearly installments through 2003. It is ironic that the first major long-term debt the company incurred was to buy out the founder. A few shares are held by other parties, but basically the ownership

A typical Maverik country store. Providence, Utah, 1995.

is split eighty/twenty with those Call family members left in the company holding the larger portion and the employees the balance.

In the five years between 1990 and 1995 (their fiscal year ends March 31), the company made remarkable growth. Sales in 1990 were just over $95 million, and by the end of 1994 they more than doubled to $202 million. Sales for 1995–96 (fiscal year ending March 31, 1996) are estimated at $217 million. Of this total, fuel accounts for 70 percent and merchandise 30 percent, close to industry averages. Merchandise sales are critical for most C-stores because fuel is typically sold at near cost after subtracting expenses, and merchandise sales carry higher gross margins (revenue minus cost of goods sold). The typical merchandise gross profit of 35 percent is at least triple that for fuel. It is not uncommon for stores to have a net loss on just fuel sales. Although the company is no longer in wholesaling, it maintains a fleet of sixteen trucks to service its own stores.

Maverik's net profits hover around one percent of sales, slightly low but in the range of most C-stores and grocery supermarkets. Because of the stock buy-back arrangement just explained, the company's debt-to-stockholders' equity ratio more than doubled beginning in 1993. This is high but not out of line considering that over half of the long-term debt is owed to Verna and Reuel. Even with this encumbrance, the company was still able to make its first major acquisition in August of 1993 when ten 7-Eleven stores in central and southern Utah were purchased. In early 1996 Maverik has 127 stores located in seven Rocky Mountain states, although 90 percent are concentrated in Utah, Idaho, and Wyoming. Plans call for increasing company holdings by about ten outlets per year.

Meanwhile, Reuel's drive to pursue new projects is as strong as ever. He now has twenty-five Trailside Country stores and is adding one or two yearly. His stores are dispersed geographically more than Maverik's with locations in Utah, Idaho, Wyoming, Nevada, Arizona, Montana, California, South Dakota, and Alaska. Many are in the same towns or along the same highways as those of his sons and his favorite nephew. His outlets have an attractive format and are on a par with Maverik's and other significant competitors'.

From the beginning when Reuel and Osborne had separate stations, it has been a family practice to treat relatives (including brothers, sisters, children, and cousins) no differently than any other customer or supplier. As demonstrated in the switch in control of Maverik from Reuel to his sons, family members have an unusual capacity to ignore blood ties when it comes to business. Under this "business is business" approach, ancestry has little significance except in providing employment opportunities. When Reuel sold Osborne his first station in Soda Springs, he arranged terms that made it possible for Osborne to survive. However, later when Osborne was behind in paying for fuel because he had large credit balances with farmers, Reuel once left him a note stating, "If you're out of gas and out of money, you're out of business." It was a lesson that Osborne never forgot, and it increased his incentive to become totally independent. When Osborne sold Jay the station in Willard, the terms were no different than those given any other buyer. When Jay purchased gasoline for his Willard station from Caribou, he received no special consideration. In return, now that Jay supplies Maverik and Trailside stations from his refinery in Woods Cross, these companies are treated like any other. In Utah, Idaho, and Wyoming, if one comes across a Maverik store, a Flying J or a Trailside is likely close by. In Cache Valley in northern Utah, Maverik has one store within two miles of a Trailside outlet, and farther north along Highway 91, a Flying J C-store is less than two miles from one of Maverik's. In Brigham City, Reuel has a station within two miles of Jay's corporate headquarters that also includes a Flying J C-store on adjacent property. Probably the most sensitive family situation is in Rexburg, Idaho, where Maverik opened a station in competition with the single Sinclair facility owned by "Uncle Bob." If anyone asks one of the Calls why they put up rival stations the response is always the same—"Competition only makes you stronger."

Many informative lessons can be learned in entrepreneurship and management from Reuel and his sons. Reuel is a self-styled entrepreneur, perhaps of the old school, but one who was extremely important in developing the rural West. He created thousands of jobs and kept communities like Afton alive during the years when farming became modernized and rural people saw their opportunities for employment plowed under by mechanization. He is an open person, willing to share his ideas and approaches with anyone—even willing to give away the majority of the stock in the largest company he founded and nurtured. He is extremely likeable, an excellent one-on-one salesman, and, according to his brother Bob, "a person who can talk to anyone." Verna attributes her husband's success to his ability to get along with people and his skill in human relations. He never gets discouraged, forgives easily, and always looks to help rather than harm. When Blake Aland called to inform him that his station in Preston had burned to the ground, Reuel paused for a moment before saying, "Well, it's time to build another one anyway." He is quicker than most to write off bad debts, making the comment "Well, I guess they need it more than I do."

Reuel is not one to flaunt his wealth or position. As one of his sons said, "He has never spent a lot on himself except for airplanes." Known for having "an idea a minute," he is well read, has a keen mind, and likes to philosophize. Successful entrepreneurship cannot be driven by greed, and Reuel Call is a prime example. True entrepreneurship is reflected in the statement he frequently makes when someone asks when he will retire: "Retire? What is retirement? I am doing what I like to do most."

Paying tribute to Reuel cannot be brought to closure without acknowledging the contributions of his wife. Verna has been extremely important in backing up him up, raising the children, and holding the family together under circumstances that were not always easy. She is a highly capable person who passed along much of this ability to her children. She has never been on the company's payroll although she has gone out of her way to assist on many occasions. She has deliberately chosen to devote most of her time to other activities. She worked fifteen years as a nurse, and in her eighties is actively engaged in various forms of community service. As do many spouses, she deserves significant credit for the success of her mate.

Their sons turned into competent professional managers. They entered the company at a time when entrepreneurship was less important in its development. They are not as interested in unbridled promotion, concentrating instead on keeping the company lean, well-organized, and efficient—driven by their overriding concern with the bottom line. Their management approach is entirely different than Reuel's. They are content to manage from the corporate offices in Afton while Reuel must be constantly on the road visiting stations, looking for new sites, and talking to customers. They have expanded the retail chain while keeping expenses down, and have developed an effective bottom-of-the-market pricing strategy. They have finely honed

Reuel and Verna, 1977.

Maverik into a respected although somewhat controversial chain of C-stores. Their effectiveness is such that the Utah Legislature, acting on pressure from Maverik's competitors, passed a law as one advocate argued to insure a "level playing field." An explanation of the action comes from the May 4, 1995 *Salt Lake Tribune:*

> An amendment applying to all gas stations, but targeting low-priced Maverik Country Stores, was added to Utah's Motor Fuel Marketing Act in the last minutes of the 1994 Legislature. The idea was to make it easier to enforce the required 6-percent markup above wholesale by prohibiting discounts for paying with cash.

Stubborn and determined like their father, the Call brothers are unlikely to change their policies because of the legislature's actions. They can justly claim they charge lower prices than most competitors because they have lower costs. Also, the 6-percent markup law has been in effect covering grocery stores and other retailers for years in Utah, but state administrators have rarely attempted to enforce it. Because of the complexities involved, it would be difficult to get the data to support legal judgments. Also, enforcement would negatively affect competition and raise consumer prices since every major grocery chain continues to have many individual items priced as loss leaders to attract customers.

An interesting enigma concerning heredity is why Reuel is the epitome of a classical entrepreneur whereas his sons fit the role of professional managers. Are the differences due to the era when they grew up, their schooling, having different parents, their role models, the varying financial pressures of their childhoods, the influence of associates, or dozens of other possible factors? As with most complex issues, no single answer is likely to be found, but undoubtedly the company's needs at the time were of major significance. Early the company required an aggressive entrepreneur and later its existence depended on strong day-to-day managers. Both Reuel and his sons have proven to be effective in the business world, and they continue in the Call tradition of making important contributions to their communities and their times.

9

Growing Up in Soda Springs and the Search for Independence

The relationship between Jay and Osborne offers an unusual opportunity to examine how a father who was an outstanding entrepreneur affected his eldest son who decided to pursue a similar career. With few exceptions, all family members and those well acquainted with the family are still alive, and they have been extremely open and willing to provide information. The array of factors influencing a person both to become an entrepreneur and to achieve success in the process are varied, but certainly family considerations must be near the top of the list. Inherited traits, early home experiences (including relationships with parents, brothers and sisters, and others), and role models all channel behavior and shape decisions regarding occupational choices.

As noted earlier, Jay's childhood was little different from his peers in Soda Springs, a small farm community in southern Idaho on the northeast slopes above Alexander Reservoir. This reservoir was created in 1924 when Utah Power and Light built a dam on the Bear River. This stretch along a bend in the river had been a favorite rest stop for those traversing the Oregon Trail one hundred years earlier. The springs along the river were then called "Beer Springs" by early trappers who said the water tasted "like lager beer—only flat." These springs, Steamboat Spring (a notable geyser named because of its rumbling sound), and other hot and cold springs were buried beneath the reservoir when the dam was completed. Remaining as a tourist

Janice with Sharon and Jay at the Miller ranch in Thayne, Wyoming.

attraction is Hooper Springs, a series of small, cold springs that seep from the ground north of the community. The water has the same effervescence as Beer Springs, but it is somewhat bitter, and the curious are normally satisfied with one sip.

When the Calls moved to Soda Springs in 1941, the only significant regional industry was nine miles northeast at Conda, a small community on a spur of the Union Pacific Railroad. In 1920, Anaconda Copper Company established this company town to support its phosphate mining operations. The ore was collected at Conda and then shipped to Montana for processing into commercial fertilizer.

Another brief industrial boom affecting Soda Springs was in 1950 when Monsanto Chemical Company started construction of a plant three miles north to mine and process phosphate ore. Soon after it opened in June of 1952, employment reached 200, boosting the community's population to 2,500, a level that remained constant until after Jay graduated from high school in 1958. Only 700 more residents have been added in the past thirty-five years.

All five of Osborne's and Janice's children have fond memories of being raised in this small community with its limited resources and diversity. They praise the people, environs, schools, and other institutions. Typical are Jay's comments when he spoke at the 1991 Soda Springs High School commencement:

I have observed the difference between people who come from rural areas and rural schools versus those who come from urban areas and schools. People from smaller schools have had more experience in leadership. They are accustomed to winning. The have had to take responsibility because their classes are small, the athletic teams are smaller, and the debate teams yet smaller. . . . People get used to being on the starting team . . . and they become very successful.

When Jay was three the family moved from the small four-room, partially-plumbed home into the three-unit apartment house Osborne purchased on Highway 30, one block west of the station. Two years later Osborne finished the eight-room brick and frame home next door to the east. The family was not particularly affluent until Jay was in high school; by then the Chevrolet agency was flourishing and Osborne's other investments were paying off. When the family first moved to Soda Springs, Osborne continued to take painting and wallpapering jobs to supplement their meager income. When Jay was twelve, he mowed the lawn around the motel as well as several neighbors' lawns to earn spending money. After Osborne purchased the Chevrolet agency, Jay owned or had access to a car, but he was expected to earn enough for fuel and incidental expenses.

Janice with Sharon and Jay.

Growing up, Jay had numerous neighborhood friends. Together they rode bicycles, hiked in the adjacent mountains, made rafts to float on Alexander Reservoir, swam in Formation Springs (now a preserve six miles northeast of Soda Springs), fished in nearby streams, and participated in school and LDS Church events. Jay had a cocker spaniel that was his constant companion. At an early age Jay was attracted by all forms of transportation. When a local police officer took Jay's bicycle for narrowly brushing a lady and knocking her down, he slipped into the police station to retrieve the bike while the officers watched in a cafe across the street,

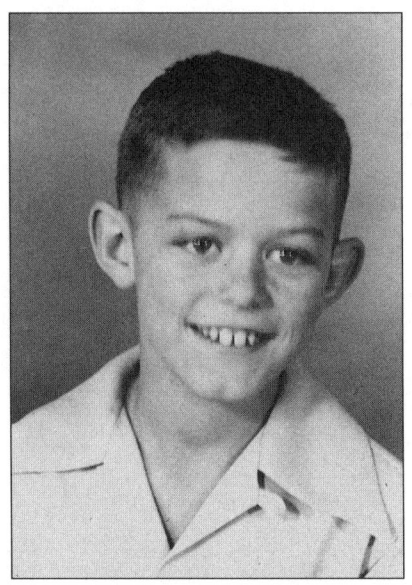
Jay when he was eight

chuckling as they sipped their coffee. Jay was not going to be without his wheels!

A few years later cars became his attraction, but here his interests were not ordinary. He liked to take one his father obtained on a trade, give it a distinctive paint job, and add novelties such as a peculiar horn, hot-wired body, and a record player behind the front seat. He refurbished several cars during high school and sold them either for income or to upgrade his transportation. Being far more adventuresome than most, Jay liked cars because they provided the mobility to explore beyond the confines of his native community.

He did little with his father because Osborne was out of town during the week, or he was tied up evenings on business matters. Saturday was no different from any other weekday, and Sundays Osborne generally devoted to church affairs. The family had few vacations. Most were short trips such as going to Yellowstone Park. Janice and the children urged Osborne several times to purchase property on Bear Lake, but he always refused, stating that it would take them away on Sundays.

Over the years the family had few contacts with Call relatives in Afton. The Calls held infrequent family reunions, probably because of the many progenies from polygamous marriages and the remaining resentment among A.V.'s descendants in the four separate family lines. When Osborne's family traveled to Star Valley they visited primarily Janice's relatives. Jay especially liked to spend one or two weeks each summer with his favorite aunt, Virginia Miller Hokanson, and her family at their Thayne ranch north of Afton.

Neighbors remember the Call children as being well behaved with little squabbling among the siblings, although members of the family note that home life was not always tranquil. Janice was an attentive mother who dutifully telephoned home in the evening if she and Osborne were away. She kept the house clean and orderly and cooked big, tasteful meals. Her emphasis on cleanliness obviously influenced Jay in how he kept his cars and other vehicles and later maintained his stations. Janice had (and still maintains for her age) a trim figure, was and is attractive, and no one finds her when she is not presentable. Some in Soda Springs mistook her quiet, reserved deportment as being snobbish. However, close acquaintances consider her a fascinating companion, although one who is frequently private and seeks to be alone. Because of her shyness, she held few church executive or teaching positions and was not considered a social climber. With a quiet mother and a father who was frequently away, communication within the family was often minimal. Due to Osborne's absences, Janice carried an extra parental load, but any form of punishment was delayed until he got home. When the youngest child, Lance, was born, Osborne was in Pocatello on business, and Sharon, their oldest child at sixteen, dropped her mother off at the hospital for the delivery.

Jay was expected to work for his father as soon as he could be of assistance. He drove the delivery truck at fourteen and tended the station when he was so young some customers thought he must be an impostor. He worked many evenings, weekends, and summers, but working never seriously inhibited his social life. Jay was always friendly, outgoing, inquisitive, and full of fun. With his charisma, rare gift for conversation, and ready access to an automobile, he always had an abundance of boy and girl friends. Patty Tipton (Smith), his long-time neighbor and classmate, declared "You will not find people who don't like Jay." Unfortunately his full work and social life had some drawbacks since he found too little time for sleep or studies.

In Soda Spring's four-year high school, Jay initially gave little hint of being a nonconformist. He was elected to several positions as a class officer, did well in school, and maintained favorable relations with his teachers, family, and other adult "overseers." Many were aware that he scored high on intelligence tests, and he was recognized as a young person with significant potential. Thus they expected him to be a high achiever as he advanced through the upper grades. Unfortunately, the further he moved along the more boring school became. For someone with a short attention span who was constantly seeking new, exciting experiences, he was easily put off by repetition or activity that seemed irrelevant. Listening to lectures and spending time memorizing data to parrot back on examinations did not fit his temperament. However, he was elected as a junior class officer and received average grades in his last two high school years, but his primary interests were friends and outside activities.

Jay's behavior was typical of many teenagers with unusual ability, potential, and zeal. They want to get on with their lives and feel they can be achievers through some route other than schooling. He yearned to be independent and in control of his own destiny, but at the same time he recognized the uncertainty of what lay ahead. He was self-assured, bordering on being cocky, but (in the words of one friend) it was "quality cockiness" or being knowledgeable for his age but less knowledgeable than he assumed. In addition, Jay had the Call strong-will and determination, was not immune to hard work, liked to challenge conventional social and religious norms, and could be verbally outspoken. He was prone to testing the limits of his cars and motorcycles which kept local law officials on the watch for his 1954 Chevrolet with the customized grill and readily identifiable maroon paint job. He enjoyed teenaged pranks, dragging Main, and interacting with the opposite sex. Drag races on the outskirts of Jackson and Montpelier were not uncommon, and he was known to traverse the sharp curves up and down Teton Pass at a record clip. But it was all in youthful fun with no serious violations of the law intended. Handsome, exciting to be around, and always on the go, his first wife Teddy referred to him as the "James Dean of Soda Springs."

With his constant yearning for adventure, he liked to get out of town when he did not have to work on weekends and evenings and, as one friend put it, "see what was across the next hill." Trips with companions to local haunts such as Jackson Hole, Pocatello, Logan, and Salt Lake City were common. Even Mexico was not out of reach when they were seeking fancy seat covers for the car and a quest for new experiences. They would often leave in the evening with little money in their pockets and a tank full of Osborne's gas, not knowing where their whims would lead them.

It should not be concluded that Jay was a mischievous teenager who had no concern for others. When he threw a firecracker into an open car on the Fourth of July not knowing anyone was inside, he apologized the next day to Mrs. Parker. When he glanced off two cars that had sideswiped on a slippery road, although he was not at fault, he was one of the first to visit an injured party. He was generous with his friends and could always be counted on for assistance.

In Jay's latter teenage years, his exciting life with friends was offset by difficulties with his parents, especially his father. As a youth, Jay always had his mother as an advocate although she acknowledges that when he was sixteen and seventeen he was "almost impossible for me to handle." Osborne was the stern disciplinarian, much like Thomas, his father. Osborne closely monitored Jay's activities and would let little go without some criticism. In many respects, it was a clash of traditional Call traits. Father and son were both headstrong, proud, and independent, and both liked to be in control. With the father's iron-handed background, sparks were sure to fly and they did. In later years, each realized that their shared traits were the underlying cause of their discord.

Osborne Call family at the time of Jay's high school graduation. Left to right: Craig, Sharon, Janice, Jay, Lance, Osborne, and Candace.

Although both parties were at fault, Osborne made the tragic mistake that fathers often do with eldest sons. Holding high expectations, the father wants the son to either follow in his path or achieve goals he has failed to attain. When the son does not move in the desired direction or is unwilling to conform, the father tends to become more strict and finds fault more quickly. To bring his offspring in line, the father adds more pressure, unknowingly ups his demands, and looks for his child to buckle under. In this psychological tug of war, the son is reluctant to lose face. He wants to show he can do it on his own, avoids contact with his antagonist, and finds comfort in his friends. In the father's determination to "teach his son a lesson," confrontation accelerates, animosity grows, and both parties let emotion rather than reason dictate their relationship.

The chasm between Jay and his father did not develop because Osborne was a poor judge of character or could not handle interpersonal relationships. To the contrary, as noted earlier, Osborne was extremely likeable and had many friends. Riley Harris, who worked as a mechanic in Osborne's Chevrolet garage, recounts, "All you had to do was be around Oz for a week or two and he knew how to read you. He knew what you were going to think before you thought it. He was a bright guy." Nor did their differences develop because Jay lacked admiration for his father. As Jay states, "I had a bitterness toward my dad and yet I had a tremendous respect for him." In growing up, Jay had watched his father multiply a variety of small businesses into larger operations and investments. As a son, he was proud that community business leaders looked up to Oz as one who could "could turn a dime into a dollar." Osborne's versatility was such that he was successful in gasoline retailing, car dealerships, construction, building and operating hotels and motels, and handling money. Jay refers to him as "aggressive and innovative," and he often quoted his father when he was out with friends. Jay also admired his dad's extraordinary drive and way with people, even though their home life was not always pleasant.

In an early incident that left scars, Osborne promised Jay he could purchase a twenty-two rifle if he earned enough money mowing lawns. Before the summer was over, Jay had saved the money, but his father now questioned whether he could handle a gun and refused to let him purchase one. As Jay grew older and moved into the teenage years, his behavior became more unbridled and his father responded by being less tolerant. Not only was Osborne quick to criticize Jay's work performance, but he paid his son less than other employees doing the same tasks. Furthermore, Osborne was annoyed with youngsters who engaged in such frivolous activities as "joy riding" or staying out late every evening with friends. Once Jay went to Irv Norcross, the tire supplier for Osborne's dealership, and asked for a job, but the next morning he withdrew his request, not wanting to create more ill will. Later, despite the fact that Jay operated his father's most profitable station in Willard, Osborne referred to his son as "one of his worst operators." After Jay acquired his small Tripacer and was landing at the airstrip east of Soda Springs, Osborne commented to one of his neighbors—half in disgust and half in pride—"What am I going to do with that boy?"

In turn, it was natural for Jay to search for something to get back at his dad, and religion provided the obvious target. Osborne regularly attended LDS Church meetings and held a variety of ecclesiastical positions. He taught Sunday school and priesthood classes for many years, served in the bishopric of the Soda Springs Third Ward, and was in charge of committees for constructing local church buildings. At the time of his death he had been called to the High Council to oversee construction of a stake center. However, it was quite widely known that he did not strictly adhere to Mormon standards including his use of alcoholic beverages (a condition quite common at the time). As Jay entered high school, he let his church attendance drop off, and he selected a group of friends who where also experiencing at least a temporary break from their parents and their religious backgrounds. Again, Osborne's reaction was to apply more pressure, but this time he compounded his mistake by attempting to impose higher standards on his son than he displayed in his own behavior.

Thus religion served as the ignitor that set off their occasionally stormy confrontations. Osborne wanted a cooperative, achievement-oriented, submissive son. Jay's response was to be defiant, and to seethe inside because of what he perceived as his father's questionable morality and two-faced behavior as it related to their LDS religion.

While their relationship was often turbulent, one should not read more into this period of their lives than is justified since few parents of large families escape having one or more of their teenage children suddenly display erratic behavior by flapping their new wings in an attempt to fly beyond parental authority. Theirs was a classic confrontation. Parents want children to carry on family traditions, accept particular values, and become members in good standing of their religious faith. Children are often determined to show they can think and act on their own, enjoy testing social and religious norms, and find reasons for rejecting parental direction. The net result is the same. The combination of a father holding unrealistic expectations for his eldest son—a son who is confident, capable, and headstrong—creates a rift that can take years to overcome.[1]

As one would anticipate, Jay's response to the growing confrontation was to avoid conflict by going to the Jackson Hole area of Wyoming during the summer between his junior and senior high school years where he worked at Jackson Lake Lodge as a dishwasher. The next summer after high school graduation he worked in his father's businesses. In the fall he enrolled at Brigham Young University in Provo at the urging of several high school classmates. Also, he wanted to get out of Soda Springs and had nothing else to do. Such motives did not result in his being studious, and he acknowledges that he essentially wasted nine months. Given Jay's recent record in high school, Osborne was not enthusiastic about his attending college but he sent him $200 a month support.

The following summer Jay returned to the Jackson area, this time to manage a station for his father. This was Osborne's way of keeping in close contact while simultaneously offering Jay a maturing opportunity. Osborne knew he was placing substantial responsibility on someone not out of his teens who was showing little sign of settling down.

---

1. It should also be noted that Jay's mother came from a tradition of parents holding high expectations for their offspring. The Millers sent all of their children to high school in Salt Lake City rather than Afton to get better schooling.

Jackson Hole, Wyoming, station that Jay managed for his father in the summer of 1959.

Osborne named the small station south of Jackson "Jays CutRate." It consisted of a 15-by-25-foot frame structure with two rest rooms and a small area for an attendant. In front was one island containing four pumps. When having breakfast at a bakery close by, Jay met a young waitress, Teddy Lou Brown, who changed his plans for the coming year. Teddy was attractive and vivacious, and she had an energy level equal to his. She planned in the fall to return to her home ten miles west of Rexburg, Idaho, and complete her senior year at the local high school. After frequent dates in the summer, Jay decided to enroll at Ricks College, also in Rexburg, rather than go back to BYU. He had few work options. Osborne always closed the station during the winter since skiing had not yet gained sufficient popularity to make Jackson a year-round resort.

Jay devoted little more time to his studies at Ricks than he had at BYU, but he had several favorable experiences. He worked part-time for his uncle Bob Call at the Sinclair dealership south of town. Bob is unlike Reuel and Osborne in that his goal has been to operate the finest station in the community and strongest distributorship in the region, but here his aspirations stop. He feels that other aspects of life are as important if not more important than business. Bob insists on keeping his facilities immaculate, even the area surrounding the grease rack, and he is a person of extremely high integrity. Jay came away from that experience with a fetish for cleanliness that has characterized him ever since and can be a source of trembling among his employees and associates. They are all concerned that circumstances might lead to his asking for a ride and, no matter how hard they try, it is difficult to meet Jay's cleanliness standards, either in their cars or in the work place.

Of more importance, Bob's approach to life caused Jay to do some introspection. He reflected on his own values and the values of others, especially his parents and friends. This assessment, coming at an important juncture in his life, had a mellowing, uplifting effect that helped shape his strong values orientation.

Another activity in Rexburg that dominated Jay's time and proved crucial to his future was his evolving relationship with Teddy. They were engaged at Christmas and married June 1, 1960, after her graduation. Both sets of parents thought Jay and Teddy were too young for marriage. However, the Calls assumed marriage would settle Jay down, and they knew he had little interest in continuing his higher education. At Osborne's insistence they were married in the Idaho Falls LDS temple. They had little time for a honeymoon since Jay had agreed to return to operate the Jackson station. As a wedding present, Jay's parents gave them a used twenty-three-foot house trailer that served as their living quarters next to the station. Jay spent many hours sanding and painting his new home. Their finances were such that Teddy took the remains of the $50 her parents had given them for their honeymoon, obtained small change at the bakery, and hoped that their first customers would not come in with large bills.

Jay's agreement with his father was to split the station's net profits. Given such an incentive, Jay quickly responded to the challenge. He and Teddy both worked long hours during a record tourist season, and when it came time to close in the fall their share was $2,000 (equivalent to $10,000 today). After noting Jay's success in Jackson, Osborne urged him to move the trailer and operate his new but failing outlet south of Willard, Utah. The station was strategically located on Highway 89 between Ogden and Brigham City. (It predated Interstate Highway 15.) During the first six months after the station was initially opened, the manager achieved only modest sales, and Osborne let him go, hoping that Jay could move in and turn the business around.

Thus in the fall of 1960 Jay took over the small modern-appearing Maverik station with three pumps in front and began searching for ways to expand sales. His first action was to improve customer service. In this pre-self-service era, Jay would fill the customer's tank, check the oil, and wash the windows, all on the run. He was fast and businesslike, and rarely had time to chat or be friendly. His hours were 7:00 A.M. to 10:00 P.M., and for the first nine months he never had a full-time employee. As he states, "For the first thirty days I never left the lot." Jay had what is known in the trade as a "B shift"—Be there in the morning, be there all day, and be there at night. Jay, not liking Teddy to pump gas, confined her duties to checking competitor prices, making bank deposits, bagging groceries, and running errands (generally in their old Chevrolet truck).

Dale Larkin (later a Maverik and currently a Flying J employee) operated a trucking business in the area. Jay offered Dale attractive rates if he would buy all of his fuel from Maverik. Dale agreed but only if he could gas up at night since his current supplier north of Willard stayed open twenty-four hours. Jay agreed although he, Teddy, and the children never became accustomed to the blast of Dale's air horn at 2:00 A.M. as they slept in the trailer south of the station.

Even with this flurry of activity, sales during the first winter never exceeded 500 gallons a day. Thus they lived on a meager income since Osborne did not provide Jay a working capital advance or other financial support. The Calls were always glad to see Teddy's parents come down from the farm in Idaho since they brought beef, potatoes, and other eatables.

Eventually their work paid off. By midsummer, sales had more than doubled. Jay still recalls the thrill of his first 1,000-gallon day. When the station later averaged 1,500 gallons per day, he hired additional help, but this did not stop him from being constantly on the run. They continued to live by the station where they could watch the pumps although they bought a larger mobile home before Thad's birth in July of 1962.

When sales eventually tripled, Jay was still not satisfied. Fortunately,

Original Maverik station Jay managed and later owned in Willard, Utah. Jay and his family lived in the trailer to the right.

Osborne had taught him that there are many ways to make money if one could identify opportunities. Relying on his experience in car sales, Jay decided to open a used-car lot next to his station if he could obtain financing. His current banker in Brigham City refused him a loan, so Fred Baugh, Jay's accountant, introduced him to officers in the Box Elder County Bank. Jay—somewhat small in stature, appearing very young for his age, and not wearing a tie—asked to borrow $3,000 to buy used cars. (Jay was always clean and neat at the time but not well-dressed. He could not even claim ownership to a suit!) Don Carlsen, the bank president, said he "looked like a fourteen-year-old kid," but "he had a determined look on his face so I invited him into my office." After listening to his story, Don said, "I think we can figure out how we can get you a couple of used cars down there" which was the start of a banking relationship that has lasted to this date.

Jay traveled as far as Denver to get the type of used cars he wanted to display. His plan was to appeal to young buyers by obtaining four-speed V-8 sports coupes. Based on his prior experience, he detailed and cleaned the cars until they sparkled. He would only stock three or four at a time, but he had constant turnover. As added advantages, he was a super salesman like his father, and he was the same age as his typical customer.

Soon a related opportunity came along that many others had previously turned down because of the narrow market. A major car accessories supplier was dropping out of the tire business and wanted to dispose of three to four hundred recap snow tires all in one size (7.50 by 14). Even though the company representative wanted to sell the entire lot for the bargain-basement price of $4.50 each, the offer was still unattractive, especially to a small

Jay's first truck.

station owner who sold at most a dozen or so tires a month. Furthermore, the 7.50 by 14 tire did not originate until 1957, and new car owners generally do not buy recaps. To most experienced station operators, opening a snow-tire business with only one size tire would not only be foolish but doomed to failure. Besides, Jay lacked an indoor or covered bay. He could not even claim ownership to a wheel balancer. In addition, his only jack was a small one that fit under the bumper.

Like most enterprising entrepreneurs, Jay found a way to exploit the situation. First he got the sellers to agree to ninety-day terms. Then he placed a large row of tires in front of the station with a chain wrapped through for security. He advertised the tires at the extremely low price of $20 a pair installed. Probably the most ingenious marketing aspect of his offer was an unconditional guarantee if the buyers purchased tubes to put inside. The tubes gave him an additional $2 to $3 profit on each tire. More important, his dealership quickly gained credence with the local populace when he replaced returned tires on a "no questions asked" basis.

The final ingredient in his tire success was one every entrepreneur invariably relies on—luck. Winter came early and it came hard. After a six-to-eight-inch snowfall in September, most dealers were out of snow tires. Dealers as well as dozens of retail customers clamored to buy them from Jay. He had well over the required $1,800 to pay his bill before the ninety-day deadline, and he still had remaining inventory. He quickly broadened his appeal by offering snow tires in different sizes. Ultimately tires became a major source of his income. Just prior to his father's death, Jay was considering putting in a large recap plant near the station.

Thus within a few years Jay was selling fuel, cars, and tires. In addition, he became involved in a partnership to mix and sell fertilize, the only one of his early ventures that failed. However, as happens with most entrepreneurs, it taught him a valuable lesson—to be cautious in moving out of his field of expertise. Jay also expanded his gasoline business. One year after he came to Willard, Reuel got him to take over a small Maverik station north of Brigham City. Jay hired an attendant to run the property while he continued as manager in Willard. Within three years Jay had become his father's largest-volume operator. This prompted Jay to consider going on his own. When he began looking for property, Osborne, reluctant to see him leave, offered him the Willard station at fair market value under the stipulation that he would pay it off within several years. After Jay agreed, they jointly purchased a tanker truck, and were considering building other stations together.

Osborne and Jay by the fuel truck they jointly owned.

The relationship between Jay and his father had improved somewhat following Jay's marriage, but it still could be contentious. At this time most of the stations owned by Osborne and Reuel were controlled under a system developed by Reuel wherein the operator was in effect a consignee. The landlord owned the fuel inventory as well as the station. The operator was charged a set amount per gallon and any revenue above that could be retained, although the operator paid all expenses other than fuel. The operator retained all income from non-fuel merchandise. This system greatly simplified the financial relationship between the owner and dealer because the only accounting necessary was to keep track of the gallons sold and maintain a record of the daily bank deposits the dealer made in the owner's name. This arrangement proved extremely effective, one Jay later adopted in his operations. Under such an agreement, the key factor for the operator was the margin between the amount per gallon charged by the owner and the retail price. Jay was naturally incensed when Osborne initially gave him 4 cents compared to 5 cents for other operators. Later Jay would bristle when Osborne came around if he assumed his purpose was to give him advice. Once when Osborne brought Mel Baird to demonstrate how a $50 punch card could be used to attract customers, Jay quickly let both his father and Mel know that he did not need their assistance. During this period, driven by the Call traits of standing on your own and vigorously protecting your independence, Jay was occasionally brash and impetuous. However, the determination and self-reliance that he displayed eventually pushed him into the forefront of the oil and hospitality industry.

After two years of managing his own station, Jay had that special feel of success that spurs someone on. He was earning $20,000 a year, significant income then for a person without a college degree, and he was starting to build equity in his business. However, the family's living conditions were far from opulent. They continued to reside in the mobile home for four years until he felt able to afford a house in Brigham City (an obvious carryover of the Thomas Call "frugality" tradition). Like Reuel, Jay's only luxury was an airplane, the Tripacer he acquired in 1962. Soon after obtaining his license, one of his initial solo flights almost resulted in his demise. When flying over Clarkston in Cache Valley, thirty miles northeast of Brigham City, the engine blew a piston, but, fortunately, he was close enough to the Logan airport to glide in safely.

Relating to these early years when Jay's entrepreneurship was beginning to sprout, several questions are relevant. Where did this drive to be an entrepreneur come from? Were there early signs that he had the interest and skill to follow in this path? How significant was his father in influencing him in this direction? Again, the answers are debatable, but some conclusions are evident.

At an early age Jay displayed the same determination, action orientation, strong work ethic, and drive to succeed that characterizes him today. Most of his high school peers assumed he would be successful in business like his father. A few viewed him as being on the fast-track to stardom in the business world consistent with his goal of being a millionaire by age thirty. One perceptive classmate wrote the following in Jay's high school yearbook when he was a junior: "Jay, you have a personality that will really take you a long way in this world and win you many friends. You have a way of doing things that no on else could think of." The last sentence identifies a characteristic that many of Jay's employees and associates consider his key attribute. Outstanding entrepreneurs are recognized as being able to "see things that escape others." Like Jay, many have the unusual capacity to identify business opportunities, evaluate risks, and break complex issues down into a few fundamentals for easy analysis. Most of Jay's associates are amazed at how quickly he gets to the heart of complex issues, and how readily he picks opportunities out of situations that appear ordinary to everyone else.

The other skill vital to Jay's continued progress is his capacity to be open and learn from experience. The occasional questionable behavior that marked him as a youth soon disappeared as he matured and accepted other values. His daring, "push to the edge" behavior when behind the wheel of a car was replaced within a few years by a pilot who is extremely cautious when at the controls of an airplane. In fact, he became so well-trained and orderly that he has been complimented by control-tower operators for his superb approaches and flying ability. His desire to control and occasionally intimidate in time became replaced by the exact opposites—giving others (notably his children) complete freedom, and letting them make their own decisions and be responsible for the results. His occasionally self-serving behavior was altered by what became one of his favorite mottos—"Always leave others better off from having associated with you." Originally reluctant to take advice from adults, now he willingly listens and actively seeks the advice of others. Rather than being self-centered, he gets some of his greatest joy out of seeing subordinates grow and develop, and he continually shuns the spotlight. Perhaps his most important trait is being able to adapt to new conditions, an attribute that has served him well as he has broadened his business horizons. (Osborne also learned from the conflict with his son. He was not nearly as demanding or critical with Jay's two younger brothers.)

As Jay matured, he came to cherish the importance of honesty. He realized that if others considered someone dishonest, everything about the person was suspect. Lack of integrity is a fatal flaw to an individual engaged in the business world because one cannot effectively operate without developing trust relationships. As he stated in his 1991 speech to the Soda Springs High School graduates, "You will find that your integrity and reputation will do more for you than all of your wealth." An example of how early in his career he bent over backwards to be fair, even when he was still struggling financially, comes from Jack Seamons, a former Soda Springs classmate. In 1963 Jack was operating Jay's Maverik station north of Brigham City under the previously described consignment arrangement. When a gas war occurred and Jack experienced losses for several months, Jay split the deficits with him even though it was not necessary under their agreement. The person most familiar with his early business transactions, his long-time secretary and office manager Marcella Hume, refers to Jay as "extremely honest. He has always tried to be very fair in his dealings with everyone—I don't care who it is."

Jay clearly displays the traditional Call traits of being strong-willed, independent, stubborn, determined, hardworking, frugal, and honest. Furthermore, he likes to be continually engaged in "building" activities where he can see quick results. He is a mixture of his parents in that he is neither as outgoing as his father nor as reserved as his mother. In one respect, for many years he patterned his life after his father's who, according to Janice, "had a one-track mind for business. That was it." However, Jay always enjoyed getting away on long motorcycle trips or flying adventures. Recently he has broadened his interests outside of the petroleum industry even more, although he still must have some "building" project underway.

Regarding Osborne's role, the observations of Warren Bennis, an acknowledged authority on leadership, are important. He concludes that leaders often "have a strong, determined set of parents" and someone in the family who said "Go for it, you can do it." While Osborne tended to criticize rather than praise, he was nevertheless an important mentor to Jay in showing how it could be done. He implanted in his son an entrepreneurial mindset, and he taught him the essence of deal making. Equally important, he gave Jay, at an early age, the opportunity to gain a feeling of accomplishment by being involved in significant business transactions. Jay still remembers selling a customer tires when he was eleven and taking the lead to get another person to buy a car when he was fourteen. Making $2,000 during the summer at Jackson went a long way toward boosting his aspirations and his confidence. With Osborne and Reuel as role models and with the early opportunity for hands-on experience, he had a jump-start in fulfilling his entrepreneurial dreams.

Osborne Call

Janice Call

Jay also learned some things *not* to do from his father, primarily the error of putting on false fronts. Several relatives, including his children, surmise that Osborne experienced internal turmoil and a loss of respect from others because he tried to make everyone happy. In attempting to play both sides of the net, he often came out the loser. One of the first comments people make about Jay is that he is genuine and refuses to be placed on a pedestal. Allen Dredge, one of Jay's closest high school friends and later a Flying J employee, notes that "Jay never would offer an excuse for anything he ever did in his life. He would just grin and bear the consequences." Jay's children agree that their "father is what he is and he doesn't make himself out to be anything else." His advice to them at an early age was that "they will always be and should always act middle class." Jay went one step further in his high school commencement speech. He told the graduates that "It is important to not be too influenced by the people around you." A person too open to influence from associates will be unwilling to take risks and challenge the conventional, both hallmarks of an entrepreneur.

Unlike Osborne, Jay is up front about his lifestyle and religion. A final coming to grips with religion can take a person many years. Jay adopted a common sense rather than doctrinaire approach. He recognizes the significance of religion in the lives of many friends, relatives, and associates. Adherence to religious values provides an important psychological anchor that is not only a source of comfort but a positive influence in the way people live. On the other hand, it can cause anxiety to sensitive individuals who find themselves unable to live up to the teachings and then receive disrespect from others. Jay approaches religion the same as he does business or any other aspect of life. People should be free to make their own decisions and be willing to be accountable for the consequences. Others should respect their right to do this and not belittle them for their views as long as outsiders are not harmed in the process. His "live and let live" attitude is based on mutual esteem. Thus he avoids trying to force others, even employees, to fit into a certain mold.

Assuming there is a judgment day, Jay feels that God will want him on his side because of his personal integrity and the way he treats employees, customers, and acquaintances. The deep concern he has for his employees and others is a fulfillment of the "love thy neighbor" concept that is the heart of Christianity and of sound human relationships. How one treats others is a better criterion to judge morality than being concerned with matters of lesser consequence such as what one eats or drinks or whether one attends church or participates in religious rituals. The difficulty with a doctrinaire religion is that it can separate rather than bring people together, an unfortunate condition found in some Call family affairs. It is natural for individuals to gravitate to those with similar beliefs and interests, and avoid others with opposite views whether it relates to religion, sports, politics, careers, ethnic backgrounds, or whatever.

Some individuals attribute Jay's success to reasons other than the ones mentioned. Most often referred to is the possibility that he was driven to exceed the accomplishments of both Reuel and his dad. Obviously he did not want to fail in comparison, but he is not one to let keeping score in this type of rivalry dominate his thinking. A few others, notably one of his sisters, point to the Napoleon syndrome. They conclude that being somewhat small in stature has given him the extra motivation to be on top.

Jay's early years provide an interesting perspective on entrepreneurship and family ties. He and his father had obvious differences, but underneath they revered one another and wanted each other's approval. The end result of a decade of occasional strife between a father and son with unyielding personalities is epitomized in the statement Jay made to Lynn "Andy" Andreason at Osborne's funeral. When Andy (a long-time friend who had also experienced difficulty with his parents) came through the funeral line, Jay whispered in his ear, "I want you to tell your father you love him tonight."

10

EARLY DEVELOPMENT OF FLYING J

*I*n the spring of 1968, fortified by his experience in working for Caribou Four Corners and operating his own stations, Jay was poised to pursue his goal of being a highly successful businessman by the age of thirty. Working for Caribou broadened his exposure to the petroleum industry, but he also learned important lessons from building his own three stations at Ontario, Oregon, in 1965; Lewiston, Idaho, in 1967; and Richland, Washington, in 1968. To finance the Ontario station, Jay first obtained a $10,000 unsecured loan from the Box Elder County Bank. By making a small down payment, he acquired the land for $10,000 after which he added an attractive, spacious building for another $17,000. Besides fuel, he sold groceries because under Oregon law the station could not be self-service, so two attendants were generally required. In Lewiston the station had four pumps with a trailer house as a pay booth. Because it was self-service, his investment and operating expenses were lower. The significant innovation at this location was using the trailer house as a live-in facility for the operators, a concept he picked up from Pat Griffin of the Gasamat chain and one Jay had verified from his experience in Willard. Using Reuel's consignment scheme, the operators were not employees. Jay owned the facility and fuel inventory, and the managers received free rent and a set amount on each gallon sold.

In 1968 soon after leaving Caribou, Jay dropped the Maverik title,

Fastway station in Richland, Washington, 1968.

incorporated as Flying J Inc., and named his stations Fastway. People familiar with Jay generally assume the corporate title came from his love of flying. However, he conceived the name as being a cattle brand or a title someone would use in ranching. It was a decade later before he named his stations Flying J.

The Fastway station in Richland was similar in design to the one in Ontario except the grocery space was converted to a live-in facility for the operators. The results at Richland provided a pleasant surprise that energized his efforts. Projected sales of forty to fifty thousand gallons per month (twice that of an average station) were eclipsed within the first thirty days. Customers purchased over 180,000 gallons monthly resulting in his first retail gusher since Willard. The facility was far too small for the traffic generated, but, as Jay said, "It really got me going."

With his keen business mind, Jay learned from all three situations. Although the Ontario site was "not the best" by his own admission, he found that with only the $10,000 loan and a small amount of personal capital, he could build a station and pay for it from cash flow. At the time, a dealer received a 1 percent discount if the bill was paid within ten days. Jay was fortunate in that most companies (especially Maverik, his major wholesaler) were slow in billing. The lag time often exceeded two or three weeks, giving Jay thirty days to make payment and still receive 1 percent off. By setting low prices his volume splurged, resulting in a quick inventory turnover. Thus, he often sold one or two loads before paying his supplier. In Richland with monthly sales of 200,000 gallons, at 30 cents a gallon, he received $60,000 in fuel receipts before he had to pay for fuel already sold. The $60,000 was more than the total cost of the station so Jay was expanding on his suppliers' money. With this excessive cash flow, after making fuel and major mortgage payments, he still had enough left to start another station. Accountants advised him of the extreme danger in funding capital facilities from cash flow, but early on Jay displayed his almost complete disregard of risk when he had confidence in his decision. Also, he was careful to fully pay off many stations so he always had collateral to back a loan.

Of the twenty-three stations he built between 1968 and 1973, nine were in California, eight in Washington, five in Oregon, and one in Nevada. Except for Portland where he had three stations, most were in medium-sized communities, such as Fresno and Bakersfield, or in smaller towns like Petaluma, Eureka, Walla Walla, and Klamath Falls.

Jay's decision to concentrate on the Northwest and California was prompted by several factors. Initially he felt it was not proper to compete with Reuel and the Maverik stores which were centered in Idaho, Utah, and Wyoming. In fact, Jay did not build a station in these three states for six years, or until 1973 when he constructed a C-store in Brigham City on the Main Street edge of the site he had selected for Flying J corporate headquarters.

Jay also chose to concentrate on the states west of Utah to avoid competition. The three-state area Maverik operated in was the hotbed in the West for cut-rate, self-service stations. Upwards of 40 percent of Utah stations were self-service whereas Washington and California had less than 10 percent. These latter areas were dominated by major-brand dealers who, at the time, charged 37 cents a gallon for regular gasoline. (The wholesale cost of fuel plus federal and state taxes accounted for 25 cents with a mark up of 12 cents). As one of the self-service pioneers in California and the Northwest, Jay priced more aggressively than his local competitors. His markup was half that of the branded dealers, and, as a result, he sold at least three times their average volume and hence was more profitable. As Lee Liberatore, one of Flying J's early employees in Washington, said, "When competitors found out how much gallonage we pumped, they said we were liars and must be doctoring the figures until they sat across the street and counted the customers."

Jay's decision to spread his operations over most of the West Coast made sense in two other ways. With limited equity, he knew that if his stations were concentrated in one area a local gas war could wipe him out. Widely dispersed operations are the best defense against this common form of commercial combat. Second, dispersed operations were not a major liability for him because of his flying capability. By air, he could reach his outlets as rapidly as those within a one or two state area could visit theirs by car.

Flying J Oil Company
P. O. Drawer 678
Brigham City, Utah 84302

DAILY SALES REPORT

Station ....

Date ....

Operator ....

Gasoline Meter Readings (In Gallons)

REGULAR GASOLINE	ETHYL GASOLINE
Finish - -	Finish - - ....
Start - -	Start - - ....
Total - -	Total - - ....
Sales - -	Sales - - ....
Finish - -	Finish - - ....
Start - -	Start - - ....
Total - -	Total - - ....
Sales - -	Sales - - ....

* * *

Cash Summary

................Gallons REGULAR Gasoline at .... - - $......................

................Gallons ETHYL Gasoline at .... - - $......................

................Gallons Other at .... - - - - - $......................

................Gallons TOTAL SALES   - - - - - - $......................

        Less. . . . . Coupons Enclosed - - $......................

        Less Credit Cards - - - - - - - - - - $......................

TOTAL DEPOSITED - - - - - - - - - - - - $......................

* * *

Gallons REGULAR Gasoline on hand at end of last report - ....

Gallons Received since last report - - - - - - - - - ....

Gallons Sold since last report - - - - - - - - - ....

TOTAL REGULAR GASOLINE - - - - - - - - - ....

Gallons by stick measurement - - - - - - - - - ....

Over or Short - - - - - - - - - - - - - - ....

* * *

Gallons ETHYL Gasoline on hand at end of last report - - ....

Gallons Received since last report - - - - - - - - ....

Gallons Sold since last report - - - - - - - - ....

Gallons by stick measurement - - - - - - - - ....

Gallons ON HAND Now - - - - - - - - - ....

Over or Short - - - - - - - - - - - - - - ....

Operator's Signature ....

(Fuel inventory on back)

Fastway station in Monterey, California, 1970.

As a bonus, it gave him an excuse to engage in his favorite activity—flying. When he left Caribou in 1968, he purchased the company's Mooney he had been using. Soon after, he replaced it with a Beechcraft Bonanza, a larger, more luxurious, five-place airplane. Within eighteen months he acquired an Aerostar, a six-place, twin-engine, turbocharged aircraft that must be piloted by someone with multi-engine instrument ratings. The casual observer would likely conclude that Jay squandered funds to satisfy his flying fancy, but those who know him well realize that he rarely splurges on unessential frills. As Bob Smith, an Oregon real estate developer and close friend stated, "Most people do not know how to use an airplane. With most businesses it is a cost. With Jay it is one of his greatest assets."

Jay started with the same strategy of his father and Reuel—minimize the investment, maintain lower prices, and keep to rural locations. However, the pivotal decision that early separated him from his two predecessors was to make volume the key. Rural sites typically get adequate volume only if they are strategically located where the traffic count is high and few if any other cut-rate stations are in the area, such as in Richland. Property in densely populated communities is more expensive and facilities generally more costly, but, depending on the competition, the potential is far greater.

The first major test of this revised strategy occurred in 1970 with Flying J's station in Monterey, California. Jay obtained property in the city just off the freeway for $100,000, by far the largest amount he had yet paid for unimproved real estate and a gamble because it represented 90 percent of the company's equity. After a long struggle to get the appropriate government approvals, he constructed a twelve-pump station and live-in facility of slump rather than cinder block. The design, combined with attractive landscaping, gave the station enormous architectural appeal and helped turn it into an instant financial success. For years after, it clearly represented the company's jewel in the crown. As Ron Brisendine, Flying J's first manager for retail operations, stated, "At Monterey, Jay was initially way over his head. Fortunately sales started off at over 200,000 gallons a month, and the station generally led the company in sales until the first truck plaza."

Every week Jay was either in the air or on the road from Tuesday through Friday visiting stations, looking for sites, or engaging in other business. He was in the corporate office only on Mondays and occasionally on weekends. The operators anxiously awaited his visits, although some were taken aback when he arrived in a black leather coat on a motorcycle. Once when making the rounds by motorcycle, he stood on the perimeter of a Flying J property viewing the facilities. An attendant who had never met him was about to call the police when another employee identified the suspicious man as their boss.

Many wondered how Flying J's business could prosper when the chief executive was rarely there. Rather than it being a problem, it was part of Jay's management strategy. By being away he forced subordinates to take responsibility and make decisions. Picking strong, committed subordinates was the key.

How Jay selected subordinates appears intuitive but, again, it is a vital business skill he learned over time. Initially he employed many of his Soda Springs High School friends. Some, such as Gerald McCammon, in charge of corporate data processing, turned out to be extremely valuable, but others proved disappointing and soon left. He strongly relied on references from business acquaintances and others; but, being a sound judge of people, he ultimately counted on his own skills. Like his father, he can quickly see through facades put up by manipulators. One technique he frequently used was to walk candidates to their cars after an interview. He calculated that if a person's car was dirty on the outside and cluttered inside, this is how the individual would maintain a station.

Initially Teddy provided the only office support. She did the bookkeeping, banking, and payroll. As business grew and Jay was away building stations, more of her time was required to answer questions from local operators and to serve as a go-between in business dealings. When away, Jay would generally keep contact by calling every evening at 7:00. Later, when office employees were hired, Teddy did most of the interior design for the corporate office and the two motels in Nevada.

Four employees played primary roles in the early development of the company. Marcella Hume, Flying J's first full-time office help, was hired in 1969 as bookkeeper. Later she became the office manager. As employees were added to the corporate staff, Marcella restricted her accounting work to payroll, insurance, and bank deposits. With Jay's frequent absences, she assumed a major role in coordinating activities within the corporate office, especially personnel matters. Jay spent time each Monday morning listening to Marcella explain the happenings of the prior week. Because of her friendliness and interest in others, one longtime employee called her "the mother of the company" and someone who "took care of everything and everybody." Paul Brown, a CPA who was controller (he also held other positions in the company), said that Marcella "had a big part in the early success of Flying J." Furthermore he added, she "had her hand on the pulse of the company and could recognize a lot of problems."

The next key employee was Ron Brisendine, a specialist in retailing. Ron attended high school in Soda Springs and worked in retail grocery stores before managing Jay's station in Ontario, Oregon. He left Flying J, returned to the grocery business for two years, and then rehired to operate the new Fastway station in Vancouver, Washington. The company had plans to build two stations near Portland when the head of construction became ill. Soon after, Jay was visiting the area and Ron volunteered to build them although he had no experience. Jay, relying on Ron's innate ability, reached in his airplane, handed him the plans, and said "Good luck." As Ron noted, "Not many people could do that." He adds, "One of the key things leading to Jay's success is his ability to let somebody else do stuff without hounding him." Jay placed such confidence in the people he worked with that they were not going to let themselves fail.

After Ron showed this initiative, Jay made him manager over the stations in the Northwest and within two years moved him back to Brigham City as director of marketing, a position involving responsibility for all retail operations. Ron was extremely likeable and a key figure in the "work hard, play hard" clan surrounding Jay that devoted almost their entire effort to the company. When Ron left in 1985, due in no small part to his ability and commitment, retail sales had been growing at over 25 percent per year and the company now had fifty-five stations.

The next employee to fulfill an extremely important initial role was Richard E. (universally known as "Buzz") Germer. Buzz joined the company in 1972 after finishing college and was soon appointed manager of retail operations in California. Buzz and his family became some of Jay's closest

Buzz Germer in the temporary Brigham City office, 1974.

friends. Buzz became an expert in refining, supply, and transportation—functions paramount to the rise of Flying J. Since 1973 Buzz has been in charge of these operations and currently is senior vice president of Refining and Supply, president of Big West Oil, and president of Flying J Transportation. (The latter two are subsidiaries of Flying J Inc.)

How Buzz was hired and trained are highly informative examples of Jay's approach to management. When Buzz graduated from Utah State University with a degree in business, Jay arranged through friends for an interview. Buzz had little interest in working in a service station, but he was enthusiastic about Jay's plans and attracted by his upbeat personality. Jay indicated he needed help in station management and construction, but said little beyond that. After Buzz agreed to come to work, Jay assigned him to manage the nine California stations and oversee construction in that area.

A few days later Jay flew him to Los Angeles on what Buzz assumed was an orientation tour. They rented a car and drove to the Fastway station in Bakersfield. Jay told Buzz that he could live in Bakersfield or at any other Southern California location. Jay noted that the Bakersfield facility needed a car wash, and made a few other suggestions before they returned to Los Angeles. Buzz kept wondering when Jay was going to outline the training program he surely had planned for him. At the airport, Buzz was astounded when Jay took out his suitcase and said he was leaving. Buzz, still in disbelief, asked "What am I supposed to do?" As Jay departed, he smiled, looked him in the eye and said, "Just learn the business. Give me a call if you need me."

Buzz did not hear from Jay for a month. Then he dropped in one day for lunch. Even then the conversation was more social than business. Jay assumed Buzz was competent to handle the job, and he knew Buzz was aware that support was available if he needed it. The only complaint Flying J employees ever express about their boss is that sometimes he is too indirect or waits too long to provide guidance or criticism; but Jay is convinced that maturity on the job comes through operating on one's own.

Jay's early personnel selections were not always on target. He had unusual difficulty in maintaining competence and consistency in the controller position. The first controller left under duress within a short period. Then, Paul Brown, a CPA of unusual ability, took over in 1973 when the company had twenty stations. He arranged for the first Flying J audit and inserted controls over the retail outlets that improved accountability and increased profits. Later he was important in helping obtain the financing to make the acquisitions that multiplied the size of the company on each occasion. Paul left Flying J twice. Each time he was hired back. In between, the financial management of the company suffered.

Starting with an airplane in 1962, Jay experimented with partnerships. He later had partners in other airplanes, motorcycles, a television cable company, gas stations, a truck plaza, apartments, restaurants, the fertilizer business, and Green Thumb, a company that sold plants. His largest partnership was with Maynard Victor, an acquaintance from Brigham City. They had two filling stations in California, a station and car wash in Ogden, an airplane, motorcycles, and property involving six restaurants in Salt Lake City. Many ventures, such as the Alpine Oil Company with his brother Craig, were means of helping others. Some partnerships were speculative or "play" projects with friends that Jay wanted to keep separate from Flying J. They also served a useful purpose by not burdening his company's already lopsided balance sheet with more debt.

By 1976 Jay had terminated the last partnership. His reasoning was that he did not have time to keep on top of each venture or, just the opposite, that he was running them with limited support. Partnerships that prospered provided few problems, but with the others he felt stymied from lack of control. And, as he stated, "When the wolves approach, partners fight" which was never to his liking. Once when he lost $300,000 in a venture where he

Fastway station in Pendleton, Oregon, 1970.

had little knowledge or input, he gracefully backed out, telling the partner and especially the partner's father that their friendship was more important than the money he lost. Jay's close associates all claim they have never heard him "bad mouth" anyone, even those who absconded with his money.

An example that clearly demonstrates Jay's skill, ingenuity, and tenacity in penetrating the retail gasoline market in California and the Northwest comes from how he started the Fastway station in Pendleton, Oregon. He had agreed with his brother Craig to share ownership in the business. Pendleton is a farming community located in the northeast portion of Oregon, forty-five miles or more from another town of any size. In 1970 the local gasoline retailers were branded dealers in the old section of town. They shared the market and marked up prices by nearly 50 percent or 12 cents a gallon. A gallon of gas was 38 cents in Pendleton versus 24 cents in Provo, Utah, where Craig attended college.

Jay saw the opportunity to grab a large share of Pendleton's market with a cut-rate station, although it could not be self-service under Oregon law. They located a small 45-by-90-foot corner lot on the right-hand side of the highway going out of town. A house on the lot was dismantled in one day. Craig then proceeded to put in the tanks for two diagonal islands that would front a trailer house serving as a pay station and live-in facility. As Craig was filling in sand around the tanks, the mayor, building inspector, and other city officials angrily gave him the order to stop construction. Likely at the behest of the local retail petroleum operators, they directed him to shut down and leave town because Flying J did not have the proper building permits, did not meet the city's fire code, and violated other regulations. The city had an ordinance, presumably based on fire safety, mandating that filling stations be serviced by bulk-plant operators, not truck transports. This ordinance gave the branded wholesalers with bulk plants control over all retail stations within city limits and in essence prohibited independent operators. (Actually, Jay was doing the general citizenry a favor by lowering fuel costs and therefore reducing their cost of living, a fact later acknowledged in the local newspaper.)

Jay hired a lawyer who was of little assistance. Not to be denied, Jay personally researched the code and discovered that a bulk plant could sell retail to the public. Hence he changed his application to building a bulk plant, received city approval, and proceeded with construction. The one obstacle provided by the ordinance was the requirement that the bulk plant be fenced. With their limited space the only solution was to locate the bulk plant on a 12-foot strip at the back of the lot, fence it, and run pipes underground to the pumps. Transports had difficulty dumping fuel in the bulk plant because of the confined space, but the station soon opened offering gas at 29.9 cents a gallon, 7 cents under the competition. As Craig stated, "We blew the fuses on every oil dealer in town." Within six months they earned back their entire investment of $25,000, and the facility was a cash cow for many years.

Jay early displayed another Call trait, that of being thrifty, and he still is adept at minimizing expenses. The tendency within the company is to work long hours and to be shorthanded. While on the road, especially in the early days, corporate officials worked from dawn to dusk and rarely got to bed before midnight. From the start and to this day employees travel in low-priced rental cars, sleep in budget motels, and fly economy class. On occasion Jay has hitchhiked from the nearest airport to one of his motels, and he takes care in obtaining favorable but fair terms in making rental or purchase agreements.

Although Jay initially skimped on operating expenses, he was more than generous in rewarding performance. Salaries were never high, often less than average, but if the company did well, bonuses more than made up the difference. For the first eight years, 25 percent of each salaried employee's income was placed in a pension fund, a figure unheard of, especially in retail industries. Cash in the fund was used to purchase Flying J capital items that were then leased back to the company, so the fund grew at an enormous pace. This continued until pension laws were passed in the mid-1970s prohibiting such generous practices. Now the company's pension plan is consistent with others in the industry.

Employees who helped Jay build his stations in the Northwest delight in telling stories about him—stories that reveal his affable nature, sense of humor, and total lack of pretention. Once when he and several coworkers got the last room in a motel and someone had to sleep on the floor, they drew straws and Jay lost. As he laid out his blanket he remarked, "Here I am the CEO and I'm sleeping on the floor." On another occasion during a downpour they drew straws to see who would go for pizza. Again he lost, and he came up with the same refrain. He has been known to ride in the back of a pickup truck while his employees sat in the front, and he likes to spend several hours in Flying J lounges talking to truck drivers. As John Lyddon, a millionaire friend marveled, "His relationship with people extends from the bluest of collars to the top tenth of 1 percent of the people in this country, and yet he can be comfortable with all of them." Buzz adds, "Jay is as comfortable in a country western place as he is in the swankiest restaurant in town." Jay prefers to deal in small groups where he can interact one-on-one. Much of his behavior toward others is dictated by how he views them. His measurement is not their wealth or position but their integrity.

Another key to his early success was being able to recruit honest, reliable, operators who generally stayed on the job for several years at a time. Retail outlets are typically at a disadvantage because most jobs start at or near minimum-wage. Thus the applicants tend to be younger persons or others who are unskilled. They typically view their positions as short-term and limited in financial rewards, and thus often have little job commitment. A common corollary is that "shrinkage" though employee theft is a major problem.

The live-in operators Flying J hired were generally married couples, usually of retirement age, who wanted something to do or found they could not live on their retirement incomes. They were enticed by the free rent and the possibility of making considerably more than minimum wage since their incomes were based on gallons sold. As independent operators, not employees, they were not affected by wage and hour laws. Many couples would keep their businesses open sixteen hours a day and then be there during the night to guard the facilities. Theft or embezzlement was difficult since the only monetary transaction between the owner and the dealer was payment for the number of gallons sold.

Jay had learned from residing in the trailer next to his Willard station that this was the optimum condition for overseeing and managing a facility. It was a formula crucial to his success in most of Flying J's first fifty stations. Then, in 1977, when the federal government declared that his operators must be considered employees, the company was fined and the practice stopped.

Fastway station in Brigham City, built in 1973.

By the close of Flying J's 1973 fiscal year (January 31, 1974), Jay had achieved an enviable record. In just five years he had expanded from four to twenty-seven stations. Annual corporate sales had increased thirteen times (from $736,000 to $10,039,000) and profits nine times ($35,000 to $316,000). Flying J owners' equity, pushed by an unbelievable average annual return-on-equity of over 50 percent, had jumped from $81,000 to $604,000, a gain beyond the dreams of all but the most optimistic investors. In 1972 his average station was making a monthly profit of nearly $1,000, he was adding five outlets annually, and nothing on the horizon stood in the way of his being a millionaire and continuing his heady advance.

Even close observers of Flying J could not determine how Jay obtained the collateral and/or financing to underwrite the twenty-three stations he built in the five years after leaving Caribou. Magazine writers speculated that his silent partners were either his mother, Reuel, Maverik, or even the Mormon Church. (Maverik was a major financing source due to the company's late billing, but that was unintended.) However, in the first two years Jay had no major financial backing other than a variety of small unsecured loans, especially those from Orin Geesey at the First National Bank of Kemmerer (the banker who acted as the white knight to save Maverik on several occasions) and from the Box Elder County Bank. For these banks even a $100,000 loan was nearing the maximum, although once Orin issued Jay an unsecured loan several times larger. In 1970 the Box Elder County Bank started satisfying his growing financial appetite by using larger Small Business Administration-backed loans. The bank could handle these more sizable borrowings because under the SBA program the bank had to guarantee only 10 percent of the total.

As much as it astonished his business associates, Jay's financing came through cash flow generated by his strategy of high volume, low prices, and an incentive to operators by making their income dependent on the gallons sold. This is verified by Fred Baugh, the Brigham City CPA who put together Flying J's financial statements each year. Baugh states that "I never did see any influx of capital from his dad or any other family source."

Profitable as the company was, its rocket-like ascent could have only been achieved through substantial borrowing. In the first few years, to make the balance sheet look more liquid (short-term assets in relation to short-term liabilities), Jay, at the end of an accounting period, would occasionally get Orin Geesey to make him a long-term loan and thus build up the cash portion of Flying J's balance sheet. The loan was normally made without collateral, something that always had bank examiners and the bank board questioning Orin's judgment. Jay would pay it off within a few months, thus drawing down his cash and, in effect, making the loan a current rather than long-term liability. It improved the appearance of his balance sheet, but bankers generally still had to issue Flying J credit based on the strength of Jay's character and management ability and overlook his precarious financial position.

Jay's willingness to walk a financial tightrope is revealed in a favorite measure of bankers—the debt-to-equity ratio. Bankers prefer a ratio of at least one-to-one. In 1971, Flying J's shot up to nearly $4 in long-term debt to $1 in equity. This ratio dropped to two-to-one the next year (although company long-term debt exceeded $1 million for the first time) after profits more than doubled to $316,000. To get on safer ground and alleviate the problem of constantly monitoring the company's cash position, Jay the next year obtained a $300,000 Small Business Administration long-term loan through the Box Elder County Bank. He hoped bankers would now stop shuddering when they reviewed his financial statements.

The following year Jay turned

Jay in the temporary Brigham City office, 1975.

to First Security Bank for financing when the Box Elder County Bank lacked the resources to meet his needs, As Bob Heiner, former president of First Security Bank, explained, "Jay was not an easy person for a banker to handle with all of this enthusiasm and confidence. Though Flying J's financial position would not justify it, it was difficult to turn Jay down based on his record. Every time he made the commitment, 'If you lend me the bucks I can make it work,' he came through on his promise." Even with Flying J's high debt load and substantial interest payments, the company still earned an impressive 10 percent return on assets.

Jay's disregard of financial constraints did not result from lack of knowledge. Although he was not a trained accountant, he soon learned the basics of analyzing financial statements, came up with many of the company's creative financing schemes, and was skilled in handling bankers. As Marcella, said "He could pick financial statements apart just like that." He was always aware of Flying J's financial condition, and although he continually pushed the company to the limit of its resources, Paul rarely had to tell him, "We can't do it. We're out of money."

No climb to the top occurs without some hitches. Jay's first major one was the 1973 international oil crisis that reached a climax in the October Israeli-Arab war, eventually resulting in a quadrupling of crude oil prices and OPEC shutting off petroleum exports to the United States. It was perhaps the closest Jay ever came to losing his company.

In the spring of 1973, Buzz telephoned from California and said he was having trouble getting fuel. Since this had never been a problem in the past, Jay was in total disbelief. He immediately flew to Bakersfield and verified that independents were having difficulty locating gasoline. Fuel shortages occurred more quickly on the West Coast than in Utah, and by October nine Fastway stations in Buzz's region had to be closed. After the war broke out in October, the shortages grew so critical that within two months half of Flying J's thirty-two stations were boarded up. Gallons sold dropped in three months from 3.2 million to 1.6 million. Fortunately the shortage caused gasoline prices to rise so Flying J sales and profits did not follow the same steep descent. Sales decreased only by 6.2 percent and profits by 3.2 percent.

The primary problem for independents was getting fuel. Obviously, branded refiners were going to service their own retailers first, and, without upstream refineries as a guaranteed source of supply, independent company owners felt totally helpless. Congress passed a law in November setting up the Federal Energy Office to allocate petroleum during the crisis. This office issued regulations requiring refineries to distribute their output to the same customers in the same proportions as of December 1, 1973. However this gave little help to the independents since their supply had already been greatly reduced by that date.

In what Teddy describes as "one of the most trying times for Jay," his first action was to bring Buzz back to the corporate office in October of 1973 and put him in charge of supply and transportation. In attempting to overcome the drastic shortages in California, Buzz had learned the ins and outs of wholesaling and refining, and trucking was an interest that dated from his youth. Maverik, Flying J's major wholesaler, had a surplus of diesel and residual fuel. Residual fuel is the "heavy" bottom component in refining and is used primarily for heating, asphalt for roads, and other purposes. The refinery manager offered Buzz more gasoline if he would take these other commodities off his hands. Flying J immediately purchased three more trucks, two for diesel and a special transport for hauling residuals. Soon contracts were obtained from Thiokol Chemical Corporation (the missile contractor twenty-five miles northwest of Brigham City) and other large companies that had need for these products.

Next Jay persuaded the banks to extend his credit lines. Then he put the company's architect-engineering staff and construction crew on projects other than building stations. They quickly fabricated one speculation house in Brigham City and were soon designing and building motels to place on property next to company stations in Carson City and Reno, Nevada. Jay assumed that the fuel crisis would be temporary, and this was a way to avoid laying off valuable employees. Fortunately he was correct as the shortage eased in April of 1974. After adding only two stations in 1974 (Idaho Falls and Carson City), the company got back on track with four outlets in 1975, three in Oregon and one in Rock Springs, Wyoming.

By the end of 1975 Jay had thirty-six stations, a fleet of seven trucks, a forty-nine-unit motel in Carson City, one with seventy-two units in Reno, three condominiums in Palm Springs, plus additional property—mainly large apartment houses in Salt Lake City, Tacoma, Portland, and Corvallis. In July the corporate headquarters were moved from a double-wide trailer house to a 5,150 square-foot modern structure in Brigham City. Ron, Buzz, and Paul were all made vice presidents, the accounting department was delighted with its first computer, and the company gave every evidence of being in business for the long haul.

In seven years Jay's retail properties nearly equaled Maverik's, and he was on safer ground by being more diversified in real estate. Jay was different in other ways from his uncle and father. Obviously he did not share their

Original Brigham City corporate office (double-wide trailer).

aversion to debt, always being highly leveraged (high debt into relation to assets and equity). However, the quality that most differentiated Jay from his earlier business relatives was an awareness that a major company cannot be built as a one-man show. He recognized that he did not have the time, desire, or breadth to direct and control every aspect of such a rapidly growing enterprise. Delegation and teamwork were the answers, and these depend on strong subordinates.

The three-fold message Jay emphasized to his first supervisors and still pounds away to disbelieving executives from other companies is to be especially carefully in selecting subordinates, then give them freedom to develop, and finally be generous in rewarding performance. Early in the company's history he became disenchanted with several trained professionals who were set in their ways, could not adapt to the Flying J's situation, and wanted to immediately step in and run the show. Accordingly, he preferred to hire individuals with high potential but more limited experience—novices who were quick to learn through the challenges he offered. Newcomers often made mistakes, but Jay's concern was whether they learned from their blunders. More than once he let a subordinate pick a bad site or make a poor investment to see if the individual could later recognize the error and correct the situation.

From 1968 to 1975 many changes occurred in Jay's home life. The family now lived in a residence he built on the hillside in the southeast section of Brigham City. Jay would spend Monday in the office, the family had dinner together that night with no friends over, and then he would be gone for the

Jay with his arm around Crystal at a Bear Lake outing.

balance of the week. Initially on weekends they traveled in a camper (later a motor home) to sites normally within a hundred miles of Brigham City. Most trips were to the southwest side of Bear Lake in Rich County, Utah, on waterfront property Teddy had located. They built a wooden floor for a tent and added showers and toilet facilities. Sometimes Jay would fly the family to Disneyland, their condo in Palm Springs, various parts of Mexico, or other locations for longer vacations; but given a choice, the children always opted for trips in the motor home, preferably to their Bear Lake retreat.

When Thad and Crystal were children, adults frequently commented on their unusual courtesy and exemplary behavior. They had certain chores to do around the house and, knowing Jay, one of the most common was to help wash and wax the cars and airplanes. When Crystal was old enough to drive, Jay bought her a car with whitewall tires. She made the mistake of visiting him when they were not clean, and he complained, "I am never going to get you another car with whitewall tires. Look at those things!"

Teddy was an excellent mother who, according to her offspring, "always put us first," completely trusted them, gave them independence, and early on treated them as adults. Both were loving parents and "fun to be around." Jay was the disciplinarian, but the children had such strong respect for him that they rarely got out of line. They liked being around their dad because "he always loved life" and wanted them to water ski, ride motor bikes, fly in his planes, and "try new things." He gave them the attitude that whatever you do in life, go for it and make it work. Teddy refers to him as "a good father when he was there, although he always had a lot on his mind."

From the beginning of their marriage, Teddy and Jay had an understanding that she would be in charge of their social life and manage the children while he took charge of developing the company. They had many friends—business associates, neighbors, and others in the community. On weekends they went dancing, rode motorcycles, and took short vacations. Besides Jay's long motorcycle trips to visit his operators throughout California and the Northwest, on occasion he, Buzz, and others (often with their wives) would motorcycle as far as the Mexico's Baja peninsula. Buzz calls these trips "some of the highlights of my life."

With Jay being away, Teddy kept busy with sorority, school, and church activities. She also was a valuable business partner, a situation that likely came to dominate too much of their relationship. Long separations never bode well for a marriage, and after thirteen years of what the children thought was the perfect match, differences started to develop. Without one another's company, it is easy for husband and wife to gradually grow apart and develop other interests, a situation that occurred in their relationship. Eventually Teddy took strong exception to some of Jay's outside activities, and a rift developed that they were unable to resolve.

Phil, Buzz and Jay on a motorcycle trip to Cabo San Lucas, Mexico, spring 1989.

Jay with Thad and Crystal.

They kept their differences private, neither criticizing the other to friends. The children said "They never argued in front of us. They just all of a sudden got thin." In the spring of 1975, the year that Thad turned thirteen and Crystal eleven, their parents decided to divorce. The decision once made was carried out in haste. Jay did not want to repeat some of the family scenes he experienced as a youth. There was no separation until the day of the dissolution of their marriage in the latter part of May. The person probably closest to both parties said, "Neither one of them wanted the divorce. It was just their pride and Call stubbornness that got in the way." For both, it was the most difficult period of their lives. Friends could not believe what had happened, for a long time expecting and hoping they would get back together. Since their separation, some contention remains over the divorce settlement and other issues, but neither expresses regret over their marriage. Teddy always strongly identified with the company and admires what Jay has accomplished. Jay is quick to tell others that he "had fourteen great years with Teddy."

The divorce sent chills throughout the company. For three or four months after, their founder and leader, widely acknowledged as the heart of the enterprise, rarely set foot on Flying J premises, spending most of his time in his Palm Desert condominium or in the Northwest, primarily Portland. Many started to wonder whether the malaise was permanent and the company would flounder.

11

GROWTH THROUGH ACQUISITION

*A*lthough Jay was in California or Oregon for most of the latter half of 1975, he kept in constant contact with Flying J's top officers by telephone. Eventually he returned to Brigham City, modified the company's double-wide trailer into comfortable living quarters, and settled back to handling business affairs, interrupted only by a severe case of hepatitis.

In 1976, Flying J resumed its plans for rapid expansion. A net of ten stations was added, bringing the total to forty-six. Five of these were in northern California, purchased from Roy Brown (Teddy's brother) and John Wallace, the Soda Springs banker. The others were new units in California, Oregon, and Washington. During the year, the company broadened its scope of services by opening its first stand-alone lubrication center, a Fastway Lube in Salt Lake City. (The name was changed to J Lube in 1979 when all company facilities were switched to the Flying J flag.) Being one of the first to offer a facility specializing in no-appointment oil change and lubrication services, it was another sign that the company was at the forefront of the industry.

In 1977, four stations were added, all first-class units with a contemporary design. The wholesale arm of the company's sales staff was strengthened by one-third when Lee Liberatore was assigned to cover the Northwest. Company sales rose 26 percent (exceeding $50 million for the first time), and net profits advanced 70 percent, to just under $700,000. Both the company and its leader were back on track and momentum was building.

From Jay's standpoint, however, the most important event during 1977 was his remarriage. Jay considered his one major failure to be the divorce, and he was reluctant to risk this occurring again. He frequently dated but never initially with the intent of searching for a new wife. One day his longtime neighbor, Jim Stone, general manager of Thiokol (the solid-propellant missile company northwest of Brigham City), told Jay he wanted him to meet a young lady at the plant, an attractive public-relations employee with considerable charm and wit—someone Jay would likely want to marry. Jay showed little interest and soon forgot the matter.

A few weeks later Jay accepted Jim's invitation to tour the plant. While waiting for lunch outside Jim's office, a striking, petite blond at the end of the hall commanded Jay's attention. As Jim came out, he said, "Come on. I want you to meet Tamra, the young lady I told you about."

"No, I just spotted a girl I would like to date," Jay responded.

Jay and Tamra at their wedding.

Jim, suspecting that it was Tamra, urged Jay to come along, agreeing to introduce him to the other young lady if Tamra would not suffice. As they walked into Tamra's office, Jay whispered to Jim who was already smiling, "It's the same girl."

Jay called Tamra that night and they dated sporadically for nearly two years. Tamra's parents, Dale and Glenda Compton, live in Thatcher, a farm community northwest of Brigham City close to the Thiokol plant. Her parents both worked for Thiokol besides running their large farm. Jay and Tamra's courtship was difficult because Tamra's parents did not want her dating a man—no matter how dashing—who was a dozen years older and divorced. He was also suspect because he was considered wealthy, drove a white Cadillac, and did not accompany the family to church. To minimize the difficulty, Tamra took a job in Salt Lake.

Jay repeatedly declared that he had little interest in marriage which was acceptable to Tamra. He surprised her one evening while she was fixing chili rellenos when suddenly he proposed. Shortly thereafter they were married on December 16 in a small family wedding at the Compton family home. Larry Call, Jay's cousin (a Mormon Bishop and vice president of Maverik at the time), performed the marriage.

By the wedding date, the Comptons were reconciled to the marriage and accepted Jay as a suitable spouse for their daughter. As they came to learn more of his genuine, caring nature, they became some of his strongest supporters. As Tamra states, "Now they take his side more than mine" and they "love and adore him."

Tamra rapidly gained the admiration of Jay's close colleagues and other acquaintances. Within a few weeks they were referring to her as "A fireball and lots of fun" and "Like Jay, a concerned, levelheaded unpretentious person." She is widely regarded as someone who is "easy to be around, sensitive, and both attractive and talented." Jay's friends acknowledge his good fortune, not only in business but in selecting wives.

Being raised on the Thatcher farm, Tamra gained an early love of the outdoors, enjoyed animals, and cherished her independence. At a young age she was photogenic and personable, resulting in her being a cheerleader and a part of the royalty in most beauty contests she entered. After graduating from Bear River High School, she attended Utah State University, finishing a bachelor's degree in business education in 1974. Following graduation she worked at Thiokol where she met Jay.

Tamra and Jay have many traits in common. Both are determined, free thinking, and willing to speak their minds. They hate losing an argument, enjoy having a good time, and tend to keep their lives private. By her own admission, Tamra "likes to be alone" and, similar to Jay, she shuns recognition and being part of any social elite. She is thoughtful to her relatives and friends, an interesting conversationalist, a charming hostess, and at ease in interacting with individuals from all social strata. Not being a sun worshiper, she appreciates cool weather, and therefore is a fan of the Northwest. Besides shopping, her other favorite activities include cooking and caring for animals, a carryover of her early fondness for farm animals and pets.

After they acquired llamas in 1987, she devoted a significant portion of her time to caring for three dozen of these unique creatures at their place in Perry just three miles south of Brigham City. Her compassion for llamas is such that she will stay up day and night if necessary when one is sick or in labor. Recently she and Jay scaled down the llama herd, and they are engaged in developing a spacious ranch along the Yellowstone River south of Livingston, Montana.

Their home in Perry was finished in 1979. It is on 30 acres of flatland below the foothills. When purchased, the land was marshy, devoid of trees, and occasionally salt-crested—suitable as pasture but unfit for productive farming. Near the middle of the property was a cattail-bordered pond known as Porter Springs. The springs and surrounding area were formerly owned by Orrin Porter Rockwell, the Mormon scout—considered both famous and infamous—who was a frequent bodyguard for Brigham Young. Tamra's grandmother, Ethel Davis Wood, was baptized in the springs as a child. Rockwell used the location as a stop on the stage line, especially valuable for its water. Teamsters would back wagons into the springs to swell the wood in the wheels, thus tightening the joints.

The land was so forbidding that locals were convinced the Calls bought it to drill for oil or other minerals. Only someone with vision could possibly consider it a potential Garden of Eden. In selecting the property, their main concerns were not having close neighbors, developing the pond into an attractive setting at the rear of the home, and being close to town and company headquarters. After arranging for tons of topsoil to be hauled in followed by considerable contouring, like the Mormon pioneers, they were able to make the "desert blossom as a rose." Now the property is filled with luxurious lawns, beautiful gardens, trimmed hedges, and wooden fences separating the barns and pens from the grazing areas for animals. Locals call it "the game preserve" because of the geese and ducks (both wild and tame) that frequent the area and the abundant fish in the pond. Initially they raised cattle, pheasants, quail, and exotic birds, but more recently the farm portion of the property has been devoted to the llamas.

In the four years following the end of the 1973 fuel shortage, Flying J sales nearly tripled, going from $23.5 million to just over $65 million. Assets also tripled to over $18 million. However, since half of this increase was funded by long-term debt, the company remained highly leveraged with debt amounting to more than twice owners' equity. Burdened by major interest payments and restricted by stagnant fuel prices due to price controls, Flying J's net income remained essentially flat. At the time refineries were highly profitable, but retailers like Flying J were struggling.

Jay, always on the lookout for other opportunities, quickly sensed the situation and aggressively moved the company into an area of investing that

Growth Through Acquisition

Jay and Tamra at their Perry, Utah, home.

was extremely profitable at the time—real estate. As noted, company assets had tripled in four years while the number of stations increased less than 50 percent, going from thirty-four to fifty-two. The balance of the asset gain was mostly in real property.

As Jay acknowledges, the majority of the bottom-line on the company's financial statements during the mid and late 1970s came from buying and selling property. This activity accounted for only 10 percent of Flying J's sales but over half its profits. With long-term capital gains taxes on real estate then being half those on other corporate earnings, brokering real estate became even more attractive. Jay did not view this as a major company shift in emphasis but as a useful hedge against the cyclical oil market. Also real estate fit hand-in-glove with his petroleum interests since property acquisition was one of the keys to retail expansion.

In building his first stations, Jay soon discovered that in buying a half-acre lot on a busy intersection or highway, he was paying 90 percent of the asking price for the entire parcel, often consisting of several acres. Hence he began purchasing the entire piece and either developing the surplus (such as with the motels in Carson City and Reno) or selling it to other commercial developers. At the pace prices were increasing (especially in the late 1970s when inflation reached 10 percent), the company frequently sold the extra

Flying J motel and restaurant on North Temple in Salt Lake City, 1978.

property surrounding a station for more than the price of the original parcel. Accordingly, beginning in 1970, Flying J always maintained a large property inventory, a situation that made its high debt-to-equity ratio not so ominous since real estate was carried on its books at the purchase price, not market value. Real estate at the time was fairly liquid and generally sellable within a few weeks. Because his real estate endeavors held up the retail end of the business in the 1970s, Jay devoted much of his energy to this activity.

As noted earlier, initially he became involved in apartment houses in Salt Lake City, Portland, Tacoma, and other cities working primarily with Bill Perry of Salt Lake City. A variety of property was bought and sold, mostly along the Wasatch Front. Initially the emphasis was on undeveloped residential property, but later office buildings were purchased, and industrial buildings were constructed at Decker Lake west of Salt Lake City. Several large housing projects were initiated though sold before construction started. After Jay terminated his ties with Bill, Flying J established a property division within the company in 1977 and hired Ron Parker to operate it.

In 1978, a local project that excited the corporate staff was construction of an eighty-four-unit motel with an adjoining restaurant at 715 West North Temple in Salt Lake City. The restaurant (leased to Perkins Cake & Steak) and the motel were on the property surrounding the original J Lube. To celebrate the completion, several days before the motel opened Flying J had a huge party for all employees, many of whom stayed in the rooms overnight.

One of the most significant years in Flying J's history was 1979. The Carter Administration had started to deregulate gasoline, and fuel prices, responding to more normal supply and demand forces, jumped by 33 percent. With fuel more abundant, Flying J increased its truck fleet to seventeen, and wholesale operations ballooned to $33 million, over one-third of total company sales. Overall sales increased by one-third, and profits by 177 percent, exceeding $1 million for the first time.

This wholesaling and retailing boom plus profitable dealings in real estate were significant, but the year's two major developments had little impact on their 1979 bottom line. The first of these was almost as momentous for the company as when Jay quit Caribou Four Corners and started on his own. It involved the construction of a major truckstop in Ogden, an event that would forever change the company's direction.

In one of his shrewd real estate moves, Jay, in the early 1970s, acquired over twenty acres west of Ogden on 21st Street. Later it became the site of an interchange when Interstate 15 was extended north from Salt Lake City. Eventually Jay bought more surrounding property bringing the total to sixty-eight acres. Initially he intended to open a large trailer park, but he also gave thought to developing an industrial park. Buzz on several occasions had suggested they develop a truckstop, but Jay said the property was too valuable for that purpose and, being "Mr. Clean," he was reluctant to become involved in what was considered the unsavory end of fuel retailing.

However, by 1979 conditions had changed. The upward explosion of gasoline prices combined with fuel economy measures imposed by the federal government made it evident that national auto fuel consumption would not only level off but decline. The same would not occur with trucks because they were continuing to displace railroads in delivering freight. Also, the I-15 extension was being completed, and no major truckstop of significance was within forty miles. Jay at first considered just putting a motel on the site since he wanted to preserve the balance for other purposes. However, a combined motel, restaurant, and truckstop complex would require only fifteen acres, leaving at least fifty more for industrial development or to sell.

Buzz's concept was to enter the truckstop business just as they had begun with self-service stations. Keep prices low, invest to a minimum (unpaved driveways, trailers as pay stations, etc.), and offer only basic services. Once Jay became convinced that Ogden was an appropriate test market for a truckstop, he envisioned a facility that he would like to visit if he were a driver. As Jay stated, "We built the stop to deal with people, not service trucks." Conditions at the typical truckstop were deplorable: they were generally in the rundown, blighted areas of a community or highway; parking was limited; trucks competed with cars for space and service; facilities were minimal, unattractive, and dirty; bathrooms were small and often lacked showers; drivers had no lounge to relax in after long stints on the road; the food was generally marginal and served in grubby surroundings; and truckers were treated as the dredges of the traveling public.

Jay insisted that Flying J's truck plaza be just the opposite: generous parking (including overnight); service islands separating trucks from cars; tiled bathrooms and showers; attractive facilities both on the interior and exterior; a television lounge; ample telephones in private booths; and top-of-the-line sleeping and restaurant facilities at budget rates. His intent was to make stops for truckers a pleasant experience where they could relax and feel at home rather than be constantly concerned about food contamination or safety. As one driver later told Dick Slater when he managed the Ogden plaza, "I love to come here. It is one of the few places I go where I can take a shower and not have to worry about something crawling up my leg."

At Jay's direction, Flying J architects designed the plaza to appeal not just to truckers, but also to local residents, tourists, and anyone else on the road. The goal was to integrate the company's real estate, motel, food, and

First Flying J travel plaza on 21st Street west of Ogden, Utah.

fuel-retailing interests, thus creating a synergy that could move Flying J one notch higher in the competitive hospitality and petroleum arenas.

When completed, the design contained the following features: eight islands equipped with twenty-nine hoses; a full-line C-store; a large recreation room and bathroom facilities for truckers, which had to meet Jay's cleanliness and privacy standards; an eighty-unit motel, the equivalent of any in Ogden at the time; and the stylish Tamarack restaurant and lounge seating 240. All facilities were of premium construction featuring brick veneer.

Such a plaza did not come without a hefty price tag—a nearly $3-million gamble representing over half of Flying J's net worth. To minimize the risk and reduce enormous interest charges (they were double-digit and rapidly rising at the time), the company applied for and received a fifteen-year Weber County Industrial Revenue Bond for $1.8 million at 8.5 percent interest. In effect, industrial revenue bonds provide a company a low-interest, public-backed loan based on the assumption that the business will create local jobs and generate significant sales and property tax revenues.

Although management had high expectations for the facility, everyone was astounded at its immediate success. Gallons sold quickly jumped to 300,000 a month. The motel and restaurant became so popular with local residents and travelers that truckers comprised only a small portion of this trade. It did not take long for Jay to realize they had uncovered a niche in the petroleum market with enormous potential. The feeling was much like a drilling crew hitting a gusher. The plaza served as the corporate flagship for the next several years and was a harbinger of things to come.

Jay's decision to build a plaza offering many amenities pleasing to truckers was the result of basic lessons he had learned through the years. With fuel products being essentially identical, a company wanting to differentiate its wares and services to attract the buying public must do so through price, location, and hospitality. The company had always been competitive on price and location, and now management's strategy was to focus on the third element—hospitality. The lesson, simple in logic but powerful in practice, was that if you cannot differentiate fuel to attract customers, differentiate the way in which it is offered or provided.

The second significant event in 1979 was also real-estate related. Through a series of fortuitous circumstances, Flying J acquired a choice 59-acre parcel in Pleasanton, California, at the junction of I-580 and I-680 in one of the most attractive regions surrounding San Francisco Bay. While visiting his sister in a community near Pleasanton, Ron Parker, at Jay's request, looked for property in the area. After making several inquiries, Ron was informed by a broker that a prime parcel would soon come on the market since Boise Cascade Credit Corporation had recently taken it back through default by a builder. After seeing the property, Ron immediately offered Boise Cascade $15,500 an acre or $900,000 with the provision that it be bought on contract with $100,000 down. By telephone he convinced Jay to put up the earnest money. Jay was attracted because it was an ideal motel site although the property had to be rezoned which took several months. After the rezoning, within days the company was receiving unsolicited offers for over $4 million.

As stated in the December 1979 Flying J *Newsletter*, acquiring the Pleasanton property was "probably the most profitable single transaction Flying J had made" to that point in time. Although Jay and Ron did not then realize it, picking up nearly $4 million in profits and cash flow helped Flying J fund its next major venture, one that again changed the direction of the company and its method of growth. Rather than adding a few stations at a time, Flying J, in one action, acquired several corporations that increased its sales by over 200 percent in two years.

Ever since the 1973 oil crisis, Jay had felt vulnerable because the company had no guaranteed fuel source. He had watched major petroleum companies weather the turbulence in world oil markets and come out unscathed. As integrated, almost self-contained suppliers, the majors had their own wells, refineries, and retail outlets. Jay yearned to get Flying J in this position, awaiting the time when assets could be added upstream (refineries and wells) to provide protection. Any such action would be a major step for a small retailer since exploration and refining require massive investments.

In the late fall of 1979, Buzz Germer and Ron Brisendine were in Spokane looking for truckstop property. While having lunch with one of Flying J's fuel suppliers, they learned that the company he represented would likely be up for sale soon. The firm, consisting of four corporations, was known as Thunderbird Resources. It was headquartered in Denver and owned by Inter-City Gas Ltd. (ICG), a Canadian corporation that was the largest propane distributor in Canada. ICG was experiencing growing dissatisfaction with its U.S. operations because of low profitability and increasingly stringent requirements imposed by the Environmental Protection Agency. ICG's divisions in the U.S. constituted 14 percent of corporate assets and contributed 28 percent of 1978 revenues but only 3 percent of operating profits. Even worse, its U.S. refineries were losing money in 1979 at a time when small refineries (such as those of Maverik) were extremely profitable because of the government-imposed small refinery bias.

Key Flying J employees reviewing the Ogden plaza design in late 1978. Left to right: John Telford (head of construction), Marcella Hume (office manager), Ron Brisendine (V.P. Retailing), Jay, Stan Weeks (controller), and Buzz Germer (V.P. Supply and Transportation).

Key Flying J employees three years later. Left to right: Jack Dailey (V.P. Propane Division), Ron Brisendine (V.P. Retailing), lower front Paul Brown (Executive Vice President), Buzz Germer (V.P. Supply and Transportation), Jay, and Ron Parker (V.P. Real Estate).

Ron and Buzz knew that Thunderbird had twice the sales and over three times the assets of Flying J, but they saw it as the possible opening Jay was seeking to become an integrated oil company. After informing Jay, he quickly called Thunderbird in Denver where officials denied any knowledge of the matter. Then he phoned ICG headquarters in Winnipeg, and they invited him up to discuss a buyout of their U.S. operations involving assets of between $30 and $40 million.

Thunderbird's fixed assets consisted of a 5,500 barrel-a-day (b/d) refinery in Cut Bank, Montana, a 4,500 b/d refinery in Williston, North Dakota, a closed refinery in Kevin, Montana, a natural gas processing plant with thirty-two propane marketing outlets, and fifty-three other marketing facilities, primarily bulk plants and small service stations. All were in Montana, North Dakota, Washington, and Oregon except for a lube oil blending plant in Louisiana. Thunderbird also operated a major wholesale business through its jobber network of 300 stations. As a bonus, Flying J gained part-ownership in over sixty oil and gas wells, and obtained lease and drilling rights in major oil-producing fields in Montana and North Dakota surrounding the two operating refineries. Thunderbird even had an auto-parts business in these areas.

After analyzing Thunderbird's holdings, Jay was convinced that the individual pieces were worth more than the whole based on the asking price. The gasoline stations in North Dakota and Montana (under such names as Thunderbird, Vista, Westco, Westland, and Domestic) were mostly small and dated. However, those in the Northwest, though aging, were generally first-class and on valuable property, often of generous proportions. The stations, wholesale business, and propane bulk plants were important, but for Flying J the real prizes would be the refineries and oil and gas fields.

For any company to take over one twice its size requires courage and aplomb, but Flying J's financial condition made it even more of a David and Goliath situation. Obtaining major loans for the acquisition would be difficult because Flying J's owners' equity was only $5.145 million or one-sixth of the asking price. Flying J's long-term debt was already $8.8 million resulting in an unfavorable debt-to-equity ratio of 1.72 to 1. The Thunderbird acquisition would boost this ratio to six dollars in long-term debt to every dollar in equity, a ratio generally deemed impossible to manage even when interest rates are low, and in 1980 they were approaching the highest level in decades. Furthermore, just before the takeover Thunderbird's refineries were losing approximately $1 million per month, losses that if continued would consume Flying J's assets within a year.

Thunderbird refinery at Cut Bank, Montana.

To get ICG to agree to the acquisition, Jay calculated he needed $10 million in hand. He hoped to obtain half from First Security Bank, at this point his major source of credit. After presenting their proposal to First Security officials, Jay, Buzz, and Paul met with George Eccles, the conservative president of the company, and, on the spot, he agreed to a $5 million loan with one proviso. Flying J must get Thunderbird's current banker, First Bank of Minneapolis, to finance the other half by granting a term loan and a line of credit. Jay realized this would be difficult because First Bank of Minneapolis was already concerned over Thunderbird's growing refinery losses. As much as the bank's loan officers admired Flying J's management team, they felt the company was too weak financially to take on such an acquisition. After a long wait and several visits, they turned Jay down.

While flying back to Brigham City after receiving the news, Jay looked at his dejected companions and said, "Let's not go home. Let's go to Winnipeg, lay our cards on the table, and see if we can negotiate a deal." Both quickly agreed, and Jay in midair had the pilot turn north for what they realized was their last opportunity to salvage any agreement.

Their only hope was for ICG to carry more of the credit. After skillful negotiation, Jay got ICG representatives to agree to finance $17,777,000 of the $31,561,000 purchase price. The debt to ICG was to be paid off in installments over ten years with $6 million payable December 31, 1980. With such favorable financing, Jay got the First Bank of Minneapolis to come back in, and Thunderbird became part of Flying J as of April 1, 1980.

Under the terms of the agreement, the first major financial challenge was to arrange for the $6 million payment at the end of December. This amount was tied to the value of the Williston refinery. Flying J quickly obtained significant financing through an industrial revenue bond issued by Williams county government in North Dakota. Although this arrangement did not reduce Flying J's debt, it made it possible to avoid violating its contract with ICG, and interest charges were lower.

Two features of the agreement ultimately made it possible for Flying J to survive. Regarding the loan, ICG gave the company the choice of a 13.5 percent fixed interest rate or a variable rate tied to the future prime. Fortunately, Flying J selected the fixed rate since prime rates jumped to over 20 percent in 1981. Also, at Flying J's insistence, an indemnity clause was included making ICG responsible for two-thirds of the refineries' cleanup costs if the EPA found the current sites in violation, a development that later proved costly to both companies.

Following the transaction, the major issue for Jay was how to handle the tremendous debt. The amount owed ICG alone was nearly three-and-a-half-times Flying J's book value. Of course, Jay had several cards to play. As noted, company assets were significantly understated, especially those of Pleasanton, since real estate was carried on the books at the purchase price, not current market value. To quickly reduce the debt, Jay sent Ron Parker to California and told him not to return until the Pleasanton site was sold. By selling Pleasanton, the Reno and Carson City motels, and other real estate, $8 million was raised to cover company obligations.

The $8 million relieved the pressure from their immediate financial crisis, but their other commitments caused their indebtedness to soon rise. Capital improvements had to be made to the refineries (although ICG had recently spent $10 million on upgrades), higher crude oil prices had to be funded, a larger debt load required servicing, and cash-flow requirements were significantly more than Flying J had estimated.

These latter problems resulted primarily from the chaotic conditions existing in the petroleum industry from 1979 through 1981. Crude prices jumped from $13 to $34 a barrel on the world market due to the overthrow of the Shah of Iran, the Iran-Iraqi war that followed, and the resultant fuel shortages brought on primarily by hoarding. Thus the crude oil inventory needed to support the refineries tripled in cost in just over a year.

Following the selling of property, company officials took several other actions to keep the company afloat. The most crucial was to stop the financial hemorrhaging associated with the refineries. It was difficult to know where to start because under ICG's inadequate cost accounting, all company retail outlets had to absorb refinery products at cost rather than at market price. Since Thunderbird's fuel exceeded market prices, the losses were passed on to their retail units, making it extremely difficult to pin down costs for each center. After intensive effort, Flying J segregated refining costs, identified the weaker units, and either sold them or shut them down. Other marketable assets—several prime retail stations, the lube plant in Louisiana, and the auto parts outlets—were put on the selling block and soon acquired by others.

The refineries were more difficult to make profitable. The problem was as much in Thunderbird's marketing as it was in the efficiency of the operations. Flying J officials had little refinery experience, but Thunderbird's management had been clearly inadequate. They even lacked an engineer to oversee the technical aspects of their operations. Flying J hired some consultants and made various changes in marketing and operations. In summarizing the situation Buzz stated, "Eventually we went from tremendous losses every month to some profits." Unfortunately, the profits could not be maintained when conditions for small refiners rapidly deteriorated in the next two years.

Unfortunately the brilliance of Flying J's acquisition was dimmed by changes in U.S. government policies and world events that were beyond its control. In 1980 U.S. crude oil prices were already being deregulated followed by the government dropping allocation regulations favoring small refineries. Within nine months of the Thunderbird transaction, only 20 percent of the crude going to Flying J refiners was subject to price and allocation controls, and on January 1, 1981, total deregulation took place. This occurred when national demand for motor fuel was decreasing for the first time in U.S. history except during the two world wars. The fall was due to higher fuel prices, improvements in engine efficiency, 55 miles-per-hour speed limits, and occasional gasoline shortages. The result was an overall national decrease of 8.8 percent in motor vehicle fuel consumption from 1979 through 1982. Only 15 percent of the decrease came from trucks with cars accounting for the balance.

This damage to small petroleum companies was intensified by the economic conditions plaguing the country as a whole. The economic depression in the three years following 1980 was the most severe since before World War II. It was driven by high interest rates, runaway inflation (nearly 30 percent in three years), peak postwar unemployment, and a slump in retail sales. The windfall profits tax hurt the majors, but their large oil inventories and reserves had been turned into black gold by price deregulation. For the small refiners, the depression put one more nail in their coffins since few pumped their own crude supply, and only the most efficient, sophisticated, and well-located could survive. One-third of all U.S. refineries closed between 1982 and 1984, most of the smaller variety.

Flying J's struggle to operate refineries soon ended. The company shutdown Williston in January of 1983 and Cut Bank two months later. As of this writing, the company still has many of the original Thunderbird properties within their production and exploration division. Also, the wholesale business acquired from Thunderbird continues to grow. Many of the retail fuel outlets obtained in the buyout contributed to Flying J profits into the 1990s, and a few still remain viable properties. The propane division was profitable but never found a comfortable niche in corporate strategy and was sold in two separate transactions in 1983 when Flying J experienced another extreme money crunch.

The pros and cons of taking over Thunderbird have been debated in the company ever since. With few exceptions Flying J participants agree that the major benefit came from gaining experience in refining, production, and exploration, thus positioning the company to make important acquisitions in the future. Without question, the biggest drawback was a delay in the timetable to expand the truckstop and travel plaza business. Like most growth companies getting into new ventures, acquiring Thunderbird was a broadening experience, valuable in terms of learning but a short-run sacrifice in profits, given other opportunities at the time. But, as Jay stated, "It put the company on the petroleum map." In effect, it forced Flying J into a sink-or-swim position where it had no alternative except to go defunct or to make the critical step of transforming from a small company into a big one and proving that it could handle the attendant problems. This maturing did not occur without considerable strife, but, as Bob Heiner, then executive vice president of First Security bank, stated, "Thunderbird kicked off some of the bigger things to come for Flying J."

Even with the strain of merging Thunderbird into the company, Flying J made a net annual after-tax profit for the next few years . However, it was a half percent or less in 1980 and 1981, a slim margin that kept company executives on edge. Cash was especially critical because with interest rates hovering around 20 percent, suppliers cut the payment cycle from thirty to ten days or even less, thus eliminating the financial windfall Jay had used since the 1960s to expand his business.

The problems in digesting Thunderbird combined with continuing difficult national economic conditions forced the company in 1983 to go through a 10 percent reduction in force. Flying J's employment at 350 more than doubled when the Thunderbird work force was acquired three years earlier. Even though many were released when facilities were sold or the refineries closed, Flying J still had a labor surplus. When the company's gallons sold dropped by 21 percent from 1982 to 1983 and sales by 10 percent (even though travel-plaza sales were up 50 percent), it was evident that changes had to be made. Besides cutting employment, the company froze wages and salaries and eliminated bonuses. These decisions were some of the most difficult for Jay because of his caring nature and concern for employees. As one employee stated, "The layoffs were a very emotional thing for Jay." It made him resolve to keep employment in check, never wanting such an occurrence to happen again.

The Thunderbird acquisition, though burdensome, did not command all of the company's attention or resources. Almost before the ink was dry on the purchase agreement, Jay again proved willing to ignore financial constraints if he spotted an opportunity he knew represented a money machine, this time the acquisition of another truck plaza. In December of 1980, a large truckstop in Boise came up for sale. It was on a desirable twenty-six-acre site but, being poorly managed and in need of remodeling, it was unprofitable and had changed owners twice in just a few months. With all his personal assets and those of the company tied up in Thunderbird, Jay knew it would be impossible to obtain adequate financing for the purchase. After evaluating his options, he offered half ownership to his friend Sterling Jardine of Jardine Petroleum based on the provision that Flying J would operate it. Once Sterling agreed, Jay was able to come up with the balance of the funding and the purchase was made. They immediately undertook a $700,000 remodeling and, within a year, sales more than doubled followed by a 27 percent climb the year after. In July of 1983, Flying J bought Sterling's share, and the Boise plaza remains as one of Flying J's valuable assets.

Thus, Flying J did not totally abandon its truckstop plans after picking up Thunderbird. The plans were pushed along somewhat by acquiring the company since a truckstop at Great Falls and one at Williston were part of the deal. Soon after, two more were purchased, one in Beach, North Dakota, in 1983, and the other on west 21st South in Salt Lake City the year after. In addition, a "mini" truckstop was constructed in Orland, California in 1983. However, the most important truckstop development of this period was to occur at Post Falls, Idaho.

The Post Falls travel plaza was significant because it replaced the one in Ogden as the company's format of the future. Buzz and Ron located the

7.5-acre lot just across the Washington border in northern Idaho, thirty miles from Spokane. The company searched for property near the state line since Washington motor fuel taxes were much higher, and truckers would fill up before entering the state. The design set a new standard for travel-plaza decor and was developed with the intent of maximizing convenience, comfort, and hospitality. It differed from Ogden in that the restaurant, C-store, and cashier station were all under one roof. The restaurant had seating for 112, and the C-store had 1,000 feet of shelf space. There were ten gas and twenty-four diesel hoses, and parking was available for eighty rigs.

A principle governing the design through each stage was to minimize required labor. In such an elaborate facility, keeping fuel prices cut-rate meant savings had to be made in labor costs. Accordingly, at Post Falls all customers pay their bills at one location in the front. This not only keeps payroll expenditures down, but the complex can be operated with very few employees if demand turns out to be less than projected. Much to Jay's relief, soon after the $2 million facility opened in October of 1982, seventy employees were required to service the growing trade.

In all, Post Falls generated another retail strike as significant as Ogden's. Business flourished and the company started to share in Jay's belief that some day Flying J would have a travel plaza network covering the entire nation.

In the early 1980s Flying J refused to mark time in other respects. A corporate annex adding executive offices and space for 105 employees was completed in 1982. In 1983 the Salt Lake motel was expanded by thirty-nine units, and an eighty-four-unit motel was built the next year at the Boise truckstop. A water slide entertainment center north of the Ogden travel plaza proved a failure, but another sideline business, rental of video equipment and movies, paid big dividends for several years.

As many entrepreneurial ventures, the opportunity to enter the video business came along almost by chance. After hearing of video successes in California, in 1982 the company introduced the "Flying J Video Club" in several of its Montana stores. These were the first rental video outlets in that area. Each store started with just one hundred titles, and the rush in business surprised Flying J executives. Within three years the company had video outlets at thirty-five Flying J locations and all of its motels plus 121 dealerships spread out over eleven states. The company's video inventory soon exceeded 37,000 tapes with nearly 2,000 VCR rental machines. In 1985, Flying J was one of the top ten national video rental chains, an indication that the business was extremely profitable. Then, as often occurs with a product or business that is on the perimeter of a company's primary interest, Flying J did not keep up with the intense competition created by soaring demand. In several years, supermarkets and stores devoted solely to video rental took the lead. However, Flying J kept its video operations in the black until the early 1990s before backing out in 1993. Thad, Jay's son, worked in the video division for several years before leaving to manage a travel plaza.

Another downside of the Thunderbird acquisition was that it not only slowed Flying J's travel-plaza development, but it also delayed the company from making necessary improvements in its self-service gasoline stations. Many facilities still contained apartments for the operators even though the government prohibited this arrangement in 1977. The company was slow to convert this space to the convenience store format that began to dominate automobile gasoline retailing, led by such companies as 7-Eleven and Circle K. Flying J, determined to catch-up, started an extensive remodeling program in 1982. Three years later, twenty-eight C-stores, mostly remodeled self-service stations, had been added..

In all, the period from 1980–84 not only tested Flying J's financial strength, but it seriously challenged its depth and capability of management. This road proved rocky in more respects than just the struggle to maintain profitability. At the time of the acquisition, Flying J's management was already thin, and they were taking over a much larger company that was struggling and especially weak in refining, expertise that Flying J also lacked. Buzz had become an expert in supply, wholesaling, and trucking, but he had limited experience in refining and exploration. Brisendine had been essential in developing the retail end of Flying J, but he had not prepared himself for more responsibility, and in 1984 he left to develop some properties on his own. Paul was a superb controller, but he had quit Flying J once and would soon leave again. It was the typical entrepreneurial problem: several members of upper management, effective at one stage of the company's growth, lacked the experience and/or capacity to be as effective at a higher level. Being lean in management and facing growing challenges, a leadership void was clearly evident given Jay's desire to shed his responsibility for day-to-day management.

At this critical juncture, it was imperative that someone step forward to coordinate company efforts in following Jay's bursts of entrepreneurial genius. Few expected this void to be filled by an accountant, still in his late twenties, who arrived on the scene during the Thunderbird acquisition. J. Phillip (Phil) Adams graduated from Brigham City's Box Elder High School in 1973 and received a degree in accounting from Utah State University five years later. Then he went to work for Paul Brown in a local CPA firm. Within

Phil Adams soon after he joined Flying J.

a year, Paul returned to work for Flying J and Phil went with him. In July of 1981, Paul was moved up to executive vice president, and Phil became the chief financial officer. The next year Phil was made vice president and treasurer. In 1983 when the company had its major downturn in sales and was overburdened with debt, Jay saw in Phil the type of take-charge executive he was looking for to direct company operations, and Jay made him vice president of retailing. Few CEOs would have thrust a young accountant into such a position, but Jay recognized that Phil had the capacity, interest, and drive to eventually head the company. Besides, he was the one who most fervently shared Jay's belief that Flying J could dominate the national truckstop and travel plaza business.

In 1984, with all aspects of Flying J operations improving, sales went up 13.3 percent. At the start of 1985, the company had sixty-five gasoline stations, twenty-eight convenience stores, seven travel plazas, seven restaurants, four motels, and a major video business. With this continuing aggregation of facilities, long-term debt was the highest in Flying J's history at approximately $40 million. However this was more than offset by improvements in owners' equity. Book value had increased nearly three times from just prior to the Thunderbird acquisition, and was now a pleasing $16 million. Thus, the debt-to-equity ratio had been reduced to a more acceptable 2.5 to 1. Even with the sell-off or closure of a significant portion of Thunderbird facilities, Flying J's fixed assets at the beginning of 1985 were just slightly lower than immediately after the acquisition.

The company was not only rapidly boosting its financial strength, but executives were again on the lookout for ways to accelerate its growth. Given Flying J's recent experiences, many would wonder whether their leaders had the will and capacity to take on an even greater acquisition. However, those knowing Jay recognized that if the right deal came along the trauma of Thunderbird would be ignored if not forgotten. Management realized that the only way to acquire the enormous capital needed to exploit its travel plaza plans was to take drastic steps aimed at multiplying Flying J's size.

This new opportunity again involved a company with extensive Rocky Mountain oil interests. The parent, Husky Oil Ltd., had major petroleum holdings in western Canada and the western U.S., although in this country its refineries were in only two states, Wyoming and Utah. Having sold its U.S. oil and production division, Husky wanted to dispose of its remaining U.S. properties. In 1984 it grouped them into a separate corporation, RMT Properties, Inc., for this purpose. Some eighteen months later Flying J acquired RMT on the last day of December in 1985.

In many respects, this purchase paralleled the acquisition of Thunderbird. RMT was centered in the western states (an area where Flying J had a presence and market expertise), and was owned by a Canadian firm that wanted to dispose of its U.S. holdings; it had truckstops, service stations, and upstream capability, namely refineries and distribution facilities; and the company had well-located retail outlets that the parent organization had been slow in updating.

The big differences between Thunderbird and RMT were in size and quality. Both had three refineries, but Husky's were over three times the size, and two were still operating; Husky's retail network was more respected, larger (400 branded dealers), and more dispersed, covering eleven western states. However, of these dealerships only twenty-four truckstops and twelve stations were owned by the company. Nevertheless, Husky's truck plazas comprised the largest single western U.S. truckstop network next to Unocal Corporation. With three refineries and a respected truckstop chain, Husky's availability was certain to gain Flying J's attention.

Of Husky's three refineries, the one in Cody, Wyoming, with a 12,000 b/d capacity was shutdown in the small refinery slaughter of 1982. The one in Cheyenne, Wyoming, with a 35,000 b/d capacity, was large for the Rocky Mountain area, but it was expensive to operate and needed upgrading. The third refinery, situated north of Salt Lake City, was half the size of the one in Cheyenne, but it could easily be upgraded to 25,000 b/d. Under normal conditions the Cheyenne refinery would command a high price, but few companies were actively trying to acquire refineries at the time. Without question, the one property that Flying J openly coveted, viewing it as the missing weapon in its battle with the regional petroleum giants, was the Salt Lake City refinery. This facility was not only in Flying J's backyard, but it was less expensive to run and was the one RMT property showing a significant profit. In addition, it had the potential of doing far better.

Husky began as a small family petroleum business under Glenn Nielsen of Cody, Wyoming. His business roots had some parallels to those of Reuel's. Nielsen started with small Wyoming refineries before expanding into surrounding states and Canada. Simultaneously, he became a major petroleum retailer in both regions, and eventually turned the company into a major public corporation. The corporation's most valuable properties turned out to be oil and gas leases in Canada. In 1978 when petroleum companies were struggling, all Husky properties were acquired in an unfriendly takeover by Nova Ltd. The price was extremely favorable, being well under $1 billion. Like Inter-City Gas, Nova was eager to get Husky out of the U.S. because of environmental protection laws, low prices, and intense competition. Many major companies were attracted by Husky's U.S. oil and gas holdings, but they did not want the unprofitable refineries and marketing properties.

In 1984 Husky Ltd. struck a deal with Marathon Oil Company (part of U.S. Steel, since renamed USX), to buy Husky's U.S. oil and gas production at an extremely favorable price. While vacationing in Palm Springs with Tamra, Jay read of the transaction in *The Wall Street Journal*. He immediately told her to pack, explaining that Husky's U.S. marketing and refining operations would soon be on the market at a bargain price, and he wanted Flying J to be on the company's doorstep with an offer.

Within a few days Jay contacted Husky officials about buying RMT (an abbreviation for refining, marketing, and transportation), but they seemed insulted at such a small company approaching them. They mentioned a selling price of $100 million, which Jay realized was not only unrealistic but far more than anything Flying J could manage. Accordingly, he temporarily let the matter drop.

Less than a year later a report appeared in newspapers and trade journals indicating that John Grambling had arranged to purchase RMT. However within a month the deal was nullified when bankers discovered that Grambling had misrepresented his financing and could not make good on the agreement. Embarrassed by what appeared to be a swindle, Husky now looked for a buyer with known integrity. The bad publicity plus continued losses by RMT resulted in few suitors, so Husky contacted Flying J, tempting them with a reduced price and seeking a quick agreement.

On June 5, 1985, Flying J and Husky signed a purchase contract with a closing date of August 1. Jay put up a nonrefundable down payment of $2 million to seal the transaction. Then Flying J officials went back to their major banks and those of RMT's to get support. Flying J's primary banker, First Security Corporation, made some promises, but would not finance more than it had with Thunderbird. Several other bankers showed interest, but on each occasion they withdrew before the settlement date. Accordingly, Flying J asked Husky for an extension while seeking other financial backing.

At this point, Husky was desperate for someone to takeover RMT's operations. Several top managers had resigned during the John Grambling fiasco, losses were accumulating, and their U.S. operations were in disarray. Husky listened to various proposals from potential owners and internal managers before settling on Flying J's plans. All other recommendations aimed to build up RMT's operations while Flying J's called for a reduction. In addition, after working for several months with Flying J's management, Husky now had full trust in Jay and the other officers. At this point, Husky was looking for integrity as much as financial strength. Accordingly, on September 1, 1985, Flying J took over management of RMT on a fee basis assuming that a switch in ownership would shortly occur. Jay was made president with Buzz and Phil as vice presidents.

Husky wanted Jay to initiate immediately the downsizing necessary to shrink required working capital, now nearly $100 million in inventories and accounts receivable. One motive for lowering the credit guarantees was to make it easier for Flying J to purchase the company. Flying J earlier had offered to buy just the truckstops and the Salt Lake refinery, but Husky wanted out of all U.S. operations. Jay's job was made difficult because Husky would not let him terminate employees even though the company was significantly overstaffed. Nevertheless, within three months the nearly $100 million needed to support operations (net working capital and letters of credit) was greatly reduced. However, even then a key financial institution in the negotiations, Bank of New England, again withdrew just before the planned closing. Flying J desperately looked for other financiers, even getting a Cheyenne refinery crude supplier to not charge RMT until revenue was earned from sale of the refined output. Still Flying J came up short.

As the end of the calendar year approached, Husky became more frantic, apparently because the company faced a major tax liability if it continued operating in the U.S. after December 31. Accordingly, at the last minute Husky stepped in to guarantee a revolving credit line at one major bank, with an agreement that Flying J would relieve it of this commitment within eighteen months. This action brought all parties back to the table, resulting in a New Year's Eve transfer of ownership that propelled Flying J into being the largest mountain west independent oil company.

The final sale figures were nearly identical to those of the Thunderbird purchase except for $39 million in revolving credit lines at two banks. The RMT purchase price was $31,969,000, within a half million of the Thunderbird agreement. The portion carried by the seller was $16,255,000, or $1.5 million less than with Thunderbird. The major difference—the larger credit guarantees from banks—was made necessary by Husky's more extensive operations, mandating huge inventories to support the refineries.

The $70 million agreement ($31 million purchase price and $39 million in guaranteed credit lines) again represented a tremendous challenge for a company with a net worth of one-fourth this total. The banks, fearful of the situation, required that both Flying J as a company and its primary owner put up the company's entire stock and all of their combined assets including Jay's home as loan guarantees. Furthermore, the company and Jay were restricted from obtaining other loans, making major capital acquisitions, or undertaking significant business expansions until the indebtedness was decreased. The company and its CEO were in a financial straitjacket until nearly $20 million in debt and loan guarantees could be eliminated.

As ominous as the figures appear, Jay and the company assumed less risk with Husky than with Thunderbird. The appraised value of RMT's twenty-four truckstops, twelve stations, three refineries, three large parcels of land, a pipeline distribution system from Cheyenne into various parts of Nebraska, and a terminal in Boise topped out at nearly $50 million versus the $20 million in fixed assets used in arriving at the purchase agreement. Furthermore, this was $19 million more than the entire purchase price, and it turned out that many of these properties were undervalued. Hence, by just selling the pieces Flying J had an approximately $25 million cushion if the company chose to liquidate.

Aware of the financial crunch that would immediately follow the takeover, Flying J sought buyers for the two most high-priced RMT assets—the Cheyenne refinery and the distribution pipeline. Both were sold on a common closing date of March 1, 1986. A group led by a top executive of Tosco Corporation bought the Cheyenne refinery for $5 million, and the distribution pipeline was dealt to Continental Pipeline Company (Conoco) for approximately the same amount. For Flying J, relieving itself of the burden to support these operations was almost as important as their sale. With the sale of other properties, including a Husky station in Denver for $1 million, Flying J had $13.3 million to help cover the initial financial obligations stipulated in the purchase agreement.

When word of the acquisition reached the streets, acquaintances were again dumbfounded at what Flying J and its CEO had accomplished. One associate outside the company declared, "My ____, how can Jay even think about doing that?" As Ed Swapp, one of Flying J's employees stated, "When you have to put even your home on the line, most multimillionaires would say, 'Hey, wait a minute,' but not Jay." Fred Greener, Flying J's primary accountant involved in the details of meshing the two companies stated, "Husky did guarantee many of the loans, but it was still an ant eating an elephant."

Unfortunately, as with Thunderbird, the timing of the acquisition could not have been worse. A few days after the New Year's Eve victory celebration, Flying J officials witnessed the price of crude drop as rapidly as it had risen in 1980. Oil on the world market was overabundant and overpriced. Saudi Arabia, holding one-third of the free world's reserves, had been hurt most by OPEC's efforts to restrict production. When the Saudis decided to let prices fluctuate on the open world market, crude dropped from $28 a barrel in January to $12 on March 31, 1986. For companies with large crude inventories that had not been hedged (agreement to buy or sell crude at a future specified price), it was a disaster of the worst proportions. For Flying J, desperate to cut Husky's operating losses and to sell properties to ease its financial strain, nothing could have been more untimely.

When the agreement was signed, even after downsizing by Flying J's management, RMT still had a fuel inventory of over a million barrels, mainly of crude oil. With crude dropping $16 a barrel and gasoline prices plummeting 36 percent, Flying J had inventory paper losses of approximately $20 million within three months of the takeover. This was offset some by the $13.3 million gained through sale of assets, but this revenue was required to meet loan guarantees. To alleviate the situation, Flying J quickly sold the Salt Lake City motel and prime real estate at a Bountiful, Utah, I-15 exit.

As many Flying J employees recall, it was the most hectic period in the company's history. Buzz, Flying J's primary transition manager who was temporarily located in Denver, Colorado, stated "I have never been so busy in my life." As Barre Burgon, vice president and corporate attorney for Flying J, described it, "We were running from one end of the continent to the other and stopping in between to get things sold, bought, and borrowed." The clamor for funding and the drawn-out uncertainty prior to the purchase, followed by the most chaotic petroleum industry conditions in at least six years, challenged the acumen and stamina of management.

Fortunately, Jay and his colleagues were equal to the test. One of the most important actions was taken by Buzz. When Flying J sold the Cheyenne

Flying J refinery in North Salt Lake City.

refinery, the buyers put $1 million down. Based on processing agreements, Flying J was to receive the balance in refined products. The new owners were most eager to dispose of the bottoms, primarily asphalt. Buzz, sensing trends in the market (asphalt demand had been low and the price weak), arranged a three-year agreement to purchase asphalt at a price tied to crude oil. Asphalt prices rose almost as rapidly as crude prices fell, and within three years the company recouped over $10 million of its losses.

Flying J was much better prepared to turn around Husky's operations than it had been Thunderbird's. Buzz, with his quick learning skills, was now well informed about refining. The entire corporate office having gone through one merger was better set to handle another. Furthermore, the company avoided the overstaffing that accompanied the absorption of Thunderbird. In what was left of RMT after the downsizing, Flying J improved performance while keeping only a fraction of RMT's employees. Even though the drop in crude prices caused major petroleum companies in 1986 to experience the worst combined profit year in their histories (3.7 percent of equity), Flying J that year had a 25 percent return on equity and net income of 2.1 percent after taxes, both its highest in over a decade. The company proved that even under extremely adverse conditions it had the management skills to be an industry leader.

How important was the Husky acquisition to the company's future? The Salt Lake refinery alone has allowed the company to grow much faster than would have been possible otherwise. The refinery has never had an annual loss since it was acquired, and it has kept the company out of the red during the costly startup of its massive retail interstate network. In fact, refinery profits have more than paid for the entire Husky acquisition and all refinery capital improvements, plus contributing millions more in profits and cash flow. Husky's 400-dealer network did not prove as valuable since many operators thought Flying J was too small to succeed and dropped their affiliation or purchased their dealership equity. The truck plaza network gave the company a considerable boost although some owners continued to operate as standoffish independent franchisees. In the two years following the acquisition, Flying J sales were up 44 percent and profits up 120 percent. Their debt-to-equity ratio declined even after acquiring a much larger company for $70 million. The experience made Flying J's management realize that they not only could compete with the majors, but they had a game plan with the potential of putting them on top. As Phil said, "It was the greatest thing that ever happened to us." Buzz's observations are similar: "The Husky acquisition got us to where we are today."

12

RISE TO DOMINANCE IN TRAVEL PLAZAS AND DIESEL

Although the Husky acquisition somewhat delayed Flying J's schedule for building truckstops, Jay never wavered in his top priority—developing a nationwide travel-plaza network. Company strategy in 1982 called for eighteen to be in place by the end of 1985. The number turned out to be larger thanks to acquiring Husky's, although many of these needed remodeling to meet Flying J standards. In 1983 with Phil at the retail helm, company travel-plaza strategy became more accelerated and grandiose. Plans were adopted to build a network of 250 plazas, fifty each for the next five years.

The rationale for such a scheme had considerable merit. The last links were being completed in the country's interstate freeway system, allowing truckers to concentrate their travel on these super highways. The interstate system comprised only 1.1 percent of national highway miles, but it carried 20.5 percent of all traffic, exceeding 60 percent for trucks with trailers. Furthermore, depending on the source, a minimum of 1,665 to a maximum of 3,000 truckstops could then be counted on the system, and few (considerably less than 10 percent), were state-of-the-art. None matched Flying J's one-stop opportunities where a traveler could obtain fuel, convenience store items, meals, and lodging in clean, attractive facilities. Truckers, most of whom spend three out of four weeks on the road, strongly appreciated Flying J's continuing efforts to make their plazas a "home away from home" for the often weary professional.

Jay's strategy to network the interstates so that truckers need fuel only at Flying J stops was not necessarily unique. Many industry analysts then held views similar to those of Forrest Baker, president of Transportation Research and Marketing, who stated in 1987 that "The future of truckstops lies in big chains." The majors were too set in their ways, too committed to oil, and too monolithic to join the competition in such a rapidly evolving industry. Flying J's primary competitors were firms like Petro Shopping Centers (a chain operating out of El Paso) and Pilot Oil (headquartered in Knoxville) that had lean organizations, youthful exuberance, and basically the right concept. However, neither strove as hard as Flying J to be the low-cost provider, and both lacked the same vital ingredient holding Jay back—adequate capital.

Although taking over Husky boosted Flying J into its 1985 *Forbes* magazine ranking as the 379th largest private U.S. corporation, the company's 2.6 to 1 debt-to-equity ratio hardly encouraged financiers to hand out significant portions of the enormous capital required to build 250 plazas. At the time, the investment in each plaza was at least $3 to $6 million. Accordingly, when taking inflation into account, nearly a billion dollars would be required to build such a network.

When Phil took over retailing, he knew from his strong financial background that some novel strategy must be concocted to attract such large sums. As he stated, "I liked to tell people we had the ideas, locations, people, and marketing to make it work. What we didn't have was the billion dollars to do it." He realized that it would be difficult to sell such a proposal to Wall Street bankers and major brokerage firms since oil was considered a stagnant business, and the truckstop industry was still looked on as an ugly duckling.

Jay early on concluded that the company's best hope was a form of franchising where each franchisee would be responsible for coming up with the capital funds. Franchising was not new to the automotive, transportation, and retail fuel industries. Hertz adopted franchising in its rental car business beginning in 1918, and several major oil companies (such as Conoco) in the 1950s constructed service stations and leased them back to dealers under a franchise arrangement. The type of franchising that became extremely popular in the 1980s was one where a franchisee funded the construction of the properties and then operated them under a franchise agreement with a major chain. Knowing that it would be difficult for most potential franchisees to independently underwrite a travel plaza, the approach Flying J pursued was one

Jay and Tamra

Jay in his office.

where financing could be obtained from third-party investors who would then lease the facilities to a franchisee approved by Flying J.

Flying J had first considered franchising in 1982. However, due to the company's financial difficulties of 1983 followed by the all-consuming Husky acquisition, no action was taken. However, Flying J conceived the possibility of converting many of the Husky truckstops into franchises and began such discussions with Husky dealers before the final takeover. At the time, based on Phil's financial background and current retailing responsibilities, Jay assigned him to pursue all franchising options.

Flying J's competitive strategy mimicked that of prominent companies in other industries that were using franchising to fund explosive growth. As stated in Flying J's fall 1986 *Newsletter*, "Flying J's primary goal through franchising will be to do for interstate travel what McDonald's had done for fast food dining by developing a nationwide marketing format designed to deliver products and service in the quickest, most economic, yet profitable way." Like most fast-food franchisors, Flying J's intent was to provide a uniform, high-quality product at low cost. Facilities were to be first class and similar in design for easy recognition. Service and cleanliness were to be hallmarks.

Three differences, however, distinguish a fast-food outlet from a travel plaza, each of which later created problems for Flying J franchisees. The cost of setting up a fast-food outlet was then about $400,000 versus at least ten times that amount for a travel plaza. In addition, with facilities as diverse as fuel stations, convenience stores, restaurants, and possibly a motel, a truckstop presents far greater management challenges. Finally, motor fuel is a commodity with essentially identical characteristics. Accordingly, fuel customers are primarily attracted by price.

Jay made the initial contact that led to the financial backing for franchising. While attending a seminar in Boise on raising business capital, he met a person associated with Morton H. Fleischer, president of Franchise Finance Corporation of America in Phoenix. FFCA in just seven years had raised over $1.2 billion through fourteen limited partnership offerings, three-fourths of which were franchises for fast-food chains. Flying J, hoping to have 70 percent of its future outlets franchised, convinced Fleischer that the company could revolutionize the interstate travel-plaza trade the way fast-food franchising had taken over that industry.

What Flying J wanted to avoid was the type of franchising common at the time with truckstop operators such as Unocal and British Petroleum. Their facilities exhibited inconsistencies similar to what customers find in many hotel and motel franchised chains. The franchisor is too often willing to take almost any lodging property owner under its wing, and customers never know what standards to expect at different locations. Many times an owner could become a truckstop franchisee by doing little more than paying a fee and agreeing to use the major's fuel in return for the right to display the logo or brand name.

Fleischer was not hard to convince, stating "There are 3,000 truckstops out there and nobody has networked them like the fast-food industry." Accordingly, FFCA got plans underway to raise through limited partnership offerings $1 billion for erecting 200 to 250 travel plazas in seven years.

The FFCA prospectus released October 10, 1986, targeted raising $50 million (50,000 units at a $1,000 per unit), although the offering could go higher if oversubscribed. Units of the limited partnership, known as "Participating Income Properties 1986, L.P.," could be bought by any investor if the individual purchased a minimum of five units. The securities were initially sold through E.F. Hutton & Company Inc., a brokerage firm with over 6,000 agents. Later Hutton became part of Shearson Lehman, and this company took over brokerage responsibilities.

The initial offering raised approximately $50 million. Minus commissions, fees, and organization costs, approximately $44 million was left for "purchase of new and existing" Flying J travel plazas. A travel-plaza franchisee could be either Flying J as a company (known in the industry as "company-ops") or an applicant that Flying J approved. Of the eleven travel plazas funded from the initial offering, only three were for independent parties. The eight Flying J company-ops were new units under design or construction, former Husky truckstops to be rebuilt, and completed plazas (such as the one at Post Falls) that were being refinanced.

With the rapid purchase of the first offering, a second one was quickly issued, this time for over $82 million ($71.5 million net). With these funds, thirteen more plazas were constructed, nine company-ops and four for new franchisees.

A third offering was issued even though at that point all seven independent franchisees had experienced operating losses and had either sold or were in the process of selling their properties to Flying J. Given this experience, early in 1990 the company decided to phase out franchising. Thus the third offering was limited to approximately $22.5 million, making a total of over $137 million raised to refinance, equip, build, and/or remodel twenty-seven travel plazas or portions of plazas such as the motel added at the Boise truckstop. All are currently Flying J properties or former Husky franchised stations that did not change their status.

Although the dream of obtaining $1 billion was not fulfilled, the net of $137 million came at a critical time in Flying J history. Bolstered by these funds, Flying J at the close of 1989 had twenty-four travel plazas and fourteen franchised properties, enabling it to leapfrog over several competitors and become number two nationwide in the truckstop/travel-plaza business.

The legal and operating details governing the relationship among Flying J, the franchisees, FFCA, and the limited partnership investors are too involved for detailed consideration. However, to understand why the seven independent franchisees failed, it is necessary to comprehend the basic ties among the parties.

Flying J was to approve applicants, oversee design and construction, evaluate sites, and train employees. Also, it was to make available its electronic point-of-sale system, inventory control forms, and other business aids. Limited partnership funds were used to equip and build facilities that were then leased to franchisees for twenty years with a purchase option at the end of ten years. The franchisee was to pay Flying J a $25,000 to $100,000 fee that guaranteed the recipient an exclusive territory, use of the Flying J name, and a variety of support services. Royalty payments to Flying J were 5 percent on gross revenues and .6 to 1 cent per gallon on fuel.

Being a "participating income" limited partnership, the investors were also to receive annual rents from Flying J or a franchisee equal to a guaranteed 10 percent minimum on invested capital. In addition to lease payments, the limited partners would receive a percentage return on all sales—3.5 percent for convenience stores and restaurants, .2 percent for fuel, and 8 percent for lodging.

Within three to six months after their openings, the seven independent franchisees were experiencing large losses, and, as is so frequently the case with new businesses, they did not have the working capital or credit lines to sustain them until they could break even. Thus they ended up selling their properties to Flying J, and several initiated lawsuits that were not entirely settled until late 1995.

The problems the franchisees experienced are textbook examples of the two most common causes of small business failure—underfinancing and weak management. Basically, most were not sufficiently experienced or financed to withstand a major competitive struggle, one that inevitably occurs when a respected rival enters a new sales territory. In retailing it is common for companies in the same local market to "heat up the ads," (cut their prices) the day a newcomer has a grand opening. Obviously, neighboring companies are not going to sit by and lose customers without a fight, and they know that single business owners often lack "staying power," so that a prolonged price war could squeeze them out.

Several reasons account for the franchisees being underfinanced: some had apparently misrepresented their financial status; Flying J could have screened applicants more thoroughly; and working capital requirements were significantly underestimated. Also in an industry noted for low margins, it was difficult to pay royalties to a franchisor and rents to limited partners and still make a profit. However, as Flying J demonstrated after taking over the properties, the main problem was that the new franchisees, eager to get short-term results, were unable or unwilling to accept Flying J's pricing philosophy and therefore did not generate projected volumes. Using its experience, pricing philosophy, and deeper pockets, Flying J turned each plaza into a profitable enterprise, generally within months after it was acquired.

A closely related problem contributing to the franchisees' demise was that most selected sites east of the Rocky Mountains in locations where Flying J currently had no travel plazas and hence a weak image. With no customer base, it often takes a new retailer a year or more to break even due to enormous start-up costs. Now Flying J has over 600,000 truckers carrying Flying J cards, and 70 percent of a new plaza's customers the first month are those who have done business with the company previously.

In addition, in several instances the franchisees lacked the experience and perhaps the desire to run what is widely known as a "a hands-on, 24-hour-a-day business." The importance of experience is clearly evident when comparing how the former Husky franchisees performed. All Husky franchisees were successful under the limited partnership arrangement whereas all of the independent franchisees failed. However, upgrading a former Husky facility required less investment than building a totally new plaza.

For FFCA and the limited partners, franchising through Flying J has been far from a disappointment. In the first few months as partnership capital was in the process of being deployed, the return to partners was only 9.5 percent. However, after all available funds were invested and Flying J was operating the plazas, annual partnership rents have never been lower than 11 percent and are generally nearer 14 percent. Important as the funding was to Flying J, this cost of capital is expensive in the current era of low interest rates. Given Flying J's present marketing and financial strengths, the company will likely seek to start purchasing the facilities once this option becomes available beginning in the fall of 1996.

Even though franchising gave Flying J what some called a "black eye," the ultimate outcome (as with Thunderbird) was positive: It was a crucial step in the company's progress, especially financially. Although burdened by many difficulties that Phil referred to as "painful and expensive," the company emerged stronger from the experience. Phil acknowledges that the primary lessons were two: restrict partners to those who have your same goals, and accept partners only under circumstances where you keep control. Flying J's primary goals were long-term—ultimately to surpass the competition and develop an interstate travel-plaza network that would dominate what was then considered an annual $26 billion industry.[1] The new franchisees' focus was more narrow and short-term—try to quickly show a profit by pricing at generous margins; totally concentrate on local concerns; and don't do anything that might increase financial insecurity.

Another development important to Flying J in the mid and late 1980s was the use of electronic data processing to enhance business operations. Two programs were started that set it apart from the balance of the truckstop/travel-plaza industry. The first was directed at improving efficiency and record keeping. The other was a marketing strategy to win truckers' allegiance, a program that ultimately became one of the most innovative and effective in the entire petroleum industry.

The initial program, conceptualized in 1984 and first tested at the Boise plaza in early 1986, focused on making the cashier's job easier and eliminating most manual operations while at the same time providing more timely, accurate information for managing. The opportunities to automate functions and improve reporting were numerous. In the retail motor fuel industry, customers use up to fifty different payment methods, many requiring pre-approval by third-party credit companies. All such transactions must be reconciled on a cash or credit basis through a variety of parties. Sales and costs are allocated to dozens of different accounts, especially when a C-store, restaurant, motel, and service center are included.

To handle these transactions and get improved reporting, Flying J first looked to purchase existing software, but found nothing adequate for a complex travel plaza. In the long run, this turned out to be extremely fortunate since Jay then authorized information specialists within the company to write their own code. This led to Flying J developing an information systems capability that pushed it at least two years ahead of the competition. It also opened opportunity doors equal to any the company had walked through in the past.

---

1. The U.S. trucking industry handles 78 percent of all national freight. Estimated annual sales are $325 to $350 billion. Truckstops likely represent 10 percent of this total.

The initial system was designed by employees in retailing, accounting, and marketing and then programmed by company data-processing experts. The goal was to automate every transaction from when an item was purchased through the final posting and payment. The designers sought to eliminate written tickets, speed credit authorizations, expedite bank and credit reconciliations, update inventories and accounts on a real-time basis, and build important data banks such as customer files.

Phil, driven by his belief that Flying J could be the industry low-cost provider only if its unit labor costs were below competitors', quickly became the major top management technology advocate. Potential savings were not hard to identify. Completing fuel-desk paperwork for a driver could take fifteen to twenty minutes. One cashier position annually required $80,000 since the fuel desk is staffed around the clock. Some large plazas had four to five employees in the back office just to keep accounts and make payments, and frequent errors due to manual processing made account reconciliations time consuming.

The Flying J point-of-sale (POS) system become the envy of other retailers and one several fuel companies are seeking to purchase. With encouragement from both inside and outside the company, Flying J is pursuing the possibility of being a clearing house for POS transactions industrywide. Quite a change for a company that in 1980 had to upgrade its small NCR computer to an IBM mainframe, retrain many of its employees, and greatly expand its accounts to accommodate the Thunderbird takeover because that company's systems were more sophisticated.

Given the complexity of Flying J's POS system, only a few of its latest features will be described, but even a brief account will show why the company is the industry's software and automation leader. After entering a fuel island and hooking up the hoses, a driver inserts a credit or fuel purchase card into a Flying J Express Pay Cardreader. High speed pumps then dispense fuel at the rate of sixty gallons a minute through hoses inserted in tanks on both sides of the cab. When the tanks are full, the plaza's dedicated electronic processing system obtains third-party billing approval in four seconds or less. (The standard telephone dial-up procedure of most other companies takes twenty to thirty seconds.) When the driver reaches the fuel desk, a credit slip or receipt is waiting for his or her signature, and the transaction is complete unless the person makes other purchases (C-store, self-service restaurant, etc.). For a Flying J cashier, each driver transaction normally takes one minute, less than one tenth the previous time. The company benefits from labor savings of least 400 percent, and the drivers leave more satisfied because of the quick, efficient service.

A driver or company can take advantage of this program by signing up for a Flying J Interstate Trucking Services (ITS) fuel-purchase card. (The company also has an Express Fuel card for smaller firms that travel mostly off the interstates—such as those involved in bread delivery, landscaping, construction, etc.). By using either card (or any third-party card that Flying J accepts), information can be obtained periodically on all transactions the company or individual has with Flying J. Summary output reports contain a breakdown of this information by driver number, place of purchase, gallons sold, license plate numbers, and even truck hub and odometer readings. Furthermore, a company can set limits on the amount and types of purchases for each driver, and can order a year-end tax report summarizing annual purchases by vehicle and state.

Since organizations are basically information processing systems, the options for using POS data are almost unlimited. Consider another example: internally each travel-plaza manager daily receives a report covering all on-site operations for the previous twenty-four hours. Sixteen different transactions are summarized on an hourly basis for fuel alone. Other hourly reports, such as those on restaurants, summarize sales by employee and the number of customers served. This information is used to schedule labor, evaluate efficiency, and identify trends or problems that need management's attention.

The second significant program started in 1986 that could only be accomplished through automation was solely marketing driven—a strategy to encourage repeat customers similar to the airlines' frequent flyer programs. Jay had a Flying J stamp program for customers going back to the 1970s when S&H Green, Gold Strike, and other stamps were common on the retail scene. Flying J stamps (given for fuel purchases) could be exchanged for merchandise out of a catalogue. Long after other stamps became unpopular, Flying J continued its program with considerable success. When the company decided to focus on truckstops, Jay conceived a offshoot program for truckers entitled "Frequent Fueler." Thanks to the POS system, Jay's new brainchild required only sixty days to design and implement.

Under the program, when a customer slides a Frequent Fueler card through Flying J's Express Pay Cardreader, Frequent Fueler points are automatically accumulated based on the gallons purchased. Points are also given for using lubrication/wash/tire centers or for buying cards to make long-distance telephone calls. A one hundred-gallon purchase awards the driver one point bearing a redemption value of $1. At the end of the month, if previous purchases exceed 500 gallons, Frequent Fueler coupons are mailed to the driver's address. These coupons are accepted at Flying J restaurants and lodging facilities, and can be exchanged for merchandise from a 200-item catalog featuring Browning sporting goods such as shotguns, fishing gear, and golf equipment. Coupons can also be applied toward vacations, household goods, and electronic items.

At last count, over 600,000 drivers are registered on the Frequent Fueler program. This is approximately 30 percent of those eligible. Of this master file, more than 355,000 are currently active. As mandated by Flying J, the awards go to the driver, not the company, although over 44,000 fleets (primarily those of private companies) come under the program. On average, 300 new applicants sign up daily. A sixteen-page publication, *The Long Haul Letter*, is mailed to each member quarterly, and hundreds of redemptions are made monthly. Without Flying J's elaborate information processing systems, such a program would be unfeasible.

The Frequent Fueler program is ideal for Flying J because its primary appeal is to common-carrier independent truckers, normally owner/operators, and to companies with small truck fleets. Larger organizations often have their own terminals and typically demand high fuel discounts, something Flying J is unwilling to grant since it conflicts with its operating philosophy of treating all customers the same. However, discounts are given if the fuel transactions involve lower costs, thus keeping the net margin approximately the same.

The success of the Frequent Fueler program has been nothing less than stunning. Essentially all professional drivers are aware of its existence. In companies where drivers are forced to use other fuel vendors, they continually badger top management to change. Richard Peterson, head of retail accounting for Flying J, a person with a long history in the industry, calls it "the most successful marketing program I have ever known." Chris Stanger, who directs POS and frequently visits plazas and talks to drivers, refers to it as "an absolutely tremendous program; drivers just love accumulating Frequent Fueler points." A group of smaller truckstop owners formed a coalition to duplicate the program, but no other company or combination of companies currently has the marketing presence or information systems needed to be a serious rival.

When franchising started to sour, Flying J was again on the lookout for ways to stabilize its financial future and still proceed with its capital-demanding travel-plaza plans. The Salt Lake refinery gave the company a secure fuel supply for those C-stores and plazas within a 400-mile radius, but not for those beyond. With most new facilities being built outside this perimeter, obtaining a guaranteed fuel supply (especially in emergencies) again became an issue. In these outlying regions, Flying J had relied primarily on the spot market (fuel a refinery sells by bid after meeting its contractual commitments). Spot market sales are often lower, but buyers cannot assume that these leftovers will always be available.

At the time, the rapid growth in Flying J diesel sales was gaining the attention of major suppliers who became more willing to make supply concessions. Flying J concentrated its purchases among two or three majors, one being Conoco Inc. Conoco (originally known as Continental Oil) was started in 1875 in the Rocky Mountain area with headquarters in Denver. A merger in 1929 with an Oklahoma company headed by E. W. Marland followed by major oil strikes in the Middle East in the late 1950s boosted Conoco into its current position as one of the large, integrated U.S. petroleum companies. In 1981 it was acquired by Du Pont (E.I. Du Pont De Nemours), the largest chemical company in the U.S. In recent years Conoco has maintained an annual national ranking of between twelfth and fifteenth on each measure used to compare the size of the integrated petroleum giants—crude oil production, refinery capacity, and gasoline motor sales. Conoco's refineries supply customers in most of the nation's regions except for the West Coast and the extreme Northeast.

As Flying J cast around for favorable long-term contractual arrangements, it found Conoco to be especially interested because it often had a diesel surplus. In addition, the relationship between the two parties was of the highest caliber leading both sides to show interest in developing closer ties. With franchising now out of the picture, Jay had in the back of his mind forming a partnership with one of the majors not only to insure supply but to gain much needed capital. He was reluctant to discuss such plans with even his closest Flying J associates since the one rumor he wanted to avoid was that the company was for sale. After several meetings between the two parties, Flying J representatives gained the impression that Conoco officials were also giving serious thought to such an arrangement. In late 1988, Conoco had purchased a dozen or so truckstops from Marathon Oil and, as one Conoco representative stated, "Our stations paled in comparison to those of Flying J."

Before eliminating other options, Flying J sent inquiries to several majors regarding a possible partnership. Most showed little interest or were slow to respond. Spurred on by their already favorable relationships, Conoco and Flying J after several weeks of negotiation agreed on January 9, 1991, to create a partnership known as CFJ Properties, formed under Utah law on February 1, 1991.

Flying J and Conoco representatives at the time of the agreement.
Left to right: Barre Burgon (FJ), Phil Fredricksen (Conoco), Ed Adwon (Conoco), Jay Call (FJ), Rich Hamm (Conoco), Phil Adams (FJ), John Barr (Conoco), and Buzz Germer (FJ).

Thirty-three facilities immediately came under the arrangement. Ten were plazas Conoco purchased from Flying J. The other twenty-three were Flying J-leased plazas built with FFCA funds. The fifty-fifty partnership required that each party initially put in $45 million, mainly in properties. Through the agreement, Flying J gained not only a large influx of capital, but also the control it wanted by being granted the exclusive right to operate the plazas and handle all trucking. Conoco did not object, noting that Flying J was the pacesetting truckstop operator in the industry and could react faster to the market. The agreement specified that both names be shown on highway signage with Flying J's listed over the diesel island and Conoco's over the gasoline lanes.

The partnership is managed by a six-person executive committee, three from each company. The committee is concerned primarily with approving plaza design, financing, and market potential plus other similar long-range concerns. Besides the thirty-three plazas then in place, eight more under design were part of the initial agreement. Both parties have the right to be a full partner in all future plazas. (Not just fuel facilities but on-site C-stores, service centers, restaurants, and lodging.) This right relates to plazas under consideration by either company. In general, Conoco has declined only when a proposed plaza would likely damage business at an existing Conoco retail outlet. The partnership covers only facilities at Flying J's interstate travel plazas. Flying J's stand-alone C-stores, motels, refineries, production properties, and other businesses are not included in the agreement.

Both parties are extremely satisfied with the arrangement. Flying J acquired a stable partner, a subsidiary of a company that for 1995 was ranked as the thirteenth largest U.S. corporation by *Fortune* magazine. In addition, Flying J finally gained access to the long-sought capital needed for financial security and for fulfilling its dream of building a travel plaza each month until a motorist could travel the entire interstate system by fueling only at Flying J outlets. As Jay stated, "It was a wonderful deal for me. It not only took off the financial strain, but it enabled the company to pursue the marketplace like we needed to." The significance to Flying J financially is demonstrated by one fact alone. Under the FFCA contractual arrangement, Flying J is paying the limited partners close to 14 percent for its leases. With Conoco as a partner, funding for travel plazas can be obtained at 7 or 8 percent.

Conoco also achieved major benefits. Company representatives refer to the partnership as the "shining star" within Conoco. Ron A. Sumner, Conoco's director of Joint Ventures, claims to be "the luckiest person in Conoco to be associated with this venture." He adds, "The partnership is profitable, growing, and dynamic, and it is changing the industry." Conoco's only complaint is that the partnership is not building plazas fast enough, but the permitting process (getting zoning approvals, etc.) now often takes two or three years, and some cases are still pending after five years. Conoco takes more of a go-slow, wait-and-see attitude on adding motels and J-Care Service Centers, but it is rare to find such compatible business bedfellows.

What the future holds for the partnership is difficult to predict. The number of plazas has grown to where Conoco in some regions cannot supply all fuel requirements. Currently Conoco provides 62 percent of Flying J's fuel needs. Also, the question will soon have to be faced of what will happen after the interstate plazas are completed? Thought is being given to building a minimum of several hundred smaller fuel stops off the freeways, but this decision is still pending. It is likely that both parties will want to participate.

As noted earlier, beginning in the mid-1980s, Jay started to pull himself away from day-to-day operations. When Phil became executive vice president in 1987, Jay distanced himself more from the details of travel-plaza development. After the Conoco partnership was completed, he knew the company was secure and pointed in the right direction. Two months later on March 26, 1991, Phil was appointed company president. Jay retained his position as chairman of the board.

Phil Adams, Flying J President.

With the future of travel-plaza development now guaranteed, Phil began to look again at opportunities the company had placed on the back burner. In 1988 Phil told a *New York Times* writer, "Our goal is to get independent truckers and trucking companies to lock into our brand name and see us a single source of information." Few people at the time understood what Phil had in mind.

When Flying J first entered the truckstop business, the industry was poorly served by a group of small, regional, marginally profitable companies. Conditions were ripe for exploitation by a firm with farsighted leaders devoted to giving better service at lower cost. In 1988 Flying J's management concluded that a similar situation existed in hauling of freight because of the disjointed, inefficient way in which the industry operated, primarily because comprehensive information systems were lacking. Trucks would often haul loads several hundred miles only to return empty on the back haul. Over 2,000 brokers were engaged in matching loads, but the complexity of hundreds of manufacturers, shippers, drivers, and trucks being serviced by a multitude of brokers, dispatchers, and company agents formed a confusing matrix with only pockets of efficiency.

Like any other market or business, the core activity (in this instance trucking) generates an information flow that identifies key industry relationships and processes. The problem is to capture these transactions and convert them into useful real-time information systems. Phil, Joe Kelley, and others surmised that if a company could centralize, systematize, and simplify the information highway relevant to trucking, such an action would not only greatly improve industry efficiency, but also prove profitable for the originator.

In the summer of 1992, Flying J established a subsidiary known as TON Services Inc., placing the talented Joseph Kelley at the helm. Joe had been one of the leaders in developing Flying J's POS system. TON's first assignment was to design an electronic system for brokering freight. The aim was to make the software sufficiently comprehensive to ultimately permit TON to serve as a central industrywide freight clearing house. Following Jay's typical approach, the scope of TON was not limited to freight brokering. It was given an open charter to develop any information systems or automated services applicable to the trucking industry and motoring public.

Within three years, this unit of under forty employees has developed an astonishing array of automated systems that are on the technology edge of the information age. Currently each Flying J travel plaza has one and sometimes two kiosks in the C-store area. A kiosk has the appearance of a video game or an oversized slot machine. Regarding the latter, the display is a computer screen rather than an opening revealing rows of numbers and/or icons. The kiosks, named RoadLink, use one common electronic network to provide a variety of services for the entire traveling public.

Typical kiosks in a Flying J plaza.

The most vital kiosk service for the trucking industry is the load matching and scanning system known as LoadPlanner. For a fee, any party can post freight availability and equipment by telephone or by using Flying J software known as DataLink. This listing on the kiosk is then available to thousands of drivers, dispatchers, brokers, and shippers who can sign up to deliver the freight or use the equipment. The big advantage for drivers is that they can search for cargo loads after fueling if they have or anticipate empty space. The process, though still highly fragmented, offers the potential of tremendous savings not just in more efficient use of equipment but in reducing unnecessary inventories, cutting down on excess warehouse space, and decreasing time lost in making contacts to optimize loads. The industry is constantly searching to improve efficiency, and this is a natural next step. U.S. shipping rates for truck transportation have dropped approximately 5 percent since 1990, due in part to better service and lower fuel prices led by Flying J as the trendsetter.

As Flying J had discovered earlier, once a broad information network is developed, it becomes relatively simple to add output reports or services. At last count, drivers could obtain a minimum of twelve services from a kiosk, and the casual motorist, business traveler, shipper, or service organization can use almost as many. One example of a service with universal appeal is Rand McNally's MileMaker. This software gives a driver a printout of the shortest route to each stop before a final destination. The printout sequentially lists the highways, cities, miles, and travel time for each segment. Totals are provided and also a summary of miles by state. Customers can also purchase prepaid long-distance calling cards, issue and receive faxes (full page in less than a second), make laser-quality photocopies, and obtain weather reports. Special driver services include getting trip permits and verifying insurance. Each kiosk also contains a call-board of local services similar to call-boards found in major airports. Motels, retail shops, truck and equipment dealers, and other service providers in the immediate area advertise on the kiosks and also on video monitors or displays located throughout the plaza.

The kiosk initially appears forbidding to those not familiar with computers. However, the user willing to experiment finds kiosk operation extremely user friendly, as easy if not easier than operating an ATM machine. Although a keyboard is positioned below the monitor, the kiosk user can generally ignore it. A person can respond to questions on the monitor by merely touching the appropriate area on the screen.

It is always difficult to predict what path technology will take, but Flying J's leadership in this area will undoubtedly become a significantly larger portion of the company's future business. It is not inconceivable that Flying J's information services will someday develop into one of the leading profit centers within the company. What TON has accomplished in four years gives Flying J a jump toward being a business applications leader in the information age. Those knowing TON representatives realize they have more goals in mind than becoming the industrywide clearing house for freight.

Enthusiasm for automation abounds throughout the company. Phil recalls that "Early we made a huge commitment to systems, and everyone around here will tell you it is the best thing we ever did." Chris Stanger claims, "Our commitment to automation is the single biggest thing that has catapulted the company to where it is today." Jim Baker, in noting Flying J's contributions to the trucking industry, argues that Flying J's "creation and implementation of advanced technology . . . have had more impact on the industry than perhaps any other single development."

At the close of Flying J's 1995 fiscal year (January 31, 1996), the company is clearly the preeminent travel-plaza operator in the United States and is formulating plans to move into Canada and possibly Mexico. The company has ninety-three travel plazas along the interstate system. Fifteen more are either under construction or in the bidding stage, making it likely that 108 will be serving customers before the end of 1996. Plans remain to add at least one per month, keeping pressure on the partnership's capital requirements since full-service plazas are now priced at nearly $6 million, $8 million with a motel. Of the ninety-three plazas currently in operation, seventy-six are full-service and seventeen are smaller units called fuel stops. Of the larger plazas, Conoco is a partner in sixty-six, seven are operated by franchisees, and three are fully owned by Flying J.

The latest design, full-sized truckstop pumps 1.5 to 2 million gallons a month and has annual sales of $20 million. As can be seen from Figure 1 (page 233), these plazas are spread throughout the country. Flying J is licensed to do business in forty states and, with plans to move into the extreme Northeast, the Flying J logo will soon be greeting customers on every segment of the nation's interstate system. Unknown to most Utah residents is that none of the latest format, full-service plazas is within 300 miles of the state. The company has added the large plazas in regions where truck-traffic flow is the most significant, such as the Midwest, the East Coast, and the Southwest.

The largest concentration of stand-alone C-stores and smaller plazas is in Utah and surrounding states because they can be supplied by the Salt Lake refinery. The company has essentially phased out of C-stores except in the

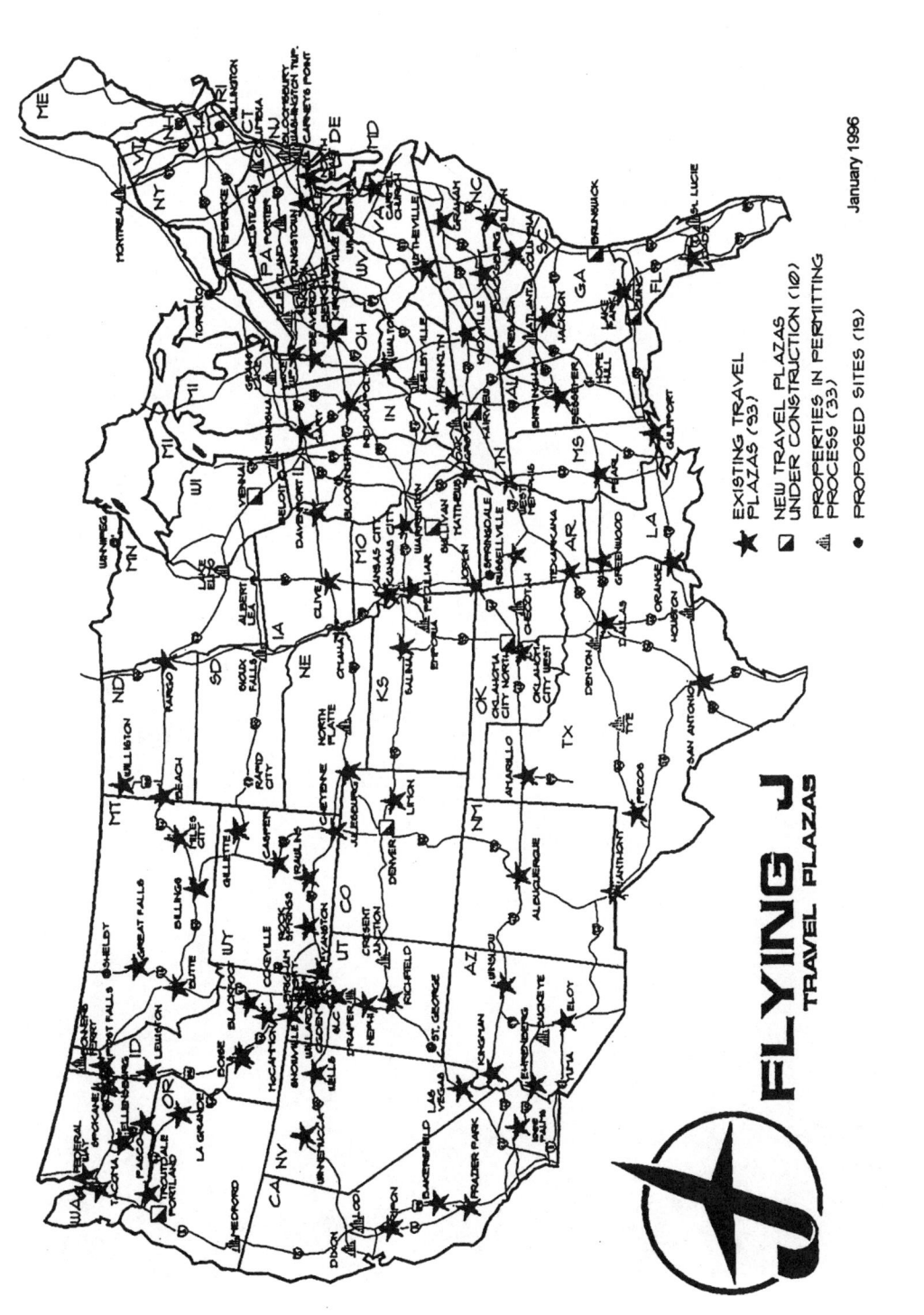

Flying J travel plaza, Frazier Park, California.

Flying J travel plaza, Dade City, Florida

Intermountain area for this reason. Flying J currently operates fourteen C-stores in addition to the travel plazas noted above.

Flying J is the largest diesel retailer in the U.S. and likely tops in the world for a private company. Diesel sales are estimated to be 13 to 15 percent of the U.S. total. The company annually sells in excess of 1.2 billion gallons of fuel, mostly diesel. By the end of 1996 this could climb to 1.7 billion gallons.

Important as fuel sales are, sales from the C-store, restaurants, and lodging facilities are becoming increasingly significant. Flying J's gross margin on fuel is well under 10 percent whereas for convenience store items it is closer to 35 percent. The big growth in recent years has been in restaurants. In 1990 the company operated only twenty-five restaurants; today it manages over one hundred and the figure is growing monthly. The most recent plaza design has a 200-seat Country Market Restaurant and Buffet and two quality fast-food counters adjacent to the C-store, one for Pepperoni's Pizza and the other for Magic Dragon Chinese food. After a recent nationwide search, the company has hired several extremely well-qualified restaurant executives headed by Bob Galentine, vice president Food Service Operations. Their intent is to give this dimension of the company the same high reputation it has in other areas. This is in line with Phil's goal to make Flying J the "premier highway hospitality company in the country." Phil knows it will not be easy since competitors, especially C-stores, are increasingly placing well-known fast-food merchants such as McDonald's and Burger King on their premises. Phil recognizes the challenge and is setting up the company to "knock heads with the best in the world."

In the race to dominate the travel-plaza industry, Flying J is currently two lengths ahead of its nearest rivals. None has the total hospitality concept of rapid fuel service, immaculate rest facilities, electronic drivers' aids, entertainment lounges, restaurants, and lodging. Of the four competitive truck-stop chains, most had sales between 40 to 60 percent of Flying J's until recently. With the large number of Flying J plazas coming on stream, the gap is rapidly widening. Pilot Corporation has as many outlets but they are smaller and have few amenities. This company is pointed directly at the trucking trade and is highly competitive in fuel pricing. Petro Shopping Centers of El Paso, Texas, has facilities more comparable with Flying J's, especially its restaurants, but they have only forty-one properties in twenty-six states. Truckstops of America, with forty-four locations mostly east of the Mississippi River, has been in business for many years and is thus burdened with a mixture of modern and dated plazas. National Auto/Truckstops, Inc. is a loosely organized marketing group of 120 former Unocal "76" dealers/franchisees with headquarters in Nashville, Tennessee. Their facilities are also a rag-tag mixture of old and new properties.

Flying J has made an enormous contribution to the traveling public. By keeping fuel prices low, providing the top travel-plaza facilities in the country, and continually adding services for the trucking industry and other travelers, it has upgraded the public's perception of truckstops and has forced competitors to work towards similar standards. What had been some of the grungiest retail facilities along the interstate highways have been turned into some of the most inviting. Just as McDonald's revolutionized the fast-food industry and Wal-Mart set new standards for how companies compete in consumer retailing, Flying J is leading the way in revamping the entire truckstop/travel-plaza business. What has others guessing is how the company can provide Cadillac facilities and services and charge Chevrolet prices.

Flying J is starting to make comparable giant strides in lodging thanks to Jay's daughter Crystal. Just three years ago the company had five budget-type motels at older plazas. Today four upscale inns have been added, and at least twenty are scheduled to be built within the next five years, some at Flying J plazas and others on separate property.

Crystal's involvement with the company follows a typical Jay Call pattern. Bob Smith, Jay's business associate and friend in Salem, Oregon, had come upon a motel/hotel design that offered considerable appeal. In the industry, this class of lodging is known as "limited service." It is above the economy classification but is not a full-service hotel with a conference center, 24-hour restaurants, etc. Bob invited Jay to join with him in financing a Phoenix Inn in Troutdale, Oregon. This property proved to be highly successful. Jay, attracted by its modular, roomy suites, concluded that the design could be adapted for a variety of lodging purposes—mini-hotels, smaller motels in rural areas, etc. Soon after while waiting for Tamra to have her hair styled at a beauty salon in Salt Lake City, Jay spotted a two-acre piece of property on Fifth South (a one-way downtown street leading to I-15) that was small but adequate for the hotel he had in mind. He purchased the land, modified the Phoenix Inn format to fit on the property, and started construction on a four-story, 175-room hotel that opened in April 1994.

Crystal two years previously had completed an MBA at Harvard Business School and was working on the East Coast in marketing, but she was looking to return to the West. Jay, not wanting to manage the hotel and hoping that Crystal would be open to the opportunity, suggested that she become part owner and manage it. (Unbeknownst to Jay, Phil was making employment offers to Crystal at the same time.) Like her father, Crystal saw the potential in such a fine facility. It was relatively inexpensive to construct, had many features attractive to business travelers, and rooms could be priced significantly lower than neighboring star-rated hotels. She quickly perceived the possibility of it being a chain and also knew the company needed a person or outside organization to vigorously pursue lodging as a part of its goal to be the hospitality leader along interstate highways. Being eager to "do her own thing," Crystal accepted her father's offer and shortly turned the property into a first-class investment with occupancy rates over 85 percent.

Soon after, she married her Harvard MBA classmate, Chuck Maggelet. Together they have formed MacCall Management LLC and have arranged to take over management of Flying J's seven inns. Several other Crystal Inns or Best Rest Inns (a name recently adopted) are in the design stage, currently under construction, or recently completed. Last year two Crystal Inns were opened, one in northeast Maryland and one in Brigham City, a mile from Flying J headquarters. Others are underway in Logan, Utah, and in Gulfport, Mississippi. A Crystal Inn similar in size to the one in Salt Lake is to be built on a Flying J-plaza site near the entrance of the new Denver airport. "All suite" Crystal Inns have business appeal because of their ample working

Crystal and Chuck Maggelet in front of the Salt Lake City Crystal Inn.

space, meeting facilities, complete breakfasts, and low prices. Thus they are appropriate adjacent to or within the boundaries of larger communities and industrial or business parks. Whether they will be equally attractive in rural areas where many Flying J plazas are located is being tested in the Maryland location.

The landlord of each motel and inn varies depending on the facility and location. Some are owned by Flying J, some by Call Investments, and others are jointly held by these two companies plus MacCall Management LLC under the Maggelets. Recently all three have combined to form Crystal Inn Company.

While building travel plazas, Flying J did not let other dimensions of its business slide. Company retail sales finally exceeded production, refinery, and other non-plaza revenues in 1989, but these upstream businesses remain strong elements of the company. After acquiring the Salt Lake City refinery in 1986, Flying J's Exploration and Production subsidiary under John Scales was given the responsibility to obtain local reserves to support the refinery. This led Flying J in the spring of 1989 to more than triple its crude output by purchasing producing properties from Houston-based Great Western Resources. The properties, containing known reserves of over eight million barrels, are in the Uinta Basin near Roosevelt, Utah. This purchase gave the Salt Lake refinery a crude source of superb quality although it is difficult to transport because of its high wax content. With the center of Flying J's exploration and production efforts switching to northeastern Utah, in 1989 the company moved the headquarters for Exploration and Production from Billings, Montana, to new offices at the Salt Lake refinery.

Like the rest of the company, Exploration and Production is constantly on the lookout for new opportunities. Accordingly, in the fall of 1995, Flying J obtained leases and properties that increased its crude production by nearly 150 percent and also added significant natural gas production. These properties and leases were obtained for $40 million from Cenex, an agricultural cooperative based in St. Paul, Minnesota. (Cenex is an abbreviation using the first letters from the last two words in the cooperative's formal title, Farmer's Union Central Exchange.) The properties Flying J obtained are primarily in North Dakota, Montana, and Wyoming. Others are more widely scattered in Colorado, Nevada, California, and Utah.

As for the key figures in Flying J, Jay keeps tabs on company developments by attending Monday morning executive meetings and chairing quarterly board of director sessions. He is involved in the expansion of the Crystal Inns, has outside joint ventures with associates such as Bob Smith in

Jay's yacht in front of a glacier in Alaska.

Jay, Laurie (Thad's wife), Thad, and Tamra.

Reuel and Jay on the yacht, 1994.

Jay with a king crab.

Fishing off Mexico.

Tamra and Jay.

*Jay's brothers and sisters with their spouses.
Alaska, July 1994. Back row left to right: Craig, Janine (Craig's wife),
Gerald Young (Candace's husband), Lance, Kathryn (Lance's wife), Sharon, Janice.
Front row: Candace, Jay, Tamra, and Larry Anderson (Sharon's husband).*

*Flying J employees and spouses.
Back row, left to right: Boat captain, cook, Barre Burgon.
Front row: Jay, Tamra, Fredee (Phil's wife), Phil, and Karen (Barre Burgon's wife).*

Tamra and Jay.

Jay with his helocopter.

Oregon, and never stops looking for business opportunities. Annually he spends many hours in his favorite activity—flying. He is highly knowledgeable about airplanes and is constantly buying, selling, and/or refurbishing them. In 1992 he purchased a 105-foot yacht that sails the North American coastline from Mexico to Alaska depending on the season. He uses the yacht to entertain family, friends, business associates, and Flying J employees. He views it as a means to acknowledge their services and/or friendship. Without exception those who are fortunate enough to spend several days on the yacht recall the experience as one of their most memorable. Jay and Tamra are currently actively involved in developing the 1,500-acre Montana ranch.

Phil continues as president with responsibilities for developing the travel plazas and making Flying J the nation's premier hospitality company for travelers. His success has been nothing short of phenomenal. In 1995 of the ten million private U.S. companies, Flying J was number 152 based on *Forbes* magazine's annual listing. In terms of job creation, employment in the company is over 8,600 and rapidly increasing. From 1987 through 1995, retail sales rose 600 percent and total sales 213 percent, just slightly under the long-standing goal of a 20 percent annual gain. Gross profits have risen faster than sales at a 25.4 percent annual clip, though profits after taxes remain under 1 percent of sales, primarily due to the major interest charges resulting from the capital-demanding, travel-plaza development. This is reflected in the company's high debt to equity ratio that remains in excess of two to one.

Phil is broadly recognized for his brilliance, aggressiveness, willingness to make hard decisions, and ability to "look at the big picture ten years down the road." As one close business associate stated, "I do not know anyone sharper and smarter or anyone who is able to deal with so many issues."

Initially when appointed as head of retailing, Phil drew some criticism for being roughshod in his relations with certain employees which led to the resignation of several high executives, but he is widely acknowledged as being the right person at the right time for the company. When the subject comes up, Jay adamantly maintains that Flying J would not be where it is today without Phil. On one occasion Jay further declared, "There are not ten executives in the United States that could have done for the company what Phil has accomplished."

What is ahead for Flying J? Just as the company has started new enterprises and frequently shifted its direction, no close observer now assumes that it will follow an even course. In addition to the company's more recent thrusts into industry software and lodging, Phil and Thad (Jay's son) are exploring other ventures involving trucking. The one conclusion all insiders agree on is that when the travel-plaza network is complete, top management will not be content to sit back and reap the rewards. Many expect the company to again place all assets on the table in a gamble for a major takeover or in pursuit of a new venture. On several occasions Phil has made known his desire to have Flying J's logo alongside those of Texaco, Mobil, Phillips, and Amoco as industry majors. If this occurs, Flying J will likely be different in two ways: it will have hospitality and service rather than petroleum as a central interest, and technology, not refining and production, will be the driving force.

Epilogue

*A*nswers to some questions raised in the preface are now so obvious, I trust, as to require little reiteration. The Call family colonists and entrepreneurs of this history had many common traits. They were (and those still alive are) hard working, honest, frugal, strong-willed (even stubborn) individuals who liked to build and create, not necessarily to enjoy financial rewards, but to be involved in projects having significance apart from them as individuals. The colonists and their offspring had the capacity to inspire trust, be purveyors of hope, and get others to join in pushing ahead when the obstacles seemed insurmountable. In general, they were not obsessed with obtaining worldly goods. Excess income was plowed back into their enterprises or was saved for their children. As a group they were gregarious, yet they wanted their personal lives kept private and unconstrained. Their intense achievement needs coupled with being strongly focused sometimes proved detrimental to their families and home lives. They were willing to take enormous risks, far more than were most of their contemporaries. They were convinced that independence was the optimum condition for personal development. Thus they encouraged their employees and their children (after they passed their teens) to make their own decisions, be responsible for the results, and learn through trial-and-error.

The one business-related trait that best typifies Call family members in recent generations is the necessity to always have a project under way where immediate progress can be observed. Before such a project is completed, the instigator is constantly on the alert for new opportunities. Thomas was building homes until he was nearly ninety, and Reuel in his late eighties is still aggressively adding stations and nurturing a business he started a decade earlier. Jay has distanced himself from daily management of his various enterprises, but he is not content unless he has in hand a new challenge such as a business venture or an activity like refurbishing an airplane, developing a ranch, or buying property. Jay tells others he is lazy and does not like to manage ongoing enterprises, but those he relates this to realize it's his excuse for getting bored with details and routine.

How these traits apply to entrepreneurship and leadership is a more difficult question. Many believe that the sources of leadership and the circumstances that develop leaders are so numerous and complex as to defy accurate analysis. Authors of related literature take the easy course of describing a leader's actions rather than attempting to explain how the person developed certain traits or why specific actions were taken. After years of study, I find it easy to conclude that we are just pecking at the edges of leadership causation. However, in completing this history, I reinforced several of my beliefs regarding leadership and entrepreneurship, and also I gained several new insights.

This history strengthened my awareness of the extreme importance early childhood experiences play in shaping the direction of a person's life. The Call colonists who struggled to survive on the frontier were strong disciplinarians, fiercely independent, frugal, determined, and enterprising. Relationships between parents and their children left lasting impressions that caused their offspring to either follow in their footsteps or branch out in other directions. Early experiences under the tutelage of a strong parent, a close family member, or an acquaintance affected priorities, determined initial work-related skills, spurred or dulled incentive, and caused the individuals to either accept or reject their elders as role models. Jay acknowledges that he started operating service stations after his marriage because that was the only occupation he knew. He also recognizes that both his father and Reuel were important role models who demonstrated how to expand a business once it was started. As these same influences relate to Jay's children, Crystal notes, "Until I was eighteen, I thought entrepreneurship was all there was."

Of those insights that modified my previous views, the most significant relates to how entrepreneurs go about starting and expanding their businesses. Classical management literature has as its core establishing goals, selecting strategies, developing detailed business or operational plans, and being careful to follow through with elaborate controls and precise implementation. It is a step-by-step, rational process dictated by management from the top. In the past decade, this bureaucratic methodology has been downplayed but not abandoned.

Jay was clearly doing essentially the opposite twenty years earlier. Rather than using detailed analysis to ferret out opportunities, or establishing meticulous five-year, long-range plans to set the company's course, he avoided and still avoids most actions that cause rigidity or limit options. He is constantly searching for opportunities in an ever-changing business environment and quickly acts once a promising light flickers though an entrepreneurial window. Flexibility not rigidity should typify the work place. Such freedom is important in dropping a project going awry or in immediately selling assets and pruning weaker elements after a takeover such as Thunderbird. On the other hand, if a project under consideration appears promising, Jay wants it to be rapidly pursued without obstacles, such as committee approval, standing in the way. These are the same reasons why he refuses to give detailed direction to employees. He does not want to wrap them in a bureaucratic cocoon that will limit their capacity to react and grow.

Planning is involved in what Jay does, but generally it is in a dynamic context, much like a gambler evaluating his odds and predetermining the next step if he wins or loses in a throw of the dice. He is never without well-considered alternatives, and he is always thinking ahead, but potential initiatives are constantly being reevaluated based on his most recent experiences. Rather than being the visionary who has in mind an end state to be achieved, Jay, like most other entrepreneurs, is the pragmatic dreamer who is led in the direction that the magnet of new opportunities pulls him. Thus leadership becomes more of an attitude and a capacity to respond rather than an ability to precisely define the future.

I found it particularly eye-opening to see how employees and his children responded when he set them loose. Management literature today stresses the importance of empowering others, but no one else I am aware of takes it as far as Jay. In recognizing that his own strengths are in finding and pursuing opportunities, and that the fun is in proving it can be done, he constantly looks for others to take over at this point. After hatching an entrepreneurial egg and getting the offspring on its feet, he seeks take-charge administrators who will continue to develop the business and multiply returns while relying on him for only minimal guidance. He realizes from his own experience that, given this freedom, talented employees will learn to perform at their highest levels. He wants others to assume control, take the lead, and be on their own. Phil turned into an extremely impressive corporate executive while still under forty, but his rapid development was made possible by the environment that Jay provided. Jay's management style is as innovative as his ability to uncover business opportunities, proving that he is far ahead of most other practitioners.

Another lesson that can be learned from observing businesses started by the Calls is the importance of the relationship between a leader and his or her followers. By definition, leaders are those who can influence others to achieve common goals. The dimension that Jay adds to this definition is that successful leadership depends on the capabilities of a leader's followers. The primary factor that differentiates Jay from the other Call entrepreneurs contained in this history is the quality of the followers that he has attracted and developed. Jay has collected a group of employees who "follow" because of their strong respect for him and the principles he represents. They are not people tagging along looking for direction, but followers who want to emulate what he has accomplished. Using this approach, he has produced a cadre of extremely capable managers to run the company.

Whenever Jay is asked what has made Flying J so successful, his response is always that it is due to "the caliber of my employees." Phil claims that the company has "as good a talent as there is anywhere in the world." Ron Sumner, the Conoco representative in the CFJ Partnership, is quick to agree: "If I had to pinpoint their success, it is the quality of their people. They just do a bang-up job of hiring top quality, highly aggressive, motivated, intelligent people to manage and run these plazas. I have told Flying J management and Conoco management that if Conoco were able to hire people with just 10 percent of this desire, we would blast by everybody else in the industry."

The employees are not only capable but they are highly committed because of how the company treats them. Crystal observes, "One thing I admire about dad is that he has always done what is best for the employees." Jay genuinely wants the people around him to be successful and this loyalty is quickly repaid. As Buzz states, "The work force has the utmost respect for him and would step in front of a bus if necessary." Dianna Hansen, a district manager over several C-stores commented (referring to the company's colors), "I would bleed orange if someone cut me." Ron Parker, vice president of Real Estate, explained it another way: "I have so much respect for him in the way he treats people that if he asked me to be on top of Mt. Timpanogos to make a deal on New Year's Eve, I'd find a way to be there."

One of my biggest surprises in conducting the research was to discover how extensively an organization takes on the characteristics of its founder, especially in the company's formative years. Jay's characteristics and philosophy can be identified in everything from the design of a plaza to how employees treat customers. The following can be clearly identified in Flying J's corporate culture: employees are confident, not arrogant; honesty and fairness are emphasized; uncleanliness is not tolerated; bathroom stalls and telephone booths are to be made private and closed in (both company signatures); chest-thumping is to be avoided and publicity limited; employees are to take risks and be willing to explore new ideas; supervisors are to generously delegate authority with the opportunity always there to take the reins; the organization is to be kept lean and free of unnecessary policies or rules; the way should be clear to make quick decisions; employees need privacy and room to grow; sanction a companywide "go for it" mentality; facilities for customers should be lasting, attractive, and comfortable, but avoid making executive offices elaborate, expensive, and ostentatious; resources should be used judiciously and business conducted in the least expensive, most efficient way.

Although most associates are fully aware of Jay's willingness to take risks, I continue to marvel at how calm and assured he can be, even when essentially everything he owns is in jeopardy. His actions confirm the statement made by Boone Pickens, king of the takeover artists: "You can't make money consistently if you are uptight." The only time Tamra noticed Jay under unusual pressure was during the long drawn out process of seeking funds to buy Husky. She said that "he did not stew a lot, but he was glad when it was finally put to bed." Jay's attitude is reflected in a conversation he had with Buzz in Winnipeg while negotiating the final high-risk arrangements to take over Thunderbird. Both agreed that should the venture fail, they would simply start over.

The above analysis and commentary should in no way suggest that just anyone could take Jay's concepts and make them work. Jay has business insights backed by sound judgment that few others display. Where these come from is debatable, but each can likely be found in all successful entrepreneurs. Essentially every Flying J manager or associate who has known Jay for several years speaks of his unusual conceptual skills. Bob Harper, longtime friend and insurance provider, claims, "He has an intelligence for business that is uncanny." Barre Burgon, vice president and corporate counsel for Flying J, after working by Jay's side during the major acquisitions and on other projects concludes, "He has a business savvy that boggles my mind." Ed Swapp, Flying J director of Convenience Stores, recalls telling his wife, "If you took Jay and put him on any street corner in America without his wallet, credit cards, and everything he owned—just put him there in street clothes and came back a year later he'd be a millionaire. He just has that touch of being able to turn everything to gold."

Sources and Bibliography

TAPED INTERVIEWS IN POSSESSION OF THE AUTHOR:

Immediate Call family and relatives: thirty-one persons interviewed.
Friends of the Call family: seventeen persons interviewed.
Business associates of Jay Call: twenty-one persons interviewed.
Business associates of Reuel Call: four persons interviewed.
Flying J employees: fifty-two persons interviewed.
Interview totals: 125 persons interviewed on tape. Since many persons were interviewed several times, the total number of taped interviews exceeds 200.

PUBLISHED FAMILY HISTORIES:

Ancestors and Descendants of Walter Covey, Dutchess County, New York (1750–1834). Compiled by Mary Lancaster Quist. Published by the Covey Family Genealogical Organization, 1971.

Anson Call and his Contributions Toward Latter-day Saint Colonization, Brigham Young University master's thesis by Duane D. Call, 1956.

Anson Vasco Call II: His Ancestors and Descendants, published by the A.V. Call family organization in 1966. Printed by Carr Printing Company, Bountiful, Utah. Contains biographical sketches of all family members.

The Descendants of Ira Call, three volumes. Collected by Joseph C. Call and Lowell E. Call. Printed by the Educational Printing Service, Logan, Utah, 1973.

A Good Long Life: The Autobiography of Anson Bowen Call, Jr. 1900-1993. Assembled and edited by Carole Call King. Published by Anson B. Call, Jr, 1994.

Joseph Holbrook Call Perpetual Family History, Collected by Lucy I. Call Osmond and Lenna Osmond Wimmer, 1964.

Osmond, George A. *George Osmond and Family Pioneers*. Published by the Osmond family in 1985.

A Tribute to Israel Call (1854–1938). Written by Thora Bergeson Watson, 1954, 24 pages.

COMMUNITY HISTORIES:

A Bend in the River. History of Thayne, Wyoming. Afton, WY: Afton Thrifty Press, 1993.

Anderson, Lavina Fielding (ed.). *Chesterfield: Mormon Outpost in Idaho.* Bancroft, ID: The Chesterfield Foundation, 1982.

Barnard, Lula, Faunda Bybee, and Lola Walker. *Tosoiba.* Soda Springs, ID: Daughters of the Utah Pioneers Camp Meads, 1958.

Carney, Ellen. *Ellis Kackley: Best Damn Doctor in the West.* Bend, OR: Maverick Publications, 1990.

Crowther, Myrle Young. *History of Three Mile Creek,* Now Perry, Utah.

Jenson, Andrew. *Encyclopedic History of the Church of Jesus Christ of Latter-day Saints.* Salt Lake City, UT: Deseret News Publishing Company, 1941.

Kennington, Forrest Weber and Kathaleen Kennington Hamblin. *A History of Star Valley formerly Salt River Valley 1800–1900.* Afton, WY: F. W. Kennington, 1989.

Star Valley and Its Communities, 128-page mimeographed collection of papers written by students in a University of Wyoming extension class in September 1951.

BOOKS AND ARTICLES ON FAMILY VENTURES OR ACTIVITIES:

"It All Started on This Corner in Afton," *Star Valley Independent,* December 15, 1977, p. 6.

"Husky Acquisition Makes Flying J Biggest Independent in Mountain West," *Petroleum News,* February 1986.

Landry, Ron. "Flying J: Branching Out in Big Sky Country," *National Petroleum News,* May 1980, pp. 60–65.

Paher, Stanley W. (ed.). *Callville, Head of Navigation, Arizona Territory.* Las Vegas, NV: Nevada Publications, 1981.

Petersen, Carl J. *The CallAir Affair: An Aeronautical History,* 1989.

"Utah's Top Ten Business Leaders," *Utah Business,* December 1989, p. 30.

TAPED INTERVIEWS, SPEECHES, AND FUNERAL RECORDINGS:

Jay Call, speech at Soda Springs High School commencement, May 23, 1991.

Osborne Papworth Call, funeral tape, September 10, 1964.

Thomas J. Call, funeral tape, June 14, 1976.

Thomas J. Call, interview by Spencer Call, January 20, 1975.

AUTOBIOGRAPHICAL DIARIES AND SKETCHES:

A Brief History of Evan Papworth Call, July 17, 1960. (Manuscript in possession of Bessie Call)

The Life and Record of Anson Call, the journal of Anson Call. Copied and published in various forms. Printed by Ethan L. Call and Christine Shaffer Call. Copies can be obtained from Shann L. Call, P.O. Box 487, Afton, WY 83110.

Rosa Emily Stayner Call. (Manuscript in possession of Bessie Call)

Thomas J. Call. (Manuscript in possession of Bessie Call)

BIOGRAPHICAL SKETCHES:

(All sketches can be found in the LDS Family History Library, Salt Lake City, Utah)

Ann Mariah Bowen Call, Life Sketch of, by Leona George Smith and Hilda Mann Condie.

"Ann Mariah Bowen Call" and "Anson Call and Mariah Call", by Lester D. Call. Contained in *Builders of Early Millard: Biographies of Pioneers of Millard County 1850 to 1875.* Sponsored by East Millard Company of the Daughters of Utah Pioneers. Printed by Art City Publishing Co., 1979.

Anson Call. Contained in *Tullidge's Histories of Utah,* vol. II, pp. 262–284.

Emma Summers Call, Life Sketch of, A.S.P., 1948.

Ethel Grace Papworth Call, written by Pamela Call for Ethel's funeral.

Margaretta Unwin Clark Call, Life Sketch of, by Willard Call.

Mary Flint Call, Life Sketch of, by Lorna Call Schlote.

Thomas John Call and Ethel Grace Papworth, Ancestral Record. Compiled, written, and printed by Pamela C. Johnson, 1986.

COMPANY PUBLICATIONS:

Caribou Quarterly, company newsletter, November 1977.

Flyer, Flying J employees' newsletter. First issue Vol. 1, No. 1, dated October 1973. Generally published two or three times yearly through Volume 21, No. 2 of 1994.

Long Haul Letter, publication sent three times yearly nationwide to drivers on the Frequent Fueler program and to other interested parties. Author's copies start with Vol. 3, No. 4, dated November 1988 and continue through Vol. 10, No. 4 of 1995.

Maverik Country Store, newsletter, 1994.

SOURCES ON THE PETROLEUM INDUSTRY:

American Petroleum Institute. *Basic Petroleum Data Book.* Washington D.C.: American Petroleum Institute. Annual volumes from 1980 thru 1994.

Anderson, Robert O. *Fundamentals of the Petroleum Industry.* Norman, OK: University of Oklahoma Press, 1984.

Glasner, David. *Politics, Prices, and Petroleum.* Cambridge, MA: Ballinger Publishing Company, 1985.

Kohl, Wilfrid (ed.). *After the Oil Price Collapse.* Baltimore, MD: Johns Hopkins University Press, 1991.

Koopmann, Georg, Klaus Matthies, and Beate Reszat. *Oil and the International Economy: Lessons from Two Price Shocks.* New Brunswick: Transaction Publishers, 1989.

Standard and Poor Industrial Surveys: Oil. 1994 and 1995.

U.S. Department of Commerce. *U.S. Industrial Outlook.* January 1994.

Yergin, Daniel. *The Prize: The Epic Quest for Oil, Money, and Power.* New York: Simon & Schuster, 1991.

INDEX

— A —

Adams, Fredee, 242
Adams, J. Phillip (Phil), 185, 205–6, 209, 213, 216, 222, 227–30, 235–37, 242, 244–45, 250
Adwon, Ed, 227
Afton Livestock Company, 94
Afton, Wyoming, 60
Aland, Blake, 119, 131, 143
Aland, Marie, 131
Alpine Oil Company, 175
Anderson, Andrew P., 53
Anderson, Herbert, 107
Anderson, Larry, 123, 242
Anderson, Sharon (Call). *See* Sharon Call
Andreason, Lynn "Andy," 166
Arrington, Leonard J., xiv

— B —

Backenstos, Sheriff, 9
Bagley, Floyd S., 85, 91
Bagley, Gerald, 93
Bagley, Rosa Vivian (Call), 85, 91
Baird, Mel, 127, 131, 137, 161
Baird, Jenny, 131
Baker, Forrest, 216
Baker, Jim, 232
Barr, John, 227
Baugh, Fred, 159, 180
Bennion, Sam, 118

Bennis, Warren, 164
Benson, Ezra T., 37
Boggs, Governor, 5, 7, 10
Boozer, John, 118
Booth, T. Y., xiv
Bountiful, Utah, 15, 22, 31, 33–35, 42, 47–48, 58–59, 64, 72
Box Elder County Bank, 159, 167, 179, 181
Box Elder Fort, 22
Brisendine, Ronald, 172, 173, 182, 196–98, 203, 205
British Petroleum, 218
Brooks, Juanita, 38
Brown, Paul, 173, 175, 181–82, 197, 199, 205–6
Brown, Roy, 118, 187
Brown, Teddy Lou (Call). *See* Teddy Lou Call
Buchanan, James (President), 28–29
Burgon, Karen, 242
Burton, Dixon, 98
Burton, Thomas F., 83
Burton, W. W., 66, 71, 73

— C —

Call, Adolphus Alvin, 60, 76
Call, Alfred, 76
Call, Alice J. (Farnham), 42, 45, 47, 59, 62–65, 71–72, 76–77, 82
Call, Alice Maud (Burton), 76

Call, Ann, 76
Call, Ann (Clark), 33, 36
Call, Ann Mariah. *See* Mariah Call
Call, Annis Janett (Barlow), 52
Call, Anson, 3, 39, 41, 90
    as a Danite, 5
    Bountiful, Utah, 15, 22, 31, 34–35
    Call's Fort, 23–25, 30, 33, 38
    Callville, settlement of, 30–33
    Carson Valley, Nevada, 25, 38
    childhood, 3
    church assignments, 16, 19, 21, 37
    colonizer skills, xi, 7–8, 24, 35, 37–38, 82
    conversion to Mormonism, 4
    death, 38
    divorce, 33
    family life/children, 15, 28, 36
    Fillmore, Utah, settlement of, 21–22
    flight across Iowa, 10–11
    in Missouri, 4–5
    in Nebraska, 12
    Kirtland, Ohio, 4
    marriages, 19–20, 27–28, 30, 36
    migration of, 6
    Mormon Trail, 11–13
    Nauvoo, Illinois, 7–10
    Parowan, Utah, settlement of, 19–20, 35, 38
    personality, 33, 35–36, 88
    rescue of hardcart companies, 25–28
    Utah War, participation in, 28–29
Call, Anson Bowen. *See* Bowen Call
Call, Anson Vasco I, 3, 15, 17, 39, 49, 52
Call, Anson Vasco II (A.V.), 3, 39–41, 82
    Afton, Wyoming, 58–80
    Bountiful, Utah, 42–44, 47
    buildings constructed, 68, 70–72
    carpentry skills, 62
    Chesterfield, Idaho, 47–54, 59–60
    childhood, 42
    church activities, 71–74
    death, 80
    family/children, 59, 65, 76–77, 95
    homesteading in Star Valley, 58–66
    marriages, 42–43, 73–74
    mission, England, 44
    partnership with Joseph Call, 65, 68–70
    personality, 75, 77, 79–80
    served as mayor 70–71, 74
Call, Anson Vasco III, 39, 60, 76
Call, Barlow, 106
Call, Bennett (Harrison), 1, 3
Call, Bessie (Warren), 85, 91
Call, Beulah, 79
Call, Bill (William Anson), 86, 124, 127, 132, 137, 139–40, 143–45
Call, Bowen, 60, 67–68
Call, Candace (Young), 93, 118–19, 123, 153, 242
Call, Caroline Charlotte (Burton), 59, 76
Call, Cecil Edmund, 76, 79
Call, Charles Stayner, 59, 64, 69, 76
Call, Charlotte (Holbrook), 3, 39–41, 49
Call, Charlotte V. (Roberts), 64, 76
Call, Charlotte Vienna. *See* Charlotte Vienna Call Nelson
Call, Cherie (Johnson), 123
Call, Chester, 15, 47, 49, 53–54, 60, 62
Call, Chester Alfred, 76
Call, Chester Vinson, 50, 52
Call, Christian Joseph, 69, 76–78, 95
Call, Claude, 76
Call, Craig, 51, 53, 93, 118, 123, 129, 153, 175–77, 242
Call, Crystal. *See* Crystal Call Maggelet
Call, Cyril, 2–4, 7, 10, 25, 36

Call, Cyril Alfred, 76, 87
Call, Cyril Moroni, 11
Call, Dan, 35, 36
Call, Dora (McCann), 106
Call, Edgar Allen, 76
Call, Eileen Ethel, 85
Call, Eliza Catherine (Kent), 39
Call, Ella (Cook), 76
Call, Emma Jane (Barlow), 52
Call, Emma Jean (Moore), 85, 91
Call, Emma (Summers), 27–28, 33, 36, 37, 91
Call, Ethel Grace (Papworth), 3, 78, 83–88
Call, Evan Papworth, 78, 85–89, 91–92, 103–4, 109
Call family characteristics, 79–80, 88–89, 102, 125, 142, 163–64, 247–48
Call, Fanny. *See* Loveland, Fanny Call
Call, Farnham Lamoni, 76
Call, Franklin, 43, 54, 71, 76
Call, Frederick William, 76
Call, George Albert, 76
Call, Gerald Papworth, 85, 111
Call, Hannah (Hatch), 50, 52
Call, Hannah (Kettell), 1, 3
Call, Harriet Louisa, 33
Call, Harvey, 11
Call, Helen (Fields), 124
Call, Henrietta Columbia (Loveland), 52
Call, Henrietta Caroline, 30, 36
Call, Horace Authur, 76, 87
Call, Hyrum, 10–11
Call, Ira Edward, 76
Call, Ira, 50, 52
Call, Israel, 33
Call Investments, 238
Call, Ivan Leon, 76, 79, 105–6
Call, Janice (Miller), 85, 91–93, 109–13, 116, 118, 123, 128–29, 137, 148–153, 164, 242
Call, Janine, 242
Call, Jay (Osborne Jay), 93, 123
  affect on organization culture, 251
  airplanes/flying, 126, 154, 162–63, 171, 243–44
  brothers and sisters, 93, 118, 123, 150, 153
  business philosophy/skills, 168–69, 171, 176–77, 181, 183, 215–16, 248–53
  Caribou Four Corners, 124–28, 137
  childhood, 89, 111, 116, 147–151
  cleanliness, emphasis on, 156, 184, 193
  Conoco joint venture, 226–228
  Crystal Inns, 236–37
  divorce, 185–86, 188
  entrepreneurial skills, xi, 125–27, 138, 162, 248–52
  family/children/home life, 125, 165, 183–85
  franchising, involvement in, 216, 218–222
  Frequent Fueler program, 224
  home (Perry, Utah), 190
  honesty, view towards, 163
  Husky acquisition, involvement in, 207–11, 251
  management style, 172–73, 175, 182–83, 248–52
  marriages, 157, 188
  motorcycles, 152, 164, 172, 185, 191
  partnerships, 175–76
  personality/values, 89, 125, 151–52, 162, 176–78, 248–53
  real estate activities, 182, 191–92, 195–96, 236
  relations with father, 120, 142, 147,

152–55, 160–61, 164–66
relations with Reuel, 125–26, 138, 142
religion, 154, 165–66
schooling, 151, 155–56
stations, development of Fastway. *See* Fastway stations
tire business, 159–60
truckstop strategy, 194–95, 206, 215
Thunderbird acquisition, involvement in, 198–203
Willard station, 125, 142, 154, 157–160, 178
working in Jackson, Wyoming, station, 155–56, 157, 164
yacht/fishing, 239–242, 244
Call, John (Captain) 1, 3
Call, John, 1, 3
Call, Joseph, 2–3
Call, Joseph Holbrook, 50, 52–53, 65, 68–70, 83
Call, Josiah Williams, 11, 29–30, 36
Call, Kathleen (Winters), 124, 131
Call, Kathryn, 242
Call, LaBerta (Wolfley), 124
Call, Lamoni, 41, 50
Call, Lamoni Farnham, 106
Call, Lance, 93, 118, 123, 151, 153, 242
Call, Larry Anson, 86–87, 89, 91, 123–24, 127, 130–32, 136–37, 139–40, 143–45, 189
Call, Laura Ann, 76
Call, Laurie, 239
Call, Lorna Louise (Scholte), 76
Call, Lucina (Sessions), 42
Call, Lucy Englesby (King), 43, 45, 47, 54, 59, 63–65, 71–72, 76, 95
Call, Lucy Margaret (Nield), 75–76, 79
Call, Margaret Ann (Hepworth), 69, 73–77, 79, 95

Call, Margaretta (Clark), 27–28, 33, 36
Call, Mariah (Bowen), 19–21, 25, 28, 30, 33, 36, 41, 68
Call, Marie (Pied), 85, 91
Call, Marius Anson, 76, 79, 103, 106
Call, Martha (Lowden), 1, 3
Call, Martha Ester (Williams), 52
Call, Mary (Sanderson), 2–3
Call, Mary Edith, 76
Call, Mary (Flint), 3, 11, 31, 32, 35–37, 39, 41–42, 45, 49, 59
Call, Mary Vashti (Muir), 15, 50, 52
Call, Mary Vashti (Low), 76
Call, Minnerette (Barlow), 52
Call, Osborne Papworth, 3, 78, 85–86, 91–92, 103, 248
automobile dealerships, 114–17, 149
builder of motels, post offices, stations, 110, 115–17
business philosophy/skills, 111–15, 117–18, 142, 154, 164
childhood, 88, 109–10
death, 121, 128, 166
entrepreneurial skills, xi, 113–15, 126
family/children, 118, 123, 148–156
friendship/partnership with Reuel, 108–9, 112, 119–20, 124
homes, 113, 116, 149
Jay, relations with, 120, 142, 152–55, 157, 160–61, 164–66
management style, 120
marriage, 109
personality/values, 111–15, 117–19, 153, 163–65
Sinclair jobber, 113
Call, Raoul, 76
Call, Reuel Thomas, 3, 78, 85–86, 91–92, 97–109, 131, 248
and airplanes, 97,104–5, 136
buyout by sons, 140

INDEX

builds Valleon Hotel, 103–4
business philosophy, 102, 130–32, 137–38, 140
childhood, 84, 88, 93, 97–98
divorce, 123
entrepreneurial skills, xi, 97–98, 120, 125, 136, 138, 142–45
family/children, relationships, 123–25, 138
family trust, 137
first service station (Afton, Wyoming), 98–99, 101
founds CallAir, 105–8,
founds Maverik, 103
founds Trailside Country Stores, 104, 139–40, 142
friendship with Jay, 125–26, 138, 240
friendship/partnership with Osborne, 109, 119–20, 142
management style, 102, 120, 129, 136
marriages, 60, 123
personality/values, 89–90, 138, 143–44
refineries, 119–20, 130, 133–35, 139
relations with father, 88, 93, 98, 138
Sinclair dealer, 99–102
wholesaling, trucking, 102, 132–35
Call, Reva Charlotte (Todd), 76, 79
Call, Robert "Bob" Papworth, 85–86, 88, 91–92, 104, 107–8, 143, 156–57
Call, Rosa Emily (Stayner), 3, 43, 45, 47, 54, 59–60, 63–65, 76–77
Call, Rosa May (Spackman), 76, 86
Call, Rosa Vivian (Bagley), 85, 88, 91–92
Call, Rosseau (Rosso), 76, 79
Call, Ruth Mary, 76
Call, Samuel, 1–3

Call, Sarah Isabel (Barlow), 52
Call, Sarah "Sally" (Tiffany), 2–3, 36
Call, Shann, 255
Call, Sharon (Anderson), 93, 109–11, 113, 118, 123, 148–49, 151, 153, 242
Call, Sidney Benajah, 50, 52
Call, Spencer Papworth, 85, 91–92, 106–108
Call, Stella (Kennington), 59, 63, 76
Call, Tamra (Compton), 188–91, 208, 217, 236, 239, 241–44, 251
Call, Teddy Lou (Brown), 123, 152, 156–58, 172, 182, 184–86
Call, Thad J., 123, 158, 184–86, 205, 239, 244
Call, Thelma Ree (Enfield), 85, 91–92
Call, Thomas, 1, 3
Call, Thomas John, 76, 78, 81–95, 248
  Afton, Wyoming residence, 84
  childhood, 44, 54, 59, 64, 82–83
  church activities, 86–88
  death, 87
  family/children, 85, 88, 91–92, 138
  frugality, 90–94
  in Logan, Utah, 86–87
  marriage, 83–84
  personality/values, 89, 93
  recollections of A.V., 73
  structures he built, 84, 86, 98, 103, 105, 108, 110, 115
Call, Tommie Loy (Schreiber), 124
Call, Val (LaVal), 86, 124, 127, 131–32, 137, 139–40, 143–45
Call, Venna Maxine (Veigel), 85, 91–92
Call, Verna (Anson), 78, 85, 91, 123–24, 131, 137, 141, 143–44
Call, Waldo, 76, 79
Call, Walter Leroy, 76
Call, Wanda F. (Haderlie), 85

CallAir, 105–8, 129–130, 139
Call's Davis County Merchantile, 28
Call's Fort, 23–24, 33, 39
Callville, 30–33, 51
Caribou Lodge, 86, 115–16, 119, 128
Caribou Four Corners, 119, 124, 128–35, 137
Carlson, Don, 159
Carson Valley, Nevada, 25, 29
Carter, Jimmy (President), 192
Cassidy, Butch, 66
Cenex, 238
CFJ Properties, 226–28, 250
Chesterfield Foundation, 53
Chesterfield, Idaho, 47–54, 60
Clawson, Rudger, 44
Colonia Juarez, Mexico, 67
Colters Lodge, 68, 104
Compton, Dale, 188–89
Compton, Glenda, 188–89
Conoco (Continental Oil), 100, 102, 210, 216, 226–28
Convenience store (C-store) concept, 136
Cook, Ella (Call). *See* Ella Call
Cooke, John, 2
Cooke, Sarah (Warren), 2
Covey, Enoch, 94
Covey Gas and Oil Company, 94, 99, 101
Covey, Grace Christy. *See* Grace Christy Covey Papworth
Covey Investment Company, 94
Covey, Stephen, 94, 99
Crystal Inns, 237
Crystal Inn Company, 238

— D —

Dailey, Jack, 197

DataLink, 231
Davids, James Henry, 50–51, 53
Davids, Ruth Piede (Call), 35, 36, 50–51, 53
Deseret News, 21
Deseret News Weekly, 37
Dredge, Allen, 165
Dripps' Brigade, 55
Drummond, W. W. (Judge), 24
DuPont, 226, 228

— E —

E. F. Hutton & Company, Inc., 219
Edmunds Act (1882), 44
Eisenhower Administration, 134
Ellsworth, George S., xiv
Enfield, Ronald, 85
Enfield, Thelma Ree (Call). *See* Thelma Ree Call
Entrepreneurship, xiii, 137–38, 142–43, 145
Evans, David, 8

— F —

Fastway stations
    Brigham City, Utah, 179
    Lewiston, Idaho, 127, 167–68
    Monterey, California, 171–72
    Ontario, Oregon, 127, 167–68
    Pendleton, Oregon, 176–77
    Richland, Washington, 167–68
Fillmore, Willard (President), 18, 21, 24
Fillmore fort, 22
First Bank of Kemmerer, 132, 179
First Bank of Minneapolis, 199
First Security Bank, 181, 209
Fleischer, Morton H., 218–20
Flygare, Ralph, 104

Flying J
    acquisitions. *See* Husky Oil Ltd., RMT Properties, Inc., and Thunderbird Resources.
    automation, use of, 222–26
    corporate culture, 251
    corporate office, 183, 204
    Exploration and Production, 238
    Express Pay CardReader, 223
    franchising, 217–22
    Frequent Fueler program, 224–25
    Interstate Trucking Services (ITS card), 224
    motels
        Boise, Idaho, 204
        Carson City, Nevada, 182, 191, 200
        Ogden, Utah, 195
        Reno, Nevada, 182, 191, 200
        Salt Lake City, Utah, 192, 204, 211
    point of sale (POS) system, 223–24
    travel plaza strategy, 206, 215–218
    Video Club, 204–05
Flying J, Inc., 168,
    diesel sales, 235
    financial leverage, 180–81, 183, 190
    Food Service Operations, 235
    profits/sales, 179, 187–88, 190, 193, 206, 244
    stations, number of, 169, 179, 182, 187, 206
    truckstops/travel plazas, 193–95, 232–33
        Boise, Idaho, 203
        Dade City, Florida, 234
        Frazier Park, California, 234
        Husky truckstops, 207, 218–19
        Ogden, Utah, 193–95
        Post Falls, Idaho, 203–04

Forbes ranking, 216, 244
Fort Hall, 47–48, 56, 67
Franchise Finance Corporation of America (FFCA), 218–21, 228
Franchising. *See* Flying J, franchising
Fredricksen, Phil, 227
Frugality, 90–93, 117, 131, 162, 177
Fuel shortages, 181

— G —

Galentine, Robert F. (Bob), 235
Geesey, Orin, 132, 137, 179–80
Germer, Richard E. (Buzz), 173–75, 178, 181–82, 185, 193, 196–99, 201, 203, 205, 209, 211–13, 227, 250–51
Graham, Neils, 53
Grambling, John, 208
Great Western Reserves, 238
Greener, Fred, 211
Griffen, Pat, 118
Gusse, Bernard, 85

— H —

Hale, Roen (Roe), 98
Hamm, Rich, 227
Handcart companies, rescue of, 25–28
Hansen, Dianna, 250
Harper, Robert, 251
Harper, Thomas, 24
Harper Ward, 24
Harris, Riley, 153
Hatch, Hannah (Call). *See* Hannah Call
Hatch, William Ansel, 52
Heiner, Robert T. "Bob," 181, 202
Heywood, Joseph L., 24
Hildreth, LaViel, 100, 115
Hokanson, Virginia (Miller), 150

Holbrook, Joseph, 30, 42
Honeyville, Utah, 24
Hooper Springs, 147
Hudson Bay trappers, 55
Hulen, Barbara, 103
Hulen, Brad, 103
Hume, Marcella, 163, 173, 181, 197
Husky Oil Ltd., acquisition of, 207–13
Hyde, Orson, 25, 37
Hyde, Wilford, A., 73

— I —

Independent Gas and Oil, 100
Independence, Missouri, 4
Indian scare of 1895, 67
Inter–City Gas Ltd., 196–201

— J —

Jardine, Sterling, 203
Jenkins, Ab, 94
Johnston's Army, 29
Journal History of the Church, 73–74

— K —

Kelley, Joseph, 230
Kennington, Stella (Call). *See* Stella Call
Kettell, Hannah, 1, 3
Kimball, Heber C., 11
Kirtland Camp, 4

— L —

Lambert, George A., 37
Lander Cut–off, 56–57, 60
Lander, Frederik West, 56
Larkin, Dale, 132, 158–59
Leadership, concept of, 248–250

Liberatore, Lee, 169, 187
Lind, Ferris, 118
Lloyd, William (Billie), 33
LoadPlanner, 231
Loveland, Chester, 25, 28, 30, 50
Loveland, Fanny (Call), 25, 50
Lyddon, John, 178
Lyman, Amasa M., 37
Lyman, Francis M., 73–75

— M —

Maggelet, Crystal (Call), 123, 184–86, 236–37, 248, 250
Maggelet, Chuck, 237
Magnum, Jeff, 107
Marathon Oil, 226
Marland, E. W., 226
Marrett, Mary, 42–43, 45, 54,
Maverik, 103, 135–36, 139–142, 167, 179, 182
Maverik Country Stores, Inc., 99, 139–141
McCall Management LLC, 237–38
McCammon, Gerald, 172
McCarty, Tom, 66
Merrill, Marriner W., 37
Miller, George, 109
Miller, Janice. *See* Janice Miller Call
Miller, Louisa, 109
Monsanto Chemical Company, 148
Mormon Trail, 11–13
Muir, Mary Vashti (Call). *See* Mary Vashti Call
Muir, Moses, 52

— N —

National Auto/Truckstops, Inc., 235
Nauvoo, Illinois, 7–10

Nelson, Charlotte Vienna (Call), 49–50, 52, 54
Nelson, Christian, 47, 49, 54
Nield, Lucy Margaret (Call). *See* Lucy Margaret Call
Nielsen, Glenn, 118, 208
Nixon, Richard (President) and price controls, 134
Norcross, Irving, 112, 154
North Canyon Ward, 15, 26–29
Nova, Ltd., 208

— O —

OPEC (Organization of Petroleum Exporting Countries), 133, 211
Oregon Trail, 47–48, 55–58, 147
Osmond, George, 71–73, 75
Osmond, Georgina, 72

— P —

Papworth, Grace Christy (Covey), 94–95
Papworth, Osborne Tavener, 83, 94
Papworth, Wilda, 86
PARCO (Producers and Refiners Company), 100
Parker, John D., 24
Parker, Ronald, 192, 195–97, 200, 250
Parowan, Utah, settlement of, 19–20
Pavant Valley, 20–21
Perpetual Immigration Fund, 23
Perry, William O. (Bill), 192
Peterson, Carl J., 106
Peterson, F. Ross, xiv
Peterson, Richard, 225
Peterson, Vernal, 115
Petro Shopping Centers, 216, 235
Petroleum, world market, 133, 200
Phoenix Inn, 236

Pickens, Boone, 251
Piede, Ruth. *See* Ruth Piede Call Davids
Pieper, Don, 118
Pierce, Franklin (President), 24
Pilot Oil, 216, 235
Pleasanton, California, property, 195–96, 200
polygamy, 20, 34, 41, 44, 48, 53, 58–59, 65, 67, 72
Pratt, Orson, 21
Preston, William B., 58

— R —

Rand McNally's MileMaker, 231
Reagan administration, 135
Refineries
    Cheyenne, Wyoming, 207, 210–12
    Cody, Wyoming, 207
    Cowley, Wyoming, 130, 133
    Cut Bank, Montana, 198–99, 202
    government programs relating to, 134, 196, 200–2
    Kevin, Montana, 198
    Kirtland, New Mexico, 130, 133
    Williston, North Dakota, 198, 200, 202
    Woods Cross, Utah, (Flying J), 142, 207, 212–13, 225, 238
    Woods Cross, Utah, (Maverik), 119–20, 130, 133
Reuel T. Call Petroleum Products, 100
Rich, Charles C., 37, 58
Rigdon, Sidney, 7
RMT Properties, Inc., acquisition of, 207–13
RoadLink, 230
Roberts, B. H., 5
Roberts, Charlotte V. (Call). *See* Charlotte V. Call

Roberts, Nora, 129
Robidoux's Brigade, 55
Rockwell, Orrin Porter, 9, 24, 190
Rocky Mountain Fur Company, 55

— S —

Salt River Valley, 54–58
Sav–On Drug Company, xi, 95
Scales, John, 238
Scholte, Lorna Louise, 76
Schreiber, Lawrence, 124
Schreiber, Tommie Loy (Call). See Tommie Loy Call
Seamons, John (Jack), 163
Sessions, Lucina (Call). See Lucina Call
Sessions, Marvin, 89–90, 98–99
Shearson Lehman, 219
Sheath, R. R., 31–32
Simmonds, A. J., xiv
Sinclair, Harry, 100
Sinclair Oil Company, 99–102, 108, 110, 113, 115, 142, 156
Slater, Dick, 194
Smith, Bob, 171, 236, 238
Smith, George A., 19, 35, 37
Smith, Hyrum, 7–9, 39
Smith, Joseph F., 69, 71
Smith, Joseph, 4, 7–11, 20, 39, 41, 82
Smith, Lot, 29
Smith, Robert, 8
Smith, William, 4
Smoot, Reed, 74
Snow, Erastus, 37
Snow, Lorenzo, 35, 37
SnowCar, 108
Soda Springs, Idaho, community of, 147–48
Spackmán, Rosa May (Call). See Rosa May Call

Spackman, Hazen, 91
Stanger, Chris, 225, 232
Star Valley, Wyoming, 55–58, 66
Star Valley Tabernacle, 69–71
Starboe, Charles, 131
Starboe, Robin, 131
State of Deseret, 17–19
Stock, Lillie Bell, 85, 98, 123
Stone, Jim, 188
Sumner, Ron A., 228, 250
Swapp, Edward M. "Ed," 211, 251–52
Swartz, Gaylord, 105

— T —

Telford, John, 197
Territory of Utah, 17–18, 35
Thatcher, Moses, 58
Thiokol Chemical Corporation, 182, 188
Thomas, Judge, 8
Thunderbird Resources Acquisition, 196–203
Tipton, Patty (Smith), 151
Todd, Reva Charlotte (Call). See Reva Charlotte Call
TON Services, 230–32
Tosco Corporation, 210
Trailside Country Stores, 104, 139–40, 142
Treaty of Guadalupe, Hidalgo, 17
Truckstops of America, 235

— U —

Uinta County, Wyoming, 58, 100
University of Deseret, 42, 67
Unocal, 218, 236
USX (U. S. Steel), 208
Utah War, 28–29, 40

INDEX

— V —

Valleon Hotel, 68, 86–87, 103–4, 109, 115
Veigel, Doyle E., 85, 91
Veigel, Venna Maxine (Call). *See* Venna Maxine Call
Victor, Maynard, 175

— W —

Walker, Clem, 112–13
Wallace, John, 104, 115, 119, 137, 140, 187
Warner, Matt, 66
Weeks, Stan, 197
Whitmer, David, 4
Williams, Colonel, 8

Winter Quarters, Nebraska (Florence), 12
Wood, Ethel Davis, 190
Woodruff, Wilford Manifesto, 48–49, 67, 72, 75
Wyoming Alaska Leasing Company, 139

— Y —

Young, Brigham, 11–13, 16–17, 19–30, 33, 35, 42
Young Brigham, Jr., 58
Young, Candace (Call). *See* Candace Call
Young, Gerald, 242

— Z —

Zion's Camp, 4